MW00638982

AQUINAS AGAINST THE AVERROISTS

Purdue University Series in the History of Philosophy

General Editors

Arion Kelkel

Joseph J. Kockelmans

Adriaan Peperzak

Calvin O. Schrag

Thomas Seebohm

A Q U I N A S
AGAINST THE
A V E R R O I S T S

On There Being
Only One Intellect

Ralph McInerny

Purdue University Press
West Lafayette, Indiana

Copyright ©1993 by Purdue University Research Foundation.
All rights reserved.

The paper used in this book meets the minimum requirements of
American National Standard for Information Sciences—Permanence of
Paper Printed Library Materials, ANSI Z39.48-1984.

Design by Anita Noble

Printed in the United States of America

97   96   95   5   4   3   2

Library of Congress Cataloging-in-Publication Data

McInerny, Ralph M.
    Aquinas against the Averroists: on there being only one intellect /
Ralph McInerny
        p.   cm. — (Purdue University series in the history of
philosophy)
    Includes Latin text and English translation of Aquinas's De unitate
intellectus contra Averroistas.
    Includes bibliographical references and index.
    ISBN 1-55753-028-9 (alk. paper)   —ISBN 1-55753-029-7 (pbk. :
alk. paper)
    1. Thomas, Aquinas, Saint, 1225?–1274. De unitate intellectus
contra Averroistas. 2. Averroës, 1126–1198. 3. Intellect. I. Thomas,
Aquinas, Saint, 1225?–1274. De unitate intellectus contra Averroistas.
English & Latin. 1992. II. Title. III. Series.
Selections. 1991. II. Title. III. Series.
B765.T53D85   1993
128' .2–dc20   92–16179 CIP

For Al Plantinga—
no foe of other minds

CONTENTS

In this book, I present a translation of a short polemical work of Saint Thomas Aquinas, written in Paris in 1270 when Thomas returned from Italy to serve a second term as Regent Master in a Dominican chair of theology. The Latin title of the opusculum is *De unitate intellectus contra Averroistas*. I have chosen to render this in English as *On There Being Only One Intellect*. In it, Thomas is intent on countering two views: first, intellect is not a faculty of the soul that animates our body; and second, there is a single intellect existing separately that suffices for all humans. Thomas argues both that Aristotle held neither of these positions and that neither of them can be rationally defended.

Selecting a minor work of a major thinker as the vehicle of that thinker's teaching on the human person is risky. The risk is compounded when the minor work is also polemical and necessarily governed by the position it would refute. Later, I will provide a number of considerations that will, I hope, make my selection seem reasonable, perhaps even inevitable. For now, I will say only that this work addresses all the significant strands of Thomas's teaching on the human person—historical, doctrinal, philosophical, and theological. Above all, it can put to rest the tired and misleading claim that Thomas "baptized Aristotle."

The Introduction of this book places the work historically and sketches the controversy to which it contributed. The second part is the text. In Part Three, I analyze the basic strategies and arguments of the five chapters of *On There Being Only One Intellect;* and in Part Four, I provide a series of interpretive essays meant to make the work more intelligible. Thomas Aquinas is, by common consent, one of the major thinkers in the history of both philosophy and theology. Thinkers are major when our interest in them is not confined to a past time or forgotten controversies. We listen to them because what they have to say seems relevant to our own pondering of similar questions. I hope this edition will contribute to making Thomas more audible today.

I am indebted to Susan Zeiter Andres and Brendan Kelly for their invaluable assistance with the manuscript.

Introduction

Thomas Aquinas's polemical work *On There Being Only One Intellect* was written in Paris in 1270 and may be said to concern the correct reading of Aristotle. Aristotle and Paris are, respectively,
continuous and recurrent factors in the life of Thomas Aquinas
(1225–74). Thomas was convinced of the complementarity of Aristotelian philosophy and his Christian faith. How could truths revealed
by God conflict with the truths gained by our God-given intellect?
The philosophy of Aristotle enabled Thomas to fashion an understanding of the human person that departed in significant ways
from the Augustinian view that had dominated Christian thought
into the thirteenth century. Thomas, though still a comparatively
young man, did not have long to live when he wrote the short work
that is the focus of this study. In it, he takes issue with Averroes's
reading of Aristotle, which, Thomas argues, is without textual support and makes Aristotle the foe of, rather than a complement and
prelude to, Christianity. Thomas's deepest convictions about the
value of Aristotle for understanding human nature and destiny
come into play in this work. This explains the sharpness with which
he opposes what Fernand Van Steenberghen wishes us to call heterodox Aristotelianism, more commonly referred to as Latin
Averroism.

Biographical Sketch

Thomas spent three years at the Dominican convent of Santa
Sabina in Rome before returning to Paris in 1269. During this time
(1265–68), he purportedly conducted a "personal *studium*" where he
was in charge of the instruction of young members of his order. It
was then that he began the *Summa theologiae*.[1] Also near the end of

this period, he commented on Aristotle's *De anima,* the first of a dozen such commentaries that he would write over the next five years. This Aristotelian work contains passages that triggered the controversy in Paris between masters of the faculty of arts and theologians, a controversy that broadened to include the general question of the compatibility of Aristotelian philosophy and Christian faith. Nonetheless, Thomas's commentary on the *De anima* has been called serene in comparison with the polemical work he wrote in Paris in 1270, *On There Being Only One Intellect,* against the Averroists. René Gauthier observed that Thomas's conviction as to the value of Aristotelian doctrine, in itself and for theology, was both doctrinal and personal.[2] It is not surprising that he reacted to what he considered distortions of Aristotle with a vigor verging on anger.

Thomas Aquinas was born in Roccasecca into a noble family often allied with the emperor against the forces of the pope. In 1231, at the age of five, Thomas was presented as an oblate at the great Benedictine abbey of Montecassino, not far from Roccasecca. There he received his first education, the rudiments of learning. When war once more engulfed the monastery in 1239, Thomas was sent to the University of Naples at the age of thirteen; he was slightly younger than others beginning the study of the arts. Among his teachers were Brother Martin, of whom we know little, and Peter of Ireland.[3] Naples was a center of Aristotelianism thanks to translations from the Arabic; therefore, Aristotle, Avicenna, and Averroes were familiar to him.

Also in Naples, Thomas met members of the Order of Preachers, founded by Dominic in 1215. Dominicans were associated with universities from the beginning, their pastoral task requiring, Dominic felt, profound intellectual training. In 1242 or 1243, Thomas became a Dominican, much to the chagrin of his family, who tried to persuade him to leave. Thomas's superiors sent him to Rome as a protective measure. This may have been his first stay at the Dominican convent of Santa Sabina. His mother, Theodora, apparently followed him to Rome and enlisted the help of the recently elected Innocent IV. Ecclesiastical honors were dangled before the young friar but without effect. The master of the order decided to send Thomas to Paris, but the family intervened, taking Thomas into custody. They put him in a family castle at Montesangiovanni, near Frosinone, where his mother urged him to leave the Dominicans. Thomas was held captive by his family from 1244 to 1245 or 1246. During this period, he read the entire Bible, may have read Peter Lombard's *Sentences,* and taught his young cousins. Except for the last activity, perhaps, it would not have been in every way a punitive sojourn. Finally, Thomas's brothers sought to weaken his resolve by sending a woman to him, but the chaste young friar chased her from the room. Then, perhaps with his mother's help, Thomas escaped and rejoined his fellow religious in Naples.

Soon Thomas resumed the long, interrupted journey north, going first to Paris, where there is reason to believe that he continued his study of the arts from 1246 to 1248. During this period, he may have attended lectures on Aristotle's *Nicomachean Ethics* and *On the Soul.* If so, it is interesting that Thomas's first contact with the latter work was on the faculty whose masters he would later oppose on Aristotle's teachings on the human soul. Then he was transferred to Cologne, where he studied under Albert the Great from 1248 to 1251. Albert was noted for his interest in Aristotle, and in Cologne, Thomas committed Albert's lectures on the *Ethics* to writing.[4]

In 1251, Thomas was sent to Paris to study theology. He was twenty-five years old. For two years he devoted himself to courses in Scripture. After his stint as *baccalaureus biblicus,* he began the study of the *Sentences* of Peter Lombard, a twelfth-century collection of theological doctrine chiefly inspired by Augustine. From 1254 to 1256, Thomas was *baccalaureus sententiarum.*[5] Occupying one of the Dominican chairs of theology, for the next three years Thomas taught as a master of theology (*magister regens*), then returned to Italy.

During this stay in Paris, Thomas felt the sting of the attacks made on the mendicant friars, Franciscan as well as Dominican, who were becoming masters in the university. William of Saint Amour likened them to the Antichrist in a work called "On the Dangers of These Last Times."[6] The secular masters successfully enlisted the help of Innocent IV, and the activities of the friars within the university were restricted. A few weeks later, Innocent IV died and was succeeded by Alexander IV, who restored the rights of the friars. But the attacks increased. It is no surprise that Thomas met opposition after he was appointed to one of the two Dominican chairs of theology in 1256 and was not welcomed into the ranks of masters of the university. It was not until a year later, in 1257, that Thomas Aquinas, a Dominican, and Bonaventure, a Franciscan, were acknowledged by the other masters.

After three years in his chair, Thomas returned to Italy. The threefold task of the master of theology was *legere, disputare, praedicare:* to lecture, to dispute, to preach. Thomas fulfilled these tasks during the next nine years. In Italy he composed his first great summary of Christian doctrine, the *Summa contra gentiles,* and began the *Summa theologiae,* the masterpiece that was, however, left unfinished at his death. Historians disagree on precisely where he was stationed from 1259 to 1262, although the assumption is that he

returned to his community in Naples. There are records of his atten-
dance at various meetings of his order during these years. In 1261,
he became lector at the Dominican priory in Orvieto, a post he held
until 1265. It was then that he completed the *Summa contra gentiles.* In 1265, he began a three-year stay at Santa Sabina, where he
is thought to have written, among other things, his *Disputed Question on the Power of God.* As stated earlier, it was at Santa Sabina
that he wrote his commentary on Aristotle's *On the Soul.*[7]

▮ The Philosopher: Aristotle

From his earliest works, Thomas exhibits an acquaintance with
Aristotle that is encyclopedic. In commenting on the *Sentences,* in
his student works, *On the Principles of Nature* and *On Being and
Essence,* he explicates Aristotelian doctrine with a sureness that is
striking. Thomas was not alone in making constant reference to
Aristotle in commenting on Peter Lombard. His great contemporary, Bonaventure, does the same in his commentary on the *Sentences.* Aristotle had come to be recognized as a vast, though
ambiguous, reservoir of philosophical wisdom that was at the dis-
posal of the theologian. But there is no work like *On Being and Essence* from the pen of Bonaventure, and in the controversy out of
which *On There Being Only One Intellect* emerged, Thomas and
Bonaventure adopt distinctively different approaches.

Aristotle had been a component of medieval education from its
beginnings in the liberal-arts curriculum, functioning as an
auctor—thus *auctoritas,* authority—in logic. He was read only in
Latin translation, and only a few of his logical works were available
in Latin. For all that, he was better off than Plato, who was known
only through a translation of the *Timaeus.* Toward the end of the
twelfth century—a century noteworthy for so many profound
changes in intellectual and cultural life—other writings of Aristotle
began to come into Latin. The *logica nova* joined the *logica vetus,*
and portions of the *Ethics* were translated. And then, at centers such
as Toledo—where Christian, Muslim, and Jew came together in un-
easy truce but in common love of the truth—Aristotelian works hith-
erto unknown to the Latins were translated from Arabic and, along
with them, the interpretations of Avicenna, Averroes, and Algazel.[8]
At the same time, translations were being made directly from the
Greek; this brought Aristotle out of oblivion, and, for the first time,
scholars had access not only to translations of the nonlogical works
but even to several translations of the same work.

This abundance of new material created difficulties. Over the
centuries, a Christian wisdom had been developed by many hands.

The twelfth century saw the codification of theology in Lombard's *Sentences,* of biblical interpretation in the *glossa ordinaria,* of canon law by Gratian. This was the century of Anselm and Abelard, of Bernard and Hugh of St. Victor, giants by any standard. If there was a dominant influence, it was Augustine, whose authority was unquestioned and whose writings animated and inspired generation after generation. If we compare a twelfth-century theologian with a thirteenth-century theologian, we are immediately struck by the difference. This is most conveniently seen by comparing the four books of Peter Lombard's *Sentences* with almost any thirteenth-century commentary on them—and such commentaries abounded, since it was the task of the fledgling theologian to explain Peter's works. The difference quite simply lies in the influence of Aristotle. In the thirteenth century, commentators ask what the subject of the science contained in the *Sentences* is, and that preliminary question, redolent of Aristotle, prepares us for the constant recourse to the Stagirite in what follows. Theology would never be the same again.

But Aristotle did not receive an immediate welcome at the University of Paris. Early on, in 1212 and in 1215, there were official prohibitions against reading his works, that is, against making them the basis of lectures. Gregory IX in 1231 softened the condemnations,[9] and by 1240 they had lost their effect. The statutes of the university of 1252 and 1255 made Aristotle a required part of the curriculum of the arts faculty.

That concern about the writings of Aristotle should be felt is not surprising. It was unclear—and the unclarity was intensified by the Avicennian and Averroistic interpretations—that Aristotle could be read with profit by a Christian. The Christian, after all, receives as truths the deliverances of revelation, and there seemed to be manifest conflicts between what Christians believe and what Aristotle taught. To take an unavoidable and incontestable instance, Aristotle clearly taught that the world had always been because it could not have come into being as the result of a change. But the clear sense of Genesis is that motion and time, the world, had a beginning. One need not be a Christian, of course, to know that one cannot regard a statement and its contradictory opposite to be simultaneously true, that the formula "p.-p" expresses an impossibility. But for the Christian, the truth of the temporal beginning of the world has the sanction of divine revelation. Its contradictory opposite must therefore be false. In short, on the eternity of the world, Aristotle is wrong if Christianity is right. It was because this could not be regarded as a small point and because the implications of the one view seemed so manifestly different from the implications of the other that this teaching of Aristotle posed a massive obstacle to the Christian mind. There were other equally momentous "errors of Aristotle" that called into question providence and the very nature and destiny of humanity.

❚ Paris, 1269–72

The regular turnover in the Dominican chairs at Paris was due to a desire to increase the number of masters who could then be assigned as lectors in the priories of the order. For Thomas to return to Paris and once more occupy the chair of a *magister regens* is thus in need of explanation. Certainly one reason was the manner in which Aristotle was being interpreted by a bumptious band in the faculty of arts. Bonaventure, now master general of the Franciscans, drew attention to the dangers to the faith from the Aristotelianism of the masters of arts.[10] Earlier, the holder of the Franciscan chair in 1266–67, William of Baglione, had opened the attack on this type of Aristotelianism and, fateful fact, had included Thomas Aquinas as his target.[11] Such an attack could not have gone unanswered, since it would eventually have implicated the Dominicans as a group.

The controversy in which *On There Being Only One Intellect* plays a role has a complicated cast. There was a growing Franciscan suspicion, first given voice by William of Baglione and then by Bonaventure, that heterodoxy was not confined to masters in the faculty of arts whose enthusiasm for Aristotle had led them astray. Simon Tugwell, O.P., describes the situation:

> By now he [Thomas] was developing a rather distinctive and original theology, which sometimes left him rather isolated among his fellows. One important factor in this theology was the conviction he shared with Albert that philosophy has to be taken seriously. The faith is not served by invoking dogmatic considerations to impose solutions to philosophical problems, nor is sound theology fostered by disowning philosophical conclusions that are genuinely cogent. Against the background of the continuing problem of heterodox philosophy, it is not surprising that Thomas was sometimes seen as conceding too much ground to the philosophers, but what was at stake in Thomas' position was the very possibility of a coherent understanding: if Christianity is true, then it must make sense and it must make sense in terms which are related to the ordinary, untheological ways in which human beings try to make sense of things.[12]

Matters were considerably complicated by the fact that the attack on the mendicants was resumed, but this time there was no longer solidarity between the Franciscans and the Dominicans. Gerald of Abbeville now led the secular attack on the friars; tensions increased when a Franciscan argued that perfection requires poverty, and poverty means not simply the abandonment of personal but also of community property. It was this view that Gerald attacked. He was answered by Bonaventure and John Pecham. Thomas was in the touchy position of disagreeing with this Franciscan view of communal property and poverty and thus agreeing with Gerald, the foe of friars. Furthermore, Thomas's opponents now included theologians in his order.[13]

The dispute that lay behind Thomas's opusculum *On There Being Only One Intellect* was not simply a dispute between master of theology and master of arts—between the faculty of theology and the faculty of arts of the university. Rather, the view Thomas defended put him between two camps: that of theologians, who were suspicious of Aristotle; and that of masters of arts, who felt that Aristotle's teachings, however much they might be opposed to faith, did not discredit him. Thomas argued that, properly understood, Aristotle provided a powerful complement to the faith. Despite the various concurrent controversies, the target of the polemical work of interest is a group of masters in the faculty of arts.

At Paris, boys began the study of the arts in their early teens and became masters of arts (*magistri artium*) in their early twenties. The medieval educational system was modeled on apprenticeship in a guild; a student was introduced by stages into the craft, spending some years listening, some years teaching under the supervision of a master, until finally being credentialed as a master himself and licensed to teach anywhere he could find a position. The faculty of arts functioned as a feeder to the further faculties of theology, law, and medicine; and at Paris, students in the faculty of theology were already masters of arts and might indeed still be functioning as such in the faculty of arts. In later years, masters of arts would remain in the initial faculty, and the arts course would no longer be seen as necessarily a prelude to further study.[14]

As the name indicates, the faculty of arts was the place where the liberal-arts tradition was continued. But under the pressure of the new learning, all those translations from Greek and Arabic, the traditional seven arts—subdivided into the trivium: grammar, rhetoric, and logic; and the quadrivium: arithmetic, geometry, music, and astronomy—could no longer contain the secular learning that was seen as a prelude to sacred studies. Despite the prohibitions mentioned above, room was soon found for Aristotle's *Ethics* and *Metaphysics* in the faculty of arts. By midcentury, there is evidence of Aristotle's being taught in the faculty of arts—that is, the new works of Aristotle. And, of course, Albert, Thomas, and Bonaventure—all theologians—employed Aristotle in sacred studies, and each exhibited a close acquaintance with his thought. While theologians had worked out a *modus vivendi* with Aristotelianism, something considerably different began to show up in the faculty of arts. An approach to the study of Aristotle came into prominence that Van Steenberghen calls heterodox Aristotelianism; it is characterized by the guidance it took from Averroes and thus is also called Latin Averroism. These are the Averroists of Thomas's title, and though he does not mention any adversary by name, Siger of Brabant is, rightly or wrongly, taken to be the champion of the view Thomas attacks.[15]

Masters of arts commented on *On the Soul,* and their attitude toward Averroes during the period from 1225 to 1250 has been characterized by Gauthier as first Averroism.[16] In these commentaries, Averroes is seen as the champion of the view that the agent and possible intellects are faculties of the soul, and he is opposed to Avicenna, who taught that the agent intellect was one substance existing separately from human souls. This Averroes is markedly different from the commentator read by the theologians. Beginning with Albert, commenting in 1250 on the *Nicomachean Ethics* and *The Divine Names* of Pseudo-Dionysius, Averroes was seen as a proponent of monopsychism. Robert Kilwardby, Bonaventure, and Thomas Aquinas continued this critique on the part of masters of theology. If there was a conflict between masters of arts and theologians at this juncture, it would have been on the correct reading of Averroes.

It has been suggested that the Averroism they attacked—monopsychism, that is, that the soul of which these are the faculties is one and separate—was an invention of the theologians and that it did not arise from a natural reading of the commentator. Was Averroes an Averroist? The question could turn on what verdict would be reached after an exhaustive study of all of his writings, or it could turn on Averroes as he was known to the men of the thirteenth century. His *Great Commentary,* which has been translated into Latin, was known in Paris from 1225 and was the main source of the judgments of masters of arts as to what Averroes taught.[17] Is monopsychism the teaching of Averroes in the *Great Commentary?* If it is, then the master of arts who missed this, and indeed attributed to Averroes the exact opposite of what he actually taught, must be convicted of a naive reading that failed to grasp the import of the text. Or did the theologians invent an opponent who cannot be found in the *Great Commentary?*

It seems clear that Averroes, in the *Great Commentary,* taught that both possible and agent intellects were separate substances and not powers of the human soul. To accuse the theological critics of

Averroes of inventing Averroism in the sense of the doctrine of the uniqueness of intellect is, therefore, misguided.[18] What Gauthier calls second Averroism begins when masters in the faculty of arts accept and defend Averroes as he is interpreted and criticized by the theologians. Prominent among them is Siger of Brabant.[19]

| Siger of Brabant

Siger was a student in the faculty of arts from 1263 to 1265, when he became a master of arts and embarked upon a teaching career. The Condemnation of 1270, involving thirteen propositions, is taken to be directed at Siger and his companions, and it may well have been, as Van Steenberghen argues, a turning point in the young man's life.[20] Nonetheless, he seems to have been one of the targets of the far more sweeping Condemnation of 1277, which involved 219 propositions, even some Thomistic ones (though Thomas had died in 1274). Siger apparently met his death in Orvieto, the victim of an attack by his mad clerk, perhaps while both were being detained at the papal court. Dante's high praise of Siger in the *Paradiso*[21] need not be thought to be based on his differences with Thomas; indeed it is Thomas who praises him, but on his later more careful expressions of the autonomy of philosophy.

On 10 December 1270, the following propositions were condemned by the bishop of Paris, Etienne Tempier, and those knowingly holding them were excommunicated:

1.   That there is numerically one and the same intellect for all humans.

2.   That this is false or improper: humans understand.

3.   That a human being's will necessarily wills or chooses.

4.   That all things here below come under the necessary control of the heavenly bodies.

5.   That the world is eternal.

6.   That there never was a first human.

7.   That the soul, which is the form of the human being insofar as the human being is human, corrupts when the body corrupts.

8.   That the soul separated by death cannot suffer from bodily fire.

9.   That free will is a passive not an active power and that it is moved necessarily by the desired object.

10.   That God does not know singulars.

11.   That God does not know things other than Himself.

12.   That human acts are not ruled by the providence of God.

13.   That God cannot grant immortality and incorruption to a mortal and corruptible thing.[22]

Sometime between 1269 and 1270, Siger commented on book 3 of Aristotle's *On the Soul,* one of the works that Thomas seems to have had in mind in writing *On There Being Only One Intellect.* Both works were written prior to 10 December 1270, though perhaps in the same year, and Siger's preceded Thomas's opusculum.[23]

Thomas's polemical work attacks the view that the possible intellect is an entity existing separately from the individual and that this single, separately existing intellect is common to all humans. That this, along with other dubious doctrines, was taught by some masters at Paris is beyond doubt. Threats of excommunication are not directed at imaginary targets. But if this is certain, it is not a simple matter to identify the specific masters whom Thomas had in mind. The passage from his adversary that he quotes in chapter 5 of the opusculum has not yet been identified with respect to work or author. Nonetheless, there seems to be no reasonable doubt that Siger of Brabant was one of the masters against whom Thomas's work was directed.

Van Steenberghen divides Siger's career into three parts. A first comprises the time from his birth, circa 1240, until the condemnation of 1270; the second is the period between the two condemnations, from 1270 to 1277; the final period extends to the death of Siger, which took place sometime between 1281 and 1284.

Siger first comes into view for the historian in 1266, and the events that were to culminate in the first condemnation can be fairly well tracked. The masters, bachelors, and students of the faculty of arts at Paris were divided into four nations:[24] the French, the Normans, the Picards, and the English. At the beginning of 1266, one John d'Ulliaco was received into the French nation, although he should have belonged to the Picard. The Picards kidnapped John and proceeded to rough up the French. It is as a leader of the Picard toughs that Siger enters the pages of history. The French elected their own chancellor and severed relations with the other nations. Two complaints against Siger are recorded in the decree of 27 August 1266, whereby the papal legate, Simon de Brion, restored peace to the university. Siger is suspected of having taken part in the kidnapping of one Canon William of the French nation and, together with his compatriot Simon of Brabant, disrupted the singing of the Office of the Dead for William of Auxerre, snatching books of hours from the hands of French participants. Siger thus appears as a troublemaker and leader of a faction. "Siger will emerge as the chief inspiration of masters and students who show disturbing rationalist tendencies and profess a radical Aristotelianism without regard for theology or even Christian orthodoxy."[25] Van Steenberghen notes, however, that the decree of the papal legate makes no mention of any heterodox teaching in the faculty of arts. Nonetheless, within months of that decree, Bonaventure is viewing with alarm the philosophy taught at Paris.

Bonaventure's sermons were preceded, as we have seen, by the criticisms of William of Baglione, holder of the Franciscan chair of theology from 1266 to 1267. William calmly discusses three dangerous doctrines: that there is but one intellect for all humanity, that the world is eternal, and that fire cannot affect the souls of the damned. All three views will figure in the Condemnation of 1270. Only when he mentions Averroes does William grow sharp, characterizing his doctrine as pestiferous, pernicious, absurd, and delirious. There is no reason to think that William was criticizing masters of arts; his apparent target, never mentioned by name, is Thomas Aquinas. The errors Bonaventure mentions are also clearly identical with those condemned in 1270.[26]

Did Siger of Brabant teach the errors that aroused Bonaventure and then Thomas and subsequently were condemned in 1270? In order to answer this question, it is first necessary to identify the writings of Siger that were composed prior to the condemnation. Bernardo Carlos Bazán places four Sigerian works in that period,[27] including the commentary on book 3 of *On the Soul.* Van Steenberghen places an unedited commentary on the *Metereology* in this period, as well as a commentary on the *Physics.*[28] That Siger taught that the world is eternal without reference to the incompatibility of this doctrine with Christianity is clear from his treatment of the puzzle, "Would 'man is animal' be true if there were no men?" According to Siger, the supposition was absurd because the human race is eternal and there never was a time when no people existed. "This conclusion must be firmly held, since when it has been pondered, the intellect acquiesces and subsides. Away with verbal vanity in this matter lest it impede knowledge."[29]

In discussing whether the intellect is eternal or created *de novo* in the second of his questions on book 3 of *On the Soul,* Siger places Aristotle in opposition to Augustine. Aristotle's view would be that making something from nothing (*de novo*) would require a change in the will of the first cause, and that is not fitting. Siger characterizes Aristotle's view as only probable but says it is more probable than the position of Augustine (Bazán, *Quaestiones,* 7, lines 81–84). In question 9 of the same work, which asks whether there is a single intellect in all people, Siger adopts the Averroist view without any allusion to its relation to revelation (ibid., 25–29). This is all the more noteworthy because in his questions on the *Physics,* in discussing whether events that are accidental or fortuitous just happen to come about with respect to God's causality, Siger remarks that an affirmative answer would be heretical.[30] Furthermore, when he asks whether the caused is always produced out of some principle, he follows the philosophers in distinguishing things generated from matter and eternal effects and answers negatively. But he appends this to the discussion:

> However I believe that every effect is new and that it is not necessary that every effect have a principle *ex quo,* since that which is made *ex nihilo* has no principle *ex quo.* And when philosophers argue that a thing does not come to be unless by its nature it is possible, it should be said that things come to be in two ways, either according to transmutation—and thus they argue well, since that which comes to be by transmutation has that out of which (*ex quo*) it comes to be—or a thing comes to be from nothing not by transmutation, and then their argument does not work. Or it could be said that the made need not come to be out of something, indeed the power of the most powerful agent suffices for it.[31]

If the questions on the *Physics* antedate the Condemnation of 1270, we have in Siger's first period a mixed situation. However, while qualifications are found in Siger's texts, there is no doubt that the sort of teaching which Thomas addresses in *On There Being Only One Intellect* was being taught by Siger of Brabant.

This is not to say that we can always locate in Siger statements which Thomas attributes to his opponents—and of course he always speaks of them in the plural—and, *a fortiori*, we need not expect to find in Siger the *implications* of the errors that Thomas draws out.

During the period between the two condemnations, 1270 to 1277, Siger avoids contradicting Christian dogmas, and if he explores heterodox views, he disavows them because they clash with revealed truth. New rifts developed in the university and continued from 1272 until 1275, and Siger was a leader of the faction questioning the authority of the rector elected by the majority. Van Steenberghen discerns a progressive growth of moderation and wisdom (from 1275) in Siger himself, but doubtless due to his political as well as his intellectual leadership, the earlier errors gained wide currency in the faculty of arts. On 23 November 1276, Siger and two of his companions were cited by the tribunal of the Inquisitor of France, and on 18 January 1277, Pope John XXI (Peter of Spain) asked the bishop of Paris, Etienne Tempier, to look into the errors being taught in the university. On 7 March 1277, Tempier, interpreting the papal charge in the most liberal fashion, condemned 219 propositions attributed to masters in the faculty of arts.

Thomas had left Paris in 1272 and returned to Naples, where he was charged with founding a *studium generale* of his order. A year later, he stopped writing, having undergone a mystical experience that led him to think of all he had written as straw. He died on 7 March 1274 at Fossanova, a Cistercian monastery south of Rome, where he had been taken when he fell ill en route to the Council of Lyon.

Siger and another of the accused, Gosvin de la Chapelle, fled France in order to avoid the Inquisitor and took refuge at the papal court in Viterbo. Absolved of the charge of heresy, Siger was nonetheless placed in forced residence in the curia. After the death of John XXI, Siger remained at the papal court. Sometime between 1281 and 1284 Siger was stabbed at Orvieto by his mad secretary.[32]

On There Being Only One Intellect is not important for its attack on one or several young masters in the faculty of arts. Ironically, Siger himself, in later works, aligns himself more and more with the views of Thomas. The charm of Dante's locating Bonaventure, Siger, and Thomas together in the *Paradiso* is that it takes us beyond their opposition at the end of the 1260s and early 1270s. What is important is not that this person was pitted against that. Rather, it is the matter of truth that is at stake. Thomas is not defending a position because it is his own nor attacking a position because it is held by these or those particular persons. This work takes its historical interest from the setting in which it was produced—a setting that is deficient of historical accounts. The philosophical and theological interest of this work is paramount. What is a human being? What is soul? What is the intellect? How do philosophical answers to these questions relate to Christian revelation? Was Aristotle merely a convenient source of quotes that could be made to mean things compatible with Christianity or is Thomas really interested in the historical meaning of the text and defending Aristotle against misinterpretations?

| NOTES

1. See Leonard Boyle, O.P., *The Setting of the* Summa Theologiae *of Saint Thomas* (Toronto: Pontifical Institute of Mediaeval Studies, 1982).

2. Cf. René Gauthier, in his introduction to volume 45, 1 of *Sancti Thomae Opera omnia, Sentencia libri De anima* (Rome: Commissio Leonina, 1984), p. 293*.

3. Michael Crowe, "Peter of Ireland: Aquinas's Teacher of the *Artes Liberales,*" in *Arts libéraux et philosophie au moyen âge* (Montreal: Institut d'études médiévales; Paris: Vrin, 1969), 617–26.

4. Albert the Great, *Opera omnia* (Monasterii Westfalorum in Aedibus Aschendorff, 1960), 14/1:v-vi.

5. On the education of theologians at the University of Paris, see Hastings Rashdall, *The Universities of Europe in the Middle Ages,* edited by E. M. Powicke and A. B. Emden (Oxford: Oxford University Press, 1936), 1:268–539.

6. See Simon Tugwell, O.P., in his introduction to the Aquinas selections in his *Albert & Thomas: Selected Writings* (New York: Paulist Press, 1988), 213–15.

7. This biographical sketch relies heavily on James Weisheipl, O.P., *Friar Thomas d'Aquino,* rev. ed. (Washington, D.C.: Catholic University of America Press, 1983); and on Tugwell's introduction to the selections of Thomas in his *Albert & Thomas: Selected Writings.*

8. In the prologue to the translation of Avicenna's *De anima* can be found a participant's description of the teamwork on the project. The writer translated the work into the vernacular and it was then turned into Latin. See *Avicenna Latinus, Liber De anima,* ed. S. Van Riet (Louvain: E. Peeters, 1972), 4, lines 21–26.

9. René Gauthier, preface to the Leonine edition of Thomas's *Sentencia libri De anima,* 235*–236*.

10. Bonaventure did this in two series of sermons, one devoted to the Decalogue, the other to the Gifts of the Holy Spirit. See *De decem praeceptis,* in *S. Bonaventurae Opera omnia* (Florence: Quarrachi, 1882–1902), 5:514, and *De donis spiritus sancti,* 5:496–98. The authoritative work on the Aristotle of the masters is Fernand Van Steenberghen, *Maître Siger de Brabant* (Louvain: Publications Universitaires, 1977).

11. See Ignatius Brady, O.F.M., "Questions at Paris, c. 1260–1270," *Archivum Franciscanum historicum* 61 (1968): 434–61; and "Background to the Condemnation of 1270: Master William of Baglione, OFM," *Franciscan Studies* 30 (1970): 6–48.

12. Tugwell, ed., *Albert & Thomas: Selected Writings,* 227.

13. See Tugwell, ed., 230–32. Among Aquinas's non-Dominican opponents was Henry of Ghent. The Augustinian Giles of Rome was a defender of Thomas.

14. For a sense of what it was like to study in Paris in the thirteenth century, see L.-J. Bataillon, O.P., "Les conditions de travail des maîtres de l'Université de Paris au xiiième siècle," *Revue des sciences philosophiques et théologiques* 67, no. 3 (1983): 417–32.

15. Thomas is taking on Averroists in the plural, and Siger is considered to be the main figure in a movement. Names of his companions are Bernier of Nivelles, John of Huy, John Fretel, and Robert of Neuville. See Van Steenberghen, *Maître Siger de Brabant,* 28 and n. 3; and "Publications récentes sur Siger de Brabant," *Historia Philosophiae Medii Aevi* 2 (1991): 1003–1010.

16. Gauthier, "Notes sur les débuts (1225–1240) du premier 'Averroisme,'" *Revue des sciences philosophiques et théologiques* 66, no. 2 (1982): 321–73. Gauthier discusses this as well in his preface to the Leonine edition of the *Sentencia libri De anima* (1984).

17. F. Stuart Crawford, ed., *Commentarium magnum in Aristotelis De anima libros* (Cambridge, Mass.: Medieval Academy, 1953).

18. Cf. Bernardo Carlos Bazán in his review of the Leonine edition of the *Sentencia, Revue des sciences philosophiques et théologiques* 69, no. 4 (1985): 528–31.

19. Fernand Van Steenberghen, *Thomas Aquinas and Radical Aristotelianism* (Washington, D.C.: Catholic University of America Press, 1980).

20. Van Steenberghen, *Maître Siger de Brabant,* 79.

21. This last, from whom thy look will pass to me
Conceals a spirit deep in meditation —
So deep, that death for him came all too slowly.
It is the light eternal of Siger,
Who, when he lectured in the Street of Straw,
Could syllogize unpalatable truths. (Canto 10)

22. Denfile and Chatelain, *Chartularium Universitatis Parisiensis* (Paris: Delalain, 1889), 1/432:486–87.

23. Bazán, *Siger de Brabant: Quaestiones in tertium De anima, De anima intellectiva, De aeternitate mundi* (Louvain: Publications Universitaires, 1972), 66*ff. (Subsequent references to this work will be abbreviated as *Quaestiones.*) See also the preface to the Leonine edition of the *De unitate intellectus,* 249–50.

24. The students at Paris were divided into "nations" indicating their country of origin. See Rashdall, 298–320.

25. Van Steenberghen, *Maître Siger de Brabant,* 33.

26. "There are three errors to be wary of in the sciences, for they put an end to Sacred Scripture, Christian faith and wisdom itself. The first concerns the cause of being, the second is contrary to the notion of understanding and the third is against orderly living. The error about the cause of being is the eternity of the world: to hold that the world is eternal. The error against the notion of understanding concerns fatal necessity: to hold that all things come about necessarily. The third is about the oneness of intellect in all" (*De donis spiritus sancti, Opera omnia,* Quarrachi, 5:498).

27. Bazán, *Quaestiones,* 67*–74*; 78*. (1) A logical exercise on the proposition "Every man is of necessity animal"; (2) the "Question where 'man is animal' would be true if no man existed?"; (3) *Compendium de generatione et corruptione;* (4) *Quaestiones in tertium De anima.*

28. Van Steenberghen, *Maître Siger de Brabant,* 50-54. He relies here on Albert Zimmermann's identification of this as a work of Siger in *Die Quaestionen des Siger von Brabant zur Physik des Aristoteles* (Cologne: Faculty of Philosophy, University of Cologne, 1956). See Bazán, *Siger de Brabant: Écrits de logique, de morale, et de physique* (Louvain: Publications Universitaires, 1974). (Subsequent references to this work will be abbreviated as *Écrits.*)

29. "Huic ergo sententiae firmiter adhaerendum est, nam cum fuerit considerata, acquiescat intellectus et sileat; recedat vanitas verborum in hac materia, ne cognitionem impediant" (Bazán, *Écrits,* 59, lines 16–18).

30. "Et hoc est haeresis" (Bazán, *Écrits,* 165, lines 8–9).

31. "Credo tamen quod omne factum novum est et quod non oportet omne factum habere principium ex quo fiat. Et cum arguunt philosophi quod non fit aliquid nisi possibile sit ipsum esse per suam naturam, dicendum quod illud quod fit est dupliciter: aut secundum transmutationem, et sic bene arguunt: illud enim quod fit per transmutationem, habet ex quo fit; aut fit aliquid ex nihilo non per transmutationem, et sic non valet eorum ratio. Vel dicendum quod non oportet factum habere ex quo fiat, immo sufficit ad hoc potentia agentis potentissimi" (Bazán, *Écrits,* 181–82, lines 58–66).

32. Van Steenberghen, *Maître Siger de Brabant,* 405.

Thomas's Latin is not easily altered; therefore, I have taken few liberties for the sake of style in the translation. I only hope that the
result is intelligible English. C. S. Lewis has observed that medieval
Latin was a living language, unlike the closet classicism of the Renaissance with its sterile attempts to mimic the style of a long-gone
day. In reviving Latin, the men of the Renaissance managed to
make it a dead language. The language of our text, on the other
hand, is alive and lively. Thomas obviously wrote his attack on the
"Averroists"—all Christian contemporaries of his in Paris—in one
compositional burst. The work is well organized and well argued,
and its language serves its purpose. The engrossing issues it covers
make the repetitiveness of phrase and syntactic construction, as
well as the limited vocabulary, less noticeable. In this sense, the
style of the opusculum is an accomplished one. It does what it is
meant to do. We are not distracted by elegant turns of phrase nor
arrested by metaphors. The task of the translator is to find a coun-
terpart in English for such a style. Consequently, I have resisted
the temptation brought on by the labors of translation to make the
language of the text "interesting." The liberties I have taken are
meant to prevent my version from obscuring the argument.

I am grateful to Father Louis Bataillon, O.P., of the Leonine
Commission, and Father Mateus Cardoso Peres, O.P., assistant to
the master of the Dominican Order for the Intellectual Life, for per-
mission to include the critical Leonine edition of the text of the *De
unitate intellectus*. I have added the paragraph numbers of the
Keeler edition to facilitate checking references.

De unitate intellectus

Capitvlvm I

(1)   Sicut omnes homines naturaliter scire desiderant
ueritatem, ita naturale desiderium inest hominibus
fugiendi errores et eos cum facultas affuerit
confutandi. Inter alios autem errores indecentior
esse uidetur error quo circa intellectum erratur, per   5
quem nati sumus deuitatis erroribus cognoscere
ueritatem. Inoleuit siquidem iam dudum circa
intellectum error apud multos, ex dictis Auerroys
sumens originem, qui asserere nititur intellectum
quem Aristotiles possibilem uocat, ipse autem   10
inconuenienti nomine materialem, esse quandam
substantiam secundum esse a corpore separatam,
nec aliquo modo uniri ei ut forma; et ulterius
quod iste intellectus possibilis sit unus omnium
hominum. Contra que iam pridem plura conscrip-   15
simus; sed quia errantium impudentia non cessat
ueritati reniti, propositum nostre intentionis est
iterato contra eundem errorem conscribere aliqua
quibus manifeste predictus error confutetur.

(2)   Nec id nunc agendum est ut positionem   20
predictam in hoc ostendamus esse erroneam
quod repugnat ueritati fidei christiane; hoc enim
satis in promptu cuique apparere potest. Subtracta
enim ab hominibus diuersitate intellectus, qui solus
inter anime partes incorruptibilis et immortalis   25
apparet, sequitur post mortem nichil de animabus
hominum remanere nisi unicam intellectus substantiam; et sic tollitur retributio premiorum et
penarum et diuersitas eorundem. Intendimus
autem ostendere positionem predictam non minus   30
contra philosophie principia esse quam contra
fidei documenta. Et quia quibusdam, ut dicunt,
in hac materia uerba Latinorum non sapiunt,
sed Peripateticorum uerba sectari se dicunt,
quorum libros numquam in hac materia uiderunt   35
nisi Aristotilis, qui fuit secte peripatetice institutor,
ostendemus primo positionem predictam eius
uerbis et sententie repugnare omnino.

On There Being Only One Intellect

Chapter 1

(1) All men by nature desire to know the truth;[1] they also have a natural desire to avoid error and to refute it when the opportunity arises. Since we have been given an intellect in order to know truth and avoid error, it seems singularly inappropriate to be mistaken about it. For a long time now there has been widespread an error concerning intellect that originates in the writings of Averroes. He seeks to maintain that what Aristotle calls the possible, but he infelicitously calls the material, intellect is a substance which, existing separately from the body, is in no way united to it as its form, and furthermore that this possible intellect is one for all men. We have already written much in refutation of this,[2] but because those mistaken on this matter continue impudently to oppose the truth, it is our intention once more to write against this error and in such a way that it is decisively refuted.

(2) There is no need now to show that the foregoing position is erroneous because repugnant to Christian faith; a moment's reflection makes this clear to anyone. Take away from men diversity of intellect, which alone among the soul's parts seems incorruptible and immortal, and it follows that nothing of the souls of men would remain after death except a unique intellectual substance, with the result that reward and punishment and their difference disappear. We intend to show that the foregoing position is opposed to the principles of philosophy every bit as much as it is to the teaching of faith. And, Latin writers on this matter not being to the taste of some, who tell us that they prefer to follow the words of the Peripatetics, though of them they have seen only the works of Aristotle, the founder of the school, we will first show the foregoing position to be in every way repugnant to his words and judgments.

---

1   *Metaphysics,* 1.1.980a22. The numbers in brackets at the beginning of paragraphs are those of Keeler, whose edition of the text provided the standard for references from its appearance in 1936. References to *On the Soul* will be identified with the Bekker page, column, and lines in parentheses.

2   For example, in his commentary on the *Sentences* of Peter Lombard, II, d. 17, q. 2, a. 1; *Summa contra gentiles,* book 2, chaps. 59–70; *Summa theologiae,* I, q. 75, articles 1 and 2; *Disputed Question on Spiritual Creatures,* articles 2 and 9; *Disputed Question on the Soul,* articles 2 and 3.

(3)   Accipienda est igitur prima diffinitio anime
quam Aristotiles in II De anima ponit, dicens   40
quod anima est "actus primus corporis phisici
organici". Et ne forte aliquis diceret hanc
diffinitionem non omni anime competere, propter
hoc quod supra sub condicione dixerat "Si
oportet aliquid commune in omni anima dicere",   45
quod intelligunt sic dictum quasi hoc esse non
possit, accipienda sunt uerba eius sequentia.
Dicit enim "Vniuersaliter quidem igitur dictum
est quid sit anima: substantia enim est que est
secundum rationem; hoc autem est quod quid   50
erat esse huiusmodi corpori", id est forma
substantialis corporis phisici organici.

(4)   Et ne forte dicatur ab hac uniuersalitate partem
intellectiuam excludi, hoc remouetur per id quod
postea dicit "Quod quidem igitur non sit anima   55
separabilis a corpore, aut partes quedam ipsius
si partibilis apta nata est, non immanifestum est:
quarundam enim partium actus est ipsarum. At
uero secundum quasdam nichil prohibet, propter
id quod nullius corporis sunt actus"; quod non   60
potest intelligi nisi de hiis que ad partem intellectiuam pertinent, puta intellectus et uoluntas. Ex
quo manifeste ostenditur illius anime, quam
supra uniuersaliter diffinierat dicens eam esse
corporis actum, quasdam partes esse que sunt   65
quarundam partium corporis actus, quasdam
autem nullius corporis actus esse. Aliud enim
est animam esse actum corporis, et aliud partem
eius esse corporis actum, ut infra manifestabitur.
Vnde et in hoc eodem capitulo manifestat   70
animam esse actum corporis per hoc quod
alique partes eius sunt corporis actus, cum dicit
"Considerare oportet in partibus quod dictum
est", scilicet in toto.

(3) Let us then take up the first definition of soul that Aristotle gives in book 2 of *On the Soul* (412b5): "the first act of a physically organized body." And lest some should say this definition does not cover every soul because of the earlier conditional remark, "If, then, we have to give a general formula applicable to all kinds of soul" (412b4), which they take to mean that it cannot be done, the words which follow should be taken into account. For he writes, "We have now given a general answer to the question, What is soul? It is substance in the sense which corresponds to the account of a thing" (412b8–12); that is, the substantial form of a physically organized body.

(4) The sequel answers those who might say that the intellective part is excluded from the range of this definition. "From this it is clear that the soul is inseparable from its body, or at any rate that certain parts of it are (if it has parts)—for the actuality of some of them is the actuality of the parts themselves. Yet some may be separable because they are not the actualities of any body at all" (413a4–7), which can only be understood of those which belong to the intellective part, namely, intellect and will. From this it is clear that some parts of the soul defined in general as being the act of the body are acts of some parts of the body, whereas others are not the acts of any body. It is one thing for the soul to be the act of body and another for some part of it to be the act of body, as will be argued below. In this same chapter he shows the soul to be the act of body because some of its parts are acts of body: "We must apply what has been said [of the whole] to the parts" (412b17).

(5)   Adhuc autem manifestius ex sequentibus apparet   75
quod sub hac generalitate diffinitionis etiam
intellectus includitur, per ea que sequntur. Nam
cum satis probauerit animam esse actum corporis
quia separata anima non est uiuens in actu, quia
tamen aliquid potest dici actu tale ad presentiam   80
alicuius, non solum si sit forma sed etiam si sit
motor, sicut combustibile ad presentiam combu-
rentis actu comburitur, et quodlibet mobile ad
presentiam mouentis actu mouetur: posset alicui
uenire in dubium utrum corpus sic uiuat actu   85
ad presentiam anime sicut mobile mouetur actu
ad presentiam motoris, an sicut materia est in
actu ad presentiam forme; et precipue quia
Plato posuit animam non uniri corpori ut formam,
sed magis ut motorem et rectorem, ut patet per   90
Plotinum et Gregorium Nissenum, quos ideo
induco quia non fuerunt Latini sed Greci. Hanc
igitur dubitationem insinuat Philosophus cum
post premissa subiungit "Amplius autem immanifestum si sic corporis actus anima sicut nauta   95
nauis".

(5) From the sequel it is even clearer that the intellect is covered by this general definition. The fact that the body no longer actually lives when the soul is separated from it is taken to be sufficient proof that soul is the act of body. However, because something could be said to be in act thanks to the presence of something other than form, of a mover, say, as the combustible actually burns when fire is present, and the moveable actually moves when the mover is present, one might wonder whether the body actually lives thanks to the presence of soul in the same way that the mobile moves at the presence of the mover, rather than as matter is in act, thanks to the presence of form. The doubt can feed on the fact that Plato said soul is united to body not as form but rather as mover and director. This is clear from Plotinus and Gregory of Nyssa—whom I mention because they were Greeks, not Latins. The Philosopher invites this doubt when, to what has been quoted, he adds, "Further, we have no light on the problem whether the soul may not be the actuality of its body in the sense in which the sailor is the actuality of the ship" (413a8–10).

(6)   Quia igitur post premissa adhuc hoc
dubium remanebat, concludit "Figuraliter quidem
igitur sic determinetur et describatur de anima",
quia scilicet nondum ad liquidum demonstrauerat
ueritatem.   100

    Ad hanc igitur dubitationem tollendam, conse-
quenter procedit ad manifestandum id quod est
secundum se et secundum rationem certius, per
ea que sunt minus certa secundum se sed magis
certa quoad nos, id est per effectus anime qui   105
sunt actus ipsius. Vnde statim distinguit opera
anime, dicens quod "animatum distinguitur ab
inanimato in uiuendo", et quod multa sunt que
pertinent ad uitam, scilicet "intellectus, sensus,
motus et status secundum locum", et motus   110
nutrimenti et augmenti, ita quod cuicumque
inest aliquod horum dicitur uiuere. Et ostenso
quomodo ista se habeant ad inuicem, id est
qualiter unum sine altero horum possit esse,
concludit in hoc quod anima sit omnium predic-   115
torum principium, et quod anima "determinatur
—sicut per suas partes—uegetatiuo, sensitiuo,
intellectiuo, motu", et quia hec omnia contingit
in uno et eodem inueniri, sicut in homine.

(6) It was because this doubt remained after what he said that he concludes, "This must suffice as our sketch or outline of the nature of soul" (413a11–13); he has not yet shown the truth with full clarity.

Therefore, in order to remove this doubt, he proceeds to make manifest that which is more certain both in itself and in definition through what is less certain in itself but more certain for us, that is, through effects of the soul which are its acts. Thus he immediately distinguishes the works of the soul, saying that "what has soul in it differs from what has not in that the former displays life" (413a21– 25), and that there are many levels of life, namely, "intellect, sense, motion, and rest according to place," the motion of nourishing and growth, such that anything in which one of these is found is said to live. Having shown how these [levels] are interrelated, that is, how one of them might be found without the other, he concludes that the soul is the principle of them all both because the soul "is specified (as by its parts) vegetative, sensitive, intellective, and motor" (413b11– 13), and because all these happen to be found in one and the same thing, for example, in man.

(7)   Et Plato posuit diuersas esse animas in homine,   120
secundum quas diuerse operationes uite ei
conueniant. Consequenter dubitationem mouet
"Vtrum unumquodque horum sit anima" per
se, uel sit aliqua pars anime; et si sint partes
unius anime, utrum differant solum secundum   125
rationem, aut etiam differant loco, id est organo.
Et subiungit quod "de quibusdam non difficile"
hoc uidetur, sed quedam sunt que dubitationem
habent. Ostendit enim consequenter quod manifestum est de hiis que pertinent ad animam   130
uegetabilem, et de hiis que pertinent ad animam
sensibilem, per hoc quod plante et animalia
quedam decisa uiuunt, et in qualibet parte
omnes operationes anime que sunt in toto
apparent. Sed de quibus dubitationem habeat,   135
ostendit subdens quod "de intellectu et perspectiua potentia nichil adhuc manifestum est".
Quod non dicit uolens ostendere quod intellectus
non sit anima, ut Commentator peruerse exponit
et sectatores ipsius: manifeste enim hoc respondet   140
ad id quod supra dixerat "Quedam enim dubitationem habent". Vnde intelligendum est:
nichil adhuc manifestum est, an intellectus sit
anima uel pars anime; et si pars anime, utrum
separata loco, uel ratione tantum.   145

(7) Plato held that, insofar as these diverse operations pertain to man, there are diverse souls in him. Consequently he [Aristotle] asks "whether each of these is a soul" by itself or a part of the soul, and, if they are parts of one soul, whether they differ in definition alone or also in place, that is, by organ. And, he adds, "of some it is not difficult" to see how it is, but there are others that give rise to doubt (413b13–26). Consequently, he shows (413b16–21) that in this regard things are clear in vegetable and sensible soul because some plants and animals go on living when divided, and all the operations that were in the whole appear in each part. When he adds that "we have no evidence as yet about mind and the power to think" (413b24–25), he makes it clear where the question arises. By saying this he does not mean to show that intellect is not soul, as the Commentator and his followers perversely interpret him, for he clearly says this in response to what was said earlier, "but some present a difficulty" (413b16). This should be understood thus: It is not yet clear whether intellect is a soul or a part of soul, and if it is a part of the soul, whether it is separate in place or in definition only.

(8)   Et quamuis dicat hoc adhuc non esse manifestum, tamen quid circa hoc prima fronte
appareat manifestat subdens "Sed uidetur genus
alterum anime esse". Quod non est intelligendum,
sicut Commentator et sectatores eius peruerse   150
exponunt, ideo dictum esse quia intellectus
equiuoce dicatur anima, uel quod predicta diffinitio
sibi aptari non possit; sed qualiter sit hoc
intelligendum apparet ex eo quod subditur "Et
hoc solum contingere separari sicut perpetuum   155
a corruptibili". In hoc ergo est alterum genus,
quod intellectus uidetur esse quoddam perpetuum,
alie autem partes anime corruptibiles. Et quia
corruptibile et perpetuum non uidentur in unam
substantiam conuenire posse, uidetur quod hoc   160
solum de partibus anime, scilicet intellectus,
contingat separari, non quidem a corpore, ut
Commentator peruerse exponit, sed ab aliis
partibus anime, ne in unam substantiam anime
conueniant.   165

(9)   Et quod sic sit intelligendum patet ex eo
quod subditur "Relique autem partes anime
manifestum est ex hiis quod non separabiles
sunt", scilicet substantia anime uel loco. De
hoc enim supra quesitum est, et hoc ex supradictis   170
probatum est. Et quod non intelligatur de
separabilitate a corpore sed de separabilitate
potentiarum ab inuicem, patet per hoc quod
subditur "Ratione autem quod altere", scilicet
sunt ad inuicem, "manifestum: sensitiuo enim   175
esse et opinatiuo alterum". Et sic manifeste
quod hic determinatur respondet questioni supra
mote: supra enim quesitum est, utrum una
pars anime ab alia separata sit ratione solum,
aut et loco. Hic dimissa questione ista quantum   180
ad intellectum, de quo nichil hic determinat, de
aliis partibus anime dicit manifestum esse quod
non sunt separabiles, scilicet loco, sed sunt
altere ratione.

(8) Although he says that it is not yet clear, he nonetheless indicates what at first blush appears to be the case by adding, "It seems to be a widely different kind of soul" (413b25–26). This should not be understood as it perversely is by the Commentator and his followers: namely, that the intellect is equivocally called soul or that the foregoing definition cannot be adapted to it. How it ought to be understood is clear from what he adds: "It alone is capable of existence in isolation from all other psychic powers, as the perpetual from the corruptible" (413b26–27). Therefore it is of another kind in the sense that intellect appears to be something perpetual, whereas the other parts of the soul are corruptible. And because the perpetual and corruptible do not seem to characterize the same substance, apparently only this part of the soul—namely, intellect—can be separated; not indeed from body, as the Commentator perversely interprets, but from other parts of the soul, lest they characterize the same substance, soul.

(9) That this is how it should be understood is clear from what he adds: "From these remarks it is clear that the other parts of the soul are not separable" (413b27–28), namely, from the substance of the soul or by place. When this was asked earlier, the question was resolved from what had just been said. That it is not to be understood as the separability from body but as the separability of the powers from one another is clear from what he adds: "that as understood they are distinguishable by definition"—namely, from one another—"is clear; for to sense and to have an opinion are different" (413b29–30). Thus what is said here is manifestly in response to the question raised earlier when he asked whether one part of the soul is separated from another in understanding alone or in place. Having set aside this question about intellect, concerning which he determines nothing here, he says it is manifest with respect to the other parts of the soul that they are not separable—that is, in place—but that they differ as understood.

(10)   Hoc ergo habito quod anima determinatur   185
uegetatiuo, sensitiuo, intellectiuo et motu, uult
ostendere consequenter quod, quantum ad omnes
istas partes, anima unitur corpori non sicut
nauta naui sed sicut forma. Et sic certificatum
erit quid sit anima in communi, quod supra   190
figuraliter tantum dictum est. Hoc autem probat
per operationes anime sic: manifestum est enim
quod illud quo primo aliquid operatur est forma
operantis, sicut dicimur scire anima et scire
scientia, per prius autem scientia quam anima,   195
quia per animam non scimus nisi in quantum
habet scientiam; et similiter sanari dicimur et
corpore et sanitate, sed per prius sanitate. Et sic
patet scientiam esse formam anime, et sanitatem
corporis.   200

(11)   Ex hoc procedit sic: "Anima est primum quo
uiuimus", quod dicit propter uegetatiuum, "quo
sentimus", propter sensitiuum, "et mouemur",
propter motiuum, "et intelligimus", propter
intellectiuum; et concludit "Quare ratio quedam   205
utique erit et species, sed non ut materia et ut
subiectum". Manifeste ergo quod supra dixerat,
animam esse actum corporis phisici, hic concludit
non solum de sensitiuo, uegetatiuo et motiuo,
sed etiam de intellectiuo. Fuit ergo sententia   210
Aristotilis quod id quo intelligimus sit forma
corporis phisici. Sed ne aliquis dicat: id quo
intelligimus non dicit hic intellectum possibilem,
sed aliquid aliud, manifeste hoc excluditur per
id quod Aristotiles in III De anima dicit, de   215
intellectu possibili loquens "Dico autem intellectum, quo opinatur et intelligit anima".

(10) It being established therefore that the soul is defined by the vegetative, sensitive, intellective, and locomotive parts, he intends to show next that, with respect to each of these, the soul is united to body as form, not as a sailor to his boat. And thus what was previously established only in outline is made certain. He proves this through the operations of the soul in this way: It is manifest that that whereby something first operates is the act of the one operating. For example, we are said to know both through the soul and through science, but first of all through science rather than through the soul—we know through the soul only insofar as it has science; similarly we are said to be healed by the body and by health, but first of all by health. Thus it is clear that science is the form of the soul and health of the body.

(11) He continues thus: "The soul is that whereby we first live," referring to the vegetative; "that whereby we sense," referring to the sensitive; "and move," referring to the locomotive; "and understand," referring to the intellective. He concludes: "It follows that the soul must be an account and essence, not matter or a subject" (414a12– 14). Manifestly, therefore, he applies here what he said above, [namely,] that the soul is the act of a physical body, not only to the sensitive, vegetative, and motive but also to the intellective. It was Aristotle's judgment, therefore, that that whereby we understand is the form of the physical body. Should someone say that that with which we understand does not here mean the possible intellect but something else, this is clearly excluded by what Aristotle says in book 3 of *On the Soul,* speaking of the possible intellect: "I call intellect that whereby the soul thinks and understands" (429a23).

(12)   Sed antequam ad uerba Aristotilis que sunt in
III De anima accedamus, adhuc amplius circa
uerba ipsius in II De anima immoremur, ut ex   220
collatione uerborum eius ad inuicem appareat
que fuerit eius sententia de anima. Cum enim
animam in communi diffinisset, incipit distinguere
potentias eius; et dicit quod potentie anime sunt
"uegetatiuum, sensitiuum, appetitiuum, motiuum   225
secundum locum, intellectiuum". Et quod intellectiuum sit intellectus, patet per id quod postea
subdit, diuisionem, explanans "Alteris autem
intellectiuum et intellectus, ut hominibus". Vult
ergo quod intellectus est potentia anime que est   230
actus corporis.

(13)   Et quod huius anime potentiam dixerit intellectum, et iterum quod supra posita diffinitio anime
sit omnibus predictis partibus communis, patet
per id quod concludit "Manifestum igitur est   235
quoniam eodem modo una utique erit ratio
anime et figure: neque enim ibi figura est preter
triangulum et que consequenter sunt, neque hic
anima preter predictas est". Non est ergo
querenda alia anima preter predictas, quibus   240
communis est anime diffinitio supra posita. Neque
plus de intellectu mentionem facit Aristotiles
in hoc secundo, nisi quod postmodum subdit quod
"ultimum et minimum" dicit esse "ratiocina-
tionem et intellectum", quia scilicet in paucioribus   245
est, ut per sequentia apparet.

(12) But before we turn to what Aristotle says in book 3 of *On the Soul,* let us linger on what he has said in book 2 so that his teaching on the soul may become apparent by comparing his statements. For, having defined the soul in general, he begins to distinguish its powers and says that the powers of the soul are "the vegetative, sensitive, appetitive, locomotive, intellective" (414a31–32). And it is evident that the intellective is the intellect from what he afterwards adds in explanation of the division: "In others, the thinking faculty and intellect, as in men" (414b18). He holds, therefore, that the intellect is a power of the soul, which is the act of body.

(13) And it is clear from his conclusion that he calls the intellect a power of this soul and, moreover, that the definition of the soul given above is common to all the aforesaid parts: "It is now evident that a single definition can be given of soul in the same way that one can be given of figure. For, as in that case, there is no figure apart from triangle and those that follow in order; here there is no soul apart from the forms of soul just enumerated" (414b19–22). One ought not then seek any soul apart from those mentioned, to which the definition of soul given above is common. Aristotle makes no further mention of intellect in the second book except when he says that "reasoning and intellect" are "ultimately and rarely" (415a7) because they are in fewer things, as the sequel makes clear.

(14)   Sed quia magna differentia est quantum ad
modum operandi inter intellectum et ymagina-
tionem, subdit quod "de speculatiuo intellectu
altera ratio est". Reseruat enim hoc inquirendum   250
usque ad tertium. Et ne quis dicat, sicut Auerroys
peruerse exponit, quod ideo dicit Aristotiles quod
de intellectu speculatiuo est alia ratio, quia
intellectus "neque est anima neque pars anime":
statim hoc excluditur in principio tertii, ubi   255
resumit de intellectu tractatum. Dicit enim "De
parte autem anime qua cognoscit anima et sapit".
Nec debet aliquis dicere quod hoc dicatur solum
secundum quod intellectus possibilis diuiditur
contra agentem, sicut aliqui sompniant; hoc   260
enim dictum est antequam Aristotiles probet
esse intellectum possibilem et agentem: unde
intellectum dicit hic partem in communi, secundum quod continet et agentem et possibilem, sicut
supra in secundo manifeste distinxit intellectum   265
contra alias partes anime, ut iam dictum est.

(15)   Est autem consideranda mirabilis diligentia et
ordo in processu Aristotilis: ab hiis enim incipit
in tertio tractare de intellectu que in secundo
reliquerat indeterminata. Duo autem supra reli-   270
querat indeterminata circa intellectum. Primo
quidem utrum intellectus ab aliis partibus anime
separetur ratione solum, aut etiam loco: quod
quidem indeterminatum dimisit cum dixit "De
intellectu autem et perspectiua potentia nichil   275
adhuc manifestum est". Et hanc questionem
primo resumit cum dicit "Siue separabili exis-
tente", scilicet ab aliis anime partibus, "siue
non separabili secundum magnitudinem, sed
secundum rationem". Pro eodem enim accipit   280
hic separabile secundum magnitudinem, pro quo
supra dixerat separabile loco.

(14) Because there is a great difference between the ways in which intellect and imagination operate, he adds that "there is another account of speculative intellect" (415a11–12). This inquiry he reserves to the third book. And lest someone suggest, as Averroes perversely does, that Aristotle speaks of another account of speculative intellect because the intellect is "neither soul nor a part of soul,"[3] this is immediately excluded at the beginning of book 3, where he takes up again the treatment of intellect, for he says, "Concerning the part of the soul whereby the soul knows and understands" (429a10–11). Nor should anyone think that this is said only insofar as the possible intellect is divided against the agent intellect, as some wildly imagine, for the remark occurs before Aristotle proves there is an agent and possible intellect. Hence, he here means by intellect that part in general, insofar as it contains both agent and possible. In much the same way, early in the second book, he manifestly distinguished intellect from the other parts of the soul, as has already been pointed out.

(15) Notice the marvelous care and order of Aristotle's procedure, beginning in book 3 with the treatment of the questions concerning intellect left undetermined in the second. There were two. First, whether intellect is separated from other parts of the soul only as understood or in place, too; which indeed he left undetermined when he said, "We have no evidence as yet about thought or the power of reflection" (413b24–25). First, he takes up this question again when he says, "Whether this is separable from the others," namely, from the other parts of the soul, "in definition only, or spatially as well" (429a11–12). "Spatially separable" here means the same as "separable in place" above.

---

3 Averroes, *In II De anima,* comm. 32 (Crawford edition), 178.34–35. The second book ends at 424b18 and the third begins at 424b22—the apparently missing lines explained by the set-off Gamma announcing the new book. The Marietti edition of Thomas's commentary on *On the Soul* distributes the Thomistic text according to this division of the books. The more recent Leonine edition makes it clear that the text Thomas used ended the second book at 429a8. He has this division in mind here in the text: the fourth chapter of book 3, with which Thomas's third book begins, deals with intellect. This is also the way the Arabs divided the second and third books. Keeler, misled perhaps by the Marietti edition, was unaware that Thomas and the Arabs divided the books in the same way, and speculated that Thomas followed the division here so that his textual points would be more easily located by his opponents.

(16)   Secundo, indeterminatum reliquerat de differentia intellectus ad alias anime partes, cum
postmodum dixit "De speculatiuo autem intellectu   285
altera ratio est". Et hoc statim querit cum dicit
"Considerandum quam habet differentiam". Hanc
autem differentiam talem intendit assignare, que
possit stare cum utroque premissorum, scilicet
siue sit separabilis anima magnitudine seu loco   290
ab aliis partibus, siue non; quod ipse modus
loquendi satis indicat. Considerandum enim dicit
quam habet intellectus differentiam ad alias anime
partes, siue sit separabilis ab eis magnitudine
seu loco, id est subiecto, siue non, sed secundum   295
rationem tantum. Vnde manifestum est quod
non intendit hanc differentiam ostendere, quod
sit substantia a corpore separata secundum esse,
hoc enim non posset saluari cum utroque
predictorum; sed intendit assignare differentiam   300
quantum ad modum operandi: unde subdit
"Et quomodo fit quidem ipsum intelligere".
Sic igitur per ea que ex uerbis Aristotilis accipere
possumus usque huc, manifestum est quod ipse
uoluit intellectum esse partem anime que est   305
actus corporis phisici.

(17)   Sed quia ex quibusdam uerbis consequentibus
Auerroyste accipere uolunt intentionem Aristotilis
fuisse, quod intellectus non sit anima que est
actus corporis, aut pars talis anime: ideo etiam   310
diligentius eius uerba sequentia consideranda
sunt. Statim igitur post questionem motam de
differentia intellectus et sensus, inquirit secundum
quid intellectus sit similis sensui, et secundum
quid ab eo differat. Duo enim supra de sensu   315
determinauerat, scilicet quod sensus est in potentia
ad sensibilia, et quod sensus patitur et corrumpitur
ab excellentiis sensibilium. Hoc ergo est quod
querit Aristotiles dicens "Si igitur est intelligere
sicut sentire, aut pati aliquid utique erit ab   320
intelligibili", ut scilicet sic corrumpatur intellectus
ab excellenti intelligibili sicut sensus ab excellenti
sensibili, "aut aliquid huiusmodi alterum": id
est aut intelligere est aliquid huiusmodi simile,
scilicet ei quod est sentire, alterum tamen quantum   325
ad hoc quod non sit passibile.

(16) Second, he left unanswered the question concerning intellect's difference from the other parts of the soul when he said later, "Reflective thought presents a different problem" (415a11–12). And he immediately begins to inquire into this when he says, "We have to inquire what differentiates this part" (429a12). He intends to express this difference in such a way that it is compatible with both possibilities mentioned; that is, whether or not it is a soul separable in extension or place from the other parts, as this way of speaking sufficiently indicates. For he says we ought to consider what the difference is between the intellect and the other parts of the soul; whether it is separable from them in size or place—that is, in subject—or not, or only in understanding. Hence, it is clear that he does not intend to give as the difference that it is a substance existing separately from the body, for this would not be compatible with the foregoing; rather, he intends to assign a difference according to the mode of operating. Hence, he adds, ". . . and how thinking takes place" (429a13). Therefore, from what we can learn from the words of Aristotle up to this point, he clearly held that intellect is a part of the soul, which is the act of a physical body.

(17) But because from some words following on these the Averroists wish to take Aristotle's intention to be that the intellect is not the soul—which is the act of the body—or a part of such a soul, we must even more carefully consider what he goes on to say. Immediately after he raised the question about the difference between intellect and sense, he asked in what intellect is like sense and how the two differ. Earlier he established two things about sense, namely, that sense is in potency to sensible objects, and that sense is affected and corrupted by excessive sensible objects. That is what Aristotle has in mind when he says, "If thinking is like perceiving, it must be either a process in which the soul is acted upon by what is capable of being thought" (429a13–15) in such a way that the intellect would be corrupted by something excessively intelligible as sense is by an excessively sensible object, "or a process different from but analogous to that." That is, understanding is something similar to sensing, but different in this, that it is not affected.

(18)   Huic igitur questioni statim respondet et
concludit, non ex precedentibus sed ex sequentibus, que tamen ex precedentibus manifestantur,
quod hanc partem anime "oportet esse impas-   330
sibilem", ut non corrumpatur sicut sensus;
est tamen quedam alia passio eius secundum quod
intelligere communi modo pati dicitur. In hoc
ergo differt a sensu. Sed consequenter ostendit
in quo cum sensu conueniat, quia scilicet oportet   335
huiusmodi partem esse "susceptiuam speciei"
intelligibilis, et quod sit in potentia ad huiusmodi
speciem, et quod non sit hoc in actu secundum
suam naturam; sicut et de sensu supra dictum
est quod est in potentia ad sensibilia, et non in   340
actu. Et ex hoc concludit quod oportet sic "se
habere sicut sensitiuum ad sensibilia sic intellectum
ad intelligibilia".

(19)   Hoc autem induxit ad excludendum opinionem
Empedoclis et aliorum antiquorum, qui posuerunt   345
quod cognoscens est de natura cogniti, utpote
quod terram terra cognoscimus, aquam aqua.
Aristotiles autem supra ostendit hoc non esse
uerum in sensu, quia sensitiuum non est actu,
sed potentia, ea que sentit; et idem hic dicit de   350
intellectu.
     Est autem differentia inter sensum et intellec-
tum, quia sensus non est cognoscitiuus omnium,
sed uisus colorum tantum, auditus sonorum, et
sic de aliis; intellectus autem est simpliciter   355
omnium cognoscitiuus. Dicebant autem antiqui
philosophi, estimantes quod cognoscens debet
habere naturam cogniti, quod anima ad hoc quod
cognoscat omnia, necesse est ex principiis omnium
esse commixtam. Quia uero Aristotiles iam   360
probauit de intellectu per similitudinem sensus,
quod non est actu id quod cognoscit sed in
potentia tantum, concludit e contrario quod
'necesse est intellectum, quia cognoscit omnia,
quod sit immixtus', id est non compositus ex   365
omnibus, sicut Empedocles ponebat.

(18) He responds to this question immediately, concluding—not from what went before but from what follows, which, however, is made clear from what went before—that this part of the soul "must be impassible" (429a15) in order that it not be corrupted like the senses. There is, however, another way of being acted upon that is characteristic of understanding according to which it can be said to suffer in a general sense of the term. In this, then, it is different from the senses. He goes on to show in what it is like the senses, namely, that this part of the soul must be "capable of receiving the intelligible form of the object" (429a15–16) and that it be in potency to this kind of form, not actually being it in its own nature; so, too, earlier it was said of sense that it is potentially, not actually, sensibles. From this he concludes that "thought must be related to what is thinkable, as sense is to what is sensible" (429a16–18).

(19) He brought this out to exclude the opinion of Empedocles (see 404b8–405b30) and other ancients who held that the knower is of the nature of the known, as if we knew earth through earth and water through water. Aristotle showed earlier (417a2–9) that this is not true of sense because the sensitive power is potentially, not actually, the things it senses, and he says the same here of intellect.

There is, however, this difference between sense and intellect, that sense is not capable of knowing everything (sight is of colors alone, hearing of sounds, and thus with the others), whereas the intellect is capable of knowing all things whatsoever. Ancient philosophers (see 405b10–17), thinking that the knower must have the nature of the known, said that in order for the soul to know all things, it was necessary that the principles of all things be mingled in it. Aristotle, having proved by analogy with sense that intellect is not actually but potentially what it knows, concludes on the contrary that "intellect, because it knows all things, must be unmixed" (429a18); that is, not composed of all things, as Empedocles held.

(20)   Et ad hoc inducit testimonium Anaxagore,
non tamen de hoc eodem intellectu loquentis,
sed de intellectu qui mouet omnia. Sicut ergo
Anaxagoras dixit illum intellectum esse immixtum   370
ut imperet mouendo et segregando, hoc nos
possumus dicere de intellectu humano, quod
oportet eum esse immixtum ad hoc ut cognoscat
omnia; et hoc probat consequenter, et habetur
sic sequens littera in Greco "Intus apparens   375
enim prohibebit extraneum et obstruet". Quod
potest intelligi ex simili in uisu: si enim esset
aliquis color intrinsecus pupille, ille color interior
prohiberet uideri extraneum colorem, et quodammodo obstrueret oculum ne alia uideret.   380

(21)   Similiter, si aliqua natura rerum que intellectus
cognoscit,puta terra aut aqua, aut calidum et frigidum, et
aliquid huiusmodi, esset intrinseca intellectui, illa
natura intrinseca impediret ipsum et quodammodo
obstrueret ne alia cognosceret.   385
      Quia ergo omnia cognoscit, concludit quod
non contingit ipsum habere aliquam naturam
determinatam ex naturis sensibilibus quas cognoscit, 'sed hanc solam naturam habet quod sit
possibilis', id est in potentia ad ea que intelligit,   390
quantum est ex sua natura; sed fit actu illa dum
ea intelligit in actu, sicut sensus in actu fit sensibile
in actu, ut supra in secundo dixerat. Concludit
ergo quod intellectus antequam intelligat in actu
"nichil est actu eorum que sunt"; quod est   395
contrarium hiis que antiqui dicebant, quod est
actu omnia.

(22)   Et quia fecerat mentionem de dicto Anaxagore
loquentis de intellectu qui imperat omnibus, ne
crederetur de illo intellectu hoc conclusisse,   400
utitur tali modo loquendi "Vocatus itaque anime
intellectus, dico autem intellectum quo opinatur
et intelligit anima, nichil est actu" etc. Ex quo
duo apparent: primo quidem quod non loquitur
hic de intellectu qui sit aliqua substantia separata,   405
sed de intellectu quem supra dixit potentiam et
partem anime, quo anima intelligit; secundo,
quod per supra dicta probauit quod intellectus
non habet naturam in actu.

(20) In support of this, he invokes the testimony of Anaxagoras (429a19), who is not, however, speaking of the same intellect but rather of the intellect that moves all things. It was in order that it might command by moving and separating that Anaxagoras said the latter intellect is unmixed. His subsequent proof of this is found in the Greek text: "For the co-presence of what is alien to its nature is a hindrance and a block" (429a20). This can be understood from what is similar in sight, for if there were some intrinsic color of the pupil, this interior color would prevent an outer color from being seen and in that way would prevent the eye from seeing others.

(21) Similarly, if one of the natures of the things that the intellect knows—earth or water, hot or cold, or some such thing—were intrinsic to intellect, that intrinsic nature would impede it and in a way obstruct it from knowing others.

Because it knows all things, therefore, he concludes that "it can have no nature of its own, other than that of having a certain capacity" (429a21–22). That is, its own nature is to be potentially those things that it understands; but it actually becomes them when it actually knows them, just as sense in act actually becomes the sensible, as was said above in the second book. Intellect, before it actually understands, he therefore concludes, "is not actually any real thing" (429a24), which is the opposite of what the ancients said, namely, that it actually is all things.

(22) Because he mentioned what Anaxagoras said in speaking of the intellect which commands all things, lest he be taken to be saying this of that intellect, he uses this manner of speaking: "That in the soul which is called intellect (by intellect I mean that whereby the soul thinks and judges) is before it thinks, not actually any real thing . . ." (429a22–24). From this two things are clear: first, that he is not speaking here of an intellect which is a separated substance but of the intellect he earlier called a power and part of the soul whereby the soul understands; second, that he proved, from what was said above, that the intellect actually has no nature.

(23)   Nondum autem
probauit quod non sit uirtus in corpore, ut   410
Auerroys dicit, sed hoc statim concludit ex
premissis, nam sequitur "Vnde neque misceri
est rationabile ipsum corpori".

   Et hoc secundum probat per primum quod
supra probauit, scilicet quod intellectus non habet   415
aliquam in actu de naturis rerum sensibilium;
ex quo patet quod non miscetur corpori, quia si
misceretur corpori, haberet aliquam de naturis
corporeis; et hoc est quod subdit "Qualis enim
aliquis utique fiet, aut calidus aut frigidus, si   420
organum aliquod erit sicut sensitiuo". Sensus
enim proportionatur suo organo et trahitur
quodammodo ad suam naturam; unde etiam
secundum immutationem organi immutatur ope-
ratio sensus. Sic ergo intelligitur istud 'non   425
misceri corpori', quia non habet organum sicut
sensus.

(24)   Et quod intellectus anime non habeat
organum, manifestat per dictum quorundam qui
dixerunt quod 'anima est locus specierum',
large accipientes locum pro omni receptiuo,   430
more platonico; nisi quod esse locum specierum
non conuenit toti anime, sed solum intellectiue:
sensitiua enim pars non recipit in se species, sed
in organo; pars autem intellectiua non recipit
eas in organo, sed in se ipsa. Item non sic est   435
locus specierum quod habeat eas in actu, sed
in potentia tantum.
   Quia ergo iam ostendit quid conueniat intellectui ex similitudine sensus, redit ad primum
quod dixerat, quod 'oportet partem intellectiuam   440
esse impassibilem'; et sic ammirabili subtilitate
ex ipsa similitudine sensus concludit dissimili-
tudinem. Ostendit ergo consequenter quod 'non
similiter sit impassibilis sensus et intellectus',
per hoc quod sensus corrumpitur ab excellenti   445
sensibili, non autem intellectus ab excellenti
intelligibili. Et huius causam assignat ex supra
probatis, 'quia sensitiuum non est sine corpore,
sed intellectus est separatus'.

(23) He has not yet proved, however, that it is not a power in the body, as Averroes says, but immediately concludes this from the foregoing: "For this reason it cannot reasonably be regarded as blended with the body" (429a25). This second conclusion he derives from the first, which he proved above, namely, that intellect does not actually have any of the natures of sensible things. It follows from this that it is not mixed with body because if it were mixed with body, it would have some corporeal nature. This is what he adds: "If so, it would acquire some quality, e.g., warmth or cold, or even have an organ like the sensitive faculty" (429a25–27). Sense is proportioned to its organ, and is in a way akin to it in nature; hence, with the immutation of the organ, the operation of sense, too, is changed. It is thus, then, that the phrase, "is not mixed with body," should be understood: intellect does not have an organ as sense does.

(24) And that the soul's intellect has no organ he manifests through the saying of those who said that "soul is the place of the forms" (429a27–29), understanding place broadly for any receiver, in the Platonic manner, except that being the place of forms is not true of the whole soul but only of intellect. For the sensitive part does not receive species in itself but in the organ; whereas the intellective does not receive them in an organ but in itself. Again, it is not the place of forms as having them actually but only in potency.

Since he has now shown what belongs to intellect from its similarity with sense, he returns to what he said first, that "the intellective part must be impassible" (429a15); and thus with wonderful subtlety, he concludes from its very similarity to sense its dissimilarity, going on to show that "sense and intellect are not impassible in the same way" (429a29–b5) because sense is destroyed by an excessive sensible, but intellect is not destroyed by the excessively intelligible. He gives as reason for this what was proved above: "The reason is that while the faculty of sensation is dependent upon the body, intellect is separable from it."

(25)   Hoc autem ultimum uerbum maxime assumunt   450
ad sui erroris fulcimentum, uolentes per hoc
habere quod intellectus neque sit anima neque
pars anime, sed quedam substantia separata.
Sed cito obliuiscuntur eius quod paulo supra
Aristotiles dixit: sic enim hic dicitur quod   455
'sensitiuum non est sine corpore et intellectus
est separatus', sicut supra dixit quod intellectus
fieret "qualis, aut calidus aut frigidus, si aliquod
organum erit ei sicut sensitiuo". Ea igitur ratione
hic dicitur quod sensitiuum non est sine corpore,   460
intellectus autem est separatus, quia sensus habet
organum, non autem intellectus.

(26)   Manifestissime igitur apparet
absque omni dubitatione ex uerbisAristotilis
hanc fuisse eius sententiam de intellectu
possibili, quod intellectus sit aliquid anime que   465
est actus corporis; ita tamen quod intellectus
anime non habeat aliquod organum corporale,
sicut habent cetere potentie anime.

(27)   Quomodo autem hoc esse possit, quod anima
sit forma corporis et aliqua uirtus anime non   470
sit corporis uirtus, non difficile est intelligere,
si quis etiam in aliis rebus consideret. Videmus
enim in multis quod aliqua forma est quidem
actus corporis ex elementis commixti, et tamen
habet aliquam uirtutem que non est uirtus   475
alicuius elementi, sed competit tali forme ex
altiori principio, puta corpore celesti: sicut quod
magnes habet uirtutem attrahendi ferrum, et iaspis
restringendi sanguinem. Et paulatim uidemus,
secundum quod forme sunt nobiliores, quod   480
habent aliquas uirtutes magis ac magis super-
gredientes materiam; unde ultima formarum,
que est anima humana, habet uirtutem totaliter
supergredientem materiam corporalem, scilicet
intellectum. Sic ergo intellectus separatus est quia   485
non est uirtus in corpore; sed est uirtus in
anima, anima autem est actus corporis.

(25) This is the favorite prop of those who want to hold the error that intellect is neither soul nor part of the soul but a separated substance. But they too quickly forget what Aristotle said only a little earlier; for just as here he says that "the sensitive faculty is not without body and intellect is separate," so above he said that intellect would "acquire some quality, e.g., warmth or cold, or even have an organ like the sensitive faculty" (429a25–26). This is the reason, therefore, why he here says that the sensitive is not without body, but the intellect is separate: because sense has an organ, but intellect does not.

(26) Quite obviously, therefore, and without any doubt so far as the text of Aristotle is concerned, it is clear that his view is that possible intellect belongs to the soul, which is the act of body, such that the soul's intellect has no bodily organ, as the other powers of the soul certainly have.

(27) It is not difficult to understand how the soul can be the form of a body yet some power of the soul not be a power of body if one takes into account other things as well. For in many things, we see that a form is indeed the act of a body of mixed elements and yet has a power which is not the power of any element but belongs to that form because of a higher principle, namely, a celestial body, e.g., the magnet has the power to attract iron, and jasper to coagulate blood. And presently we shall see that insofar as forms are nobler, they have powers which more and more surpass matter. Hence, the ultimate form, the human soul, has a power—namely, intellect—that wholly surpasses corporeal matter. Thus, the intellect is separate because it is not a power in the body but in the soul, and soul is the act of the body.

(28)   Nec dicimus quod anima, in qua est intellectus,
sic excedat materiam corporalem quod non habeat
esse in corpore; sed quod intellectus, quem   490
Aristotiles dicit potentiam anime, non est actus
corporis: neque enim anima est actus corporis
mediantibus suis potentiis, sed anima per se
ipsam est actus corporis dans corpori esse
specificum. Alique autem potentie eius sunt   495
actus partium quarundam corporis, perficientes
ipsas ad aliquas operationes; sic autem potentia
que est intellectus nullius corporis actus est, quia
eius operatio non fit per organum corporale.

(28) Nor do we say that the soul, in which the intellect is, so exceeds corporeal matter that it does not exist in the body, but rather that intellect, which Aristotle calls a power of the soul, is not the act of the body. For the soul is not the act of the body through the mediation of its powers but is through itself (per se) the act of body, giving to body its specific existence. Some of its powers are acts of certain parts of the body, perfecting them for definite operations, but the power which is intellect is not the act of any body because its operation does not take place by means of a bodily organ.

(29)   Et ne alicui uideatur quod hoc ex nostro   500
sensu dicamus preter Aristotilis intentionem,
inducenda sunt uerba Aristotilis expresse hoc
dicentis. Querit enim in II Phisicorum "usque
ad quantum oporteat cognoscere speciem et quod
quid est"; non enim omnem formam considerare   505
pertinet ad phisicum. Et soluit subdens "Aut
quemadmodum medicum neruum et fabrum es,
usquequo", id est usque ad aliquem terminum.
Et usque ad quem terminum ostendit subdens
"Cuius enim causa unumquodque", quasi dicat: 510
in tantum medicus considerat neruum in quantum
pertinet ad sanitatem, propter quam medicus
neruum considerat, et similiter faber es propter
artificium. Et quia phisicus considerat formam
in quantum est in materia, sic enim est forma   515
corporis mobilis, similiter accipiendum quod
naturalis in tantum considerat formam in quantum
est in materia.

(30)   Terminus ergo considerationis
phisici de formis est in formis que sunt in materia
quodammodo, et alio modo non in materia;   520
iste enim forme sunt in confinio formarum
separatarum et materialium. Vnde subdit "Et circa
hec", scilicet terminatur consideratio naturalis
de formis, "que sunt separate quidem species,
in materia autem". Que autem sint iste forme,   525
ostendit subdens "Homo enim hominem generat
ex materia, et sol". Forma ergo hominis est in
materia et separata: in materia quidem secundum
esse quod dat corpori, sic enim est terminus
generationis, separata autem secundum uirtutem   530
que est propria homini, scilicet secundum intellectum. Non est ergo impossibile quod aliqua forma
sit in materia, et uirtus eius sit separata, sicut
expositum est de intellectu.

(29) And lest it seem to anyone that we give this as our own reading, not Aristotle's meaning, the words of Aristotle expressly stating this must be cited. For in book 2 of the *Physics* he asks "to what degree it is necessary to know the species and quiddity,"[4] for it is not the natural philosopher's task to consider every form. And he solves this, adding, "to the degree that the doctor must know sinew and the smith bronze," that is, up to a point. And up to what point he shows, adding, "until he understands the cause of each," as if to say, the doctor considers the nerve insofar as it pertains to health, and so, too, the artisan bronze for the sake of the artifact. And because the natural philosopher considers form insofar as it is in matter—for such is the form of mobile body—so, too, it should be understood that the naturalist considers form insofar as it is in matter.

(30) The term of the physicist's consideration of form is of forms that are in some way in matter and, in another way, not in matter; for these forms are on the border of material and separated forms. Hence he adds, "and concerning these," namely, those forms that terminate the natural philosopher's consideration, "which are separable but which do not exist apart from matter."[5] He goes on to show what these forms are: "For man is generated by man and by the sun as well." Man's form, therefore, is in matter and separate: in matter indeed insofar as it gives existence to body, for thus it is the term of generation; separate, however, because of the power that is proper to man, namely, intellect. Therefore, it is not impossible for a form to be in matter yet its power be separate, as was shown concerning intellect.

---

4 *Physics,* 2.4.194b9–12.
5 *Physics,* 2.4.194b12–13.

(31)   Adhuc autem alio modo procedunt ad osten-   535
dendum quod Aristotilis sententia fuit, quod
intellectus non sit anima uel pars anime que
unitur corpori ut forma. Dicit enim Aristotiles
in pluribus locis, intellectum esse perpetuum et
incorruptibilem, sicut patet in II De anima, ubi   540
dixit "Hoc solum contingere separari sicut
perpetuum a corruptibili"; et in primo, ubi
dixit quod intellectus uidetur esse substantia
quedam, "et non corrumpi"; et in tertio, ubi
dixit "Separatus autem est solum hoc quod   545
uere est, et hoc solum immortale et perpetuum
est", quamuis hoc ultimum quidam non exponant
de intellectu possibili, sed de intellectu agente.
Ex quibus omnibus uerbis apparet quod Aristotiles
uoluit intellectum esse aliquid incorruptibile.   550

(32)   Videtur autem quod nichil incorruptibile possit
esse forma corporis corruptibilis. Non enim est
accidentale forme sed per se ei conuenit esse in
materia, alioquin ex materia et forma fieret unum
per accidens; nichil autem potest esse sine eo   555
quod inest ei per se: ergo forma corporis non
potest esse sine corpore. Si ergo corpus sit
corruptibile, sequitur formam corporis corrupti-
bilem esse. Preterea, forme separate a materia,
et forme que sunt in materia, non sunt eedem   560
specie, ut probatur in VII Methaphisice; multo
ergo minus una et eadem forma numero potest
nunc esse in corpore, nunc autem sine corpore:
destructo ergo corpore, uel destruitur forma
corporis, uel transit ad aliud corpus. Si ergo   565
intellectus est forma corporis, uidetur ex necessi-
tate sequi quod intellectus sit corruptibilis.

(31) There is yet another way in which they go about showing that Aristotle taught that the intellect is not a soul nor a part of the soul united to body as its form. For Aristotle says in several places that the intellect is perpetual and incorruptible, as is clear in book 2 of *On the Soul* (413b26–27), where he says, ". . . differing as what is eternal from what is perishable; it alone is capable of being separated"; and book 1, where he says that intellect seems to be a substance "incapable of being destroyed" (408b17–18). And, in book 3, he says, "This alone is truly separate and it alone is immortal and perpetual" (430a22–23), although some do not understand this last to be about the possible intellect but about the agent intellect. From all these texts, it is clear that Aristotle means that intellect is something incorruptible.

(32) However, it seems that nothing incorruptible could be the form of a corruptible body. It is not accidental to form but belongs to it per se that it be in matter, otherwise what comes to be from matter and form would be accidentally one. But nothing can exist without that which belongs to it as such; therefore, the form of body cannot be without body. If, then, the body is corruptible, it follows that the form of body is corruptible. Moreover, forms separate from matter and forms that exist in matter are not of the same kind, as is proved in book 7 of the *Metaphysics*.[6] Much less can numerically one form be now in body and now apart from body. With the destruction of the body, therefore, either the form of body is destroyed, or it passes to another body. If, then, intellect is the form of body, it seems necessarily to follow that intellect is corruptible.

---

6 *Metaphysics,* 7.11.1036b22–24; 1037a1–2; 16.1040b28–1041a4. Gauthier suggests that *Metaphysics* 10.1058b26–29 more expressly makes the point. Indeed, this text is invoked by the *Anonymus averroista* (*In de anima,* II, q. 4, a. 5, in *Trois commentaires anonymes sur le Traité de l'âme d'Aristote,* ed. M. Giele (Louvain: Publications Universitaires, 1971).

(33)   Est autem sciendum quod hec ratio plurimos
mouit: unde Gregorius Nissenus imponit
Aristotili e conuerso quod, quia posuit animam   570
esse formam, quod posuerit eam esse corrupti-
bilem; quidam uero posuerunt propter hoc
animam transire de corpore in corpus; quidam
etiam posuerunt quod anima haberet corpus
quoddam incorruptibile, a quo numquam sepa-   575
raretur. Et ideo ostendendum est per uerba
Aristotilis, quod sic posuit intellectiuam animam
esse formam quod tamen posuit eam incorruptibilem.

(34)   In XI enim Methaphisice, postquam ostenderat   580
quod forme non sunt ante materias, quia "quando
sanatur homo tunc est sanitas, et figura enee
spere simul est cum spera enea", consequenter
inquirit utrum aliqua forma remaneat post mate-
riam; et dicit sic secundum translationem Boetii   585
"Si uero aliquid posterius remaneat", scilicet post
materiam, "considerandum est: in quibusdam
enim nichil prohibet, ut si anima huiusmodi
est, non omnis sed intellectus; omnem enim
impossibile est fortasse". Patet ergo quod ani-   590
mam, que est forma, quantum ad intellectiuam
partem dicit nichil prohibere remanere post
corpus, et tamen ante corpus non fuisse. Cum
enim absolute dixisset quod cause mouentes sunt
ante, non autem cause formales, non quesiuit   595
utrum aliqua forma esset ante materiam, sed
utrum aliqua forma remaneat post materiam; et
dicit hoc nichil prohibere de forma que est
anima, quantum ad intellectiuam partem.

(33) It should be noted that this argument convinces many: thus, Gregory of Nyssa, making the reverse point, understood Aristotle to teach that the soul is corruptible because he made the soul a form. Some maintain because of this that soul passes from body to body. Others held that the soul has a certain incorruptible body from which it is never separate. It must be shown, therefore, from Aristotle's words, that he held that the intellective soul is form and nonetheless held it to be incorruptible.

(34) In book 11 of the *Metaphysics*,[7] after he had shown that forms do not exist before their matters because "when man is healed then health exists, and the shape of the bronze sphere at the same time as the bronze sphere," he then asks whether any form remains after matter. In Boethius's translation, "It should be considered whether anything remains afterward," namely, after matter, "for nothing stands in the way of this in some things, as if the soul were of this kind, not all but intellect, or perhaps it is impossible for them all." What he clearly says, therefore, is that nothing prevents the soul, which is a form, from remaining after the body, thanks to its intellective part, although it did not exist prior to body. For when he said absolutely that moving causes are prior but not formal causes, he did not ask whether any form were prior to matter, and he says that nothing prevents this in the case of the form which is soul with respect to its intellective part.

---

7   Actually *Metaphysics,* 12.1.1069a21–22.

(35)   Cum igitur, secundum premissa Aristotilis   600
uerba, hec forma que est anima post corpus
remaneat, non tota sed intellectus, considerandum
restat quare magis anima secundum partem
intellectiuam post corpus remaneat, quam secundum alias partes, et quam alie forme post suas   605
materias. Cuius quidem rationem ex ipsis
Aristotilis uerbis assumere oportet: dicit enim
"Separatum autem est solum hoc quod uere est,
et hoc solum immortale et perpetuum est".
Hanc igitur rationem assignare uidetur quare hoc   610
solum immortale et perpetuum esse uidetur, quia
hoc solum est separatum.

(36)   Sed de quo hic loquatur
dubium esse potest, quibusdam dicentibus quod
loquitur de intellectu possibili, quibusdam quod
de agente: quorum utrumque apparet esse falsum,   615
si diligenter uerba Aristotilis considerentur, nam
de utroque Aristotiles dixerat ipsum esse separatum. Restat igitur quod intelligatur de tota
intellectiua parte, que quidem separata dicitur
quia non est ei aliquod organum, sicut ex uerbis   620
Aristotilis patet.

(35) When then, in accordance with the foregoing words of Aristotle, this form which is the soul remains after the body—not the whole but intellect—we must yet ask why the soul remains after the body with respect to its intellective part rather than to its other parts, and why other forms do not remain after their matters. The reason is to be found in the text of Aristotle. He says, "This alone is truly separate and this alone immortal and perpetual" (430a22–23). Thus, the reason he gives that it alone seems to be immortal and perpetual is that it alone is separate.

(36) But a question arises as to what he is here speaking of, for some say he means possible intellect, and others [say] that he means the agent intellect. But both of these are seen to be false when Aristotle's words are carefully considered, for Aristotle says that both are separate. It is clear from the words of Aristotle that it is the whole intellective part which is said to be separate because it has no organ.

(37)   Dixerat autem Aristotiles in principio libri De
anima quod "si est aliquid anime operum aut
passionum proprium, continget utique ipsam
separari; si uero nullum est proprium ipsius,   625
non utique erit separabilis". Cuius quidem
consequentie ratio talis est, quia unumquodque
operatur in quantum est ens; eo igitur modo
unicuique competit operari quo sibi competit
esse. Forme igitur que nullam operationem   630
habent sine communicatione sue materie, ipse
non operantur, sed compositum est quod operatur
per formam; unde huiusmodi forme ipse quidem
proprie loquendo non sunt, sed eis aliquid est.
Sicut enim calor non calefacit, sed calidum, ita   635
etiam calor non est proprie loquendo, sed calidum
est per calorem; propter quod Aristotiles dicit
in XI Methaphisice quod de accidentibus non
uere dicitur quod sunt entia, sed magis quod
sunt entis.

(38)   Et similis ratio est de formis   640
substantialibus que nullam operationem habent
absque communicatione materie, hoc excepto
quod huiusmodi forme sunt principium essendi
substantialiter. Forma igitur que habet opera-
tionem secundum aliquam sui potentiam uel   645
uirtutem absque communicatione sue materie,
ipsa est que habet esse, nec est per esse compositi
tantum sicut alie forme, sed magis compositum
est per esse eius. Et ideo destructo composito
destruitur illa forma que est per esse compositi;   650
non autem oportet quod destruatur ad destruc-
tionem compositi illa forma per cuius esse
compositum est, et non ipsa per esse compositi.

(37) In the beginning of *On the Soul,* Aristotle said that "if there is any way of acting or being acted upon proper to soul, soul will be capable of separate existence" (403a10–12). The reason for the consequence is this: since anything acts according to the kind of being that it is, activity will belong to anything in the same way in which it exists. Therefore, forms, which have no activity without the participation of their matter, do not themselves operate, but the composite acts through the form. Hence, forms of this kind do not themselves exist, but something exists because of them. Heat does not warm, but rather the hot thing does; so, too, heat does not exist properly speaking, but the thing is warm thanks to heat. Because of this, Aristotle says in book 11 of the *Metaphysics*[8] that one does not truly say of accidents that they are beings, but that they are *of* beings.

(38) The same reasoning applies to substantial forms having no operation in which matter does not take part, except that such forms are principles of being substantially. Therefore, a form that has an activity thanks to one of its powers or faculties in which its matter does not participate has existence of itself. It does not exist simply in virtue of the existence of the composite, as is the case with other forms; but rather the composite exists in virtue of its existence. Therefore, the composite being destroyed, a form that exists thanks to the existence of the composite is destroyed; whereas a form through whose existence the composite exists, not vice versa, need not be destroyed when the composite is destroyed.

---

8   Actually *Metaphysics,* 12.1.1069a21–22.

(39)   Si quis autem contra hoc obiciat quod Aristotiles
dicit in I De anima, quod "intelligere et amare   655
et odire non sunt illius passiones, id est anime,
sed huius habentis illud secundum quod illud
habet; quare et hoc corrupto neque memoratur
neque amat, non enim illius erant sed communis,
quod quidem destructum est": patet responsio   660
per dictum Themistii hoc exponentis, qui dicit
"Nunc dubitanti magis quam docenti assimilatur"
Aristotiles. Nondum enim destruxerat opinionem
dicentium non differre intellectum et sensum;

(40)   unde in toto illo capitulo loquitur de intellectu   665
sicut de sensu: quod patet precipue ubi probat
intellectum incorruptibilem per exemplum sensus,
qui non corrumpitur ex senectute. Vnde et per
totum sub conditione et sub dubio loquitur
sicut inquirens, semper coniungens ea que sunt   670
intellectus hiis que sunt sensus: quod precipue
apparet ex eo quod in principio solutionis dicit
"Si enim et quam maxime dolere et gaudere et
intelligere" etc. Si quis autem pertinaciter dicere
uellet quod Aristotiles ibi loquitur determinando;   675
adhuc restat responsio, quia intelligere dicitur
esse actus coniuncti non per se sed per accidens,
in quantum scilicet eius obiectum, quod est
fantasma, est in organo corporali, non quod iste
actus per organum corporale exerceatur.   680

(39) Against this might be pointed out what Aristotle says in book 1 of *On the Soul:* "Thinking, loving, and hating are affections not of mind, but of that which has mind, so far as it has it. That is why, when this vehicle decays, memory and love cease; they were activities not of mind but of the composite which has perished" (408b25–29). The answer is clear from Themistius, who, in explaining this text, says that Aristotle "now is more in the mode of the doubter than the teacher." For he has not yet destroyed the opinion of those saying that intellect and sense do not differ.

(40) Hence, in that whole chapter he speaks of intellect in the same way he does of sense. This is especially evident where he proves the intellect to be incorruptible using the example of sense, which is not corrupted by age. Hence, throughout he speaks conditionally and problematically as one inquiring, always conflating intellect and sense. This is chiefly apparent because, in the beginning of the solution, he says, "We may admit to the full that being pained or pleased, or thinking, are movements, etc." (408b5–6). Were anyone adamantly to insist that Aristotle speaks decisively here, another response remains. Understanding is said to be the act of the composite, not essentially but accidentally, insofar as its object, the phantasm, is in a bodily organ and not because this activity is exercised through a bodily organ.

(41)   Si quis autem querat ulterius: si intellectus sine
fantasmate non intelligit, quomodo ergo anima
habebit operationem intellectualem postquam
fuerit a corpore separata? Scire autem debet
qui hoc obicit, quod istam questionem soluere   685
non pertinet ad naturalem. Vnde Aristotiles in
II Phisicorum dicit de anima loquens "Quomodo
autem separabile hoc se habeat et quid sit,
philosophie prime opus est determinare". Esti-
mandum est enim quod alium modum intelligendi   690
habebit separata quam habeat coniuncta, similem
scilicet aliis substantiis separatis. Vnde non sine
causa Aristotiles querit in III De anima 'utrum
intellectus non separatus a magnitudine intelligat
aliquid separatum': per quod dat intelligere quod   695
aliquid poterit intelligere separatus, quod non
potest non separatus.

(42)   In quibus etiam uerbis ualde notandum est
quod, cum superius utrumque intellectum, scilicet
possibilem et agentem, dixerit separatum, hic   700
tamen dicit eum non separatum. Est enim
separatus in quantum non est actus organi, non
separatus uero in quantum est pars siue potentia
anime que est actus corporis, sicut supra dictum
est. Huiusmodi autem questiones certissime col-   705
ligi potest Aristotilem soluisse in hiis que patet
eum scripsisse de substantiis separatis, ex hiis
que dicit in principio XII Methaphisice; quos
etiam libros uidi numero X, licet nondum in
lingua nostra translatos.   710

(41) A further question might be asked: If intellect does not understand without the phantasm, how can the soul have an intellectual operation after it is separated from the body? The questioner ought to know that it is not the natural philosopher's task to solve this question. That is why Aristotle, speaking of the soul in book 2 of the *Physics,* writes, "It is the business of First Philosophy to resolve how this is separable and what it is."[9] For it should be seen that the soul, when separated, has a different way of understanding than it does when conjoined, a way similar to that of separate substances. Hence, it is not surprising that Aristotle should say, in book 3 of *On the Soul,* "Whether it is possible for it while not existing separate from spatial conditions to think anything that is separate or not, we must consider later" (431b17–19). This suggests that it can understand something in a separated state that it cannot when unseparated.

(42) What is especially to be noticed in these words is that while he said earlier that both intellects, namely, the possible and the agent, are separate, here he says that intellect is not separate. For it is separate insofar as it is not the act of an organ, and it is nonseparate inasmuch as it is a part or power of the soul, which is the act of body, as has been said. Aristotle's resolution of such questions can be more certainly gathered from what he wrote of separate substances at the beginning of book 12 of the *Metaphysics,*[10] ten books of which I have seen, though they are not yet translated into our language.

---

9 *Physics,* 2.4.194b14–15.

10 Actually *Metaphysics,* 13.1.1076a10–13. (Gauthier refers to his own preface to the text in §37c.)

(43)   Secundum hoc igitur patet quod rationes
inducte in contrarium necessitatem non habent.
Essentiale enim est anime quod corpori uniatur;
sed hoc impeditur per accidens, non ex parte
sua sed ex parte corporis quod corrumpitur: 715
sicut per se competit leui sursum esse, et 'hoc
est leui esse ut sit sursum', ut Aristotiles dicit
in VIII Phisicorum, "contingit tamen per aliquod
impedimentum quod non sit sursum".

       Ex hoc etiam patet solutio alterius rationis.   720
Sicut enim quod habet naturam ut sit sursum,
et quod non habet naturam ut sit sursum, specie
differunt; et tamen idem et specie et numero
est quod habet naturam ut sit sursum, licet
quandoque sit sursum et quandoque non sit   725
sursum propter aliquod impedimentum: ita
differunt specie due forme, quarum una habet
naturam ut uniatur corpori, alia uero non habet;
sed tamen unum et idem specie et numero esse
potest habens naturam ut uniatur corpori, licet   730
quandoque sit actu unitum, quandoque non actu
unitum propter aliquod impedimentum.

(44)   Adhuc autem ad sui erroris fulcimentum
assumunt quod Aristotiles dicit in libro De
generatione animalium, scilicet "intellectum   735
solum deforis aduenire et diuinum esse solum";
nulla autem forma que est actus materie aduenit
deforis, sed educitur de potentia materie:
intellectus igitur non est forma corporis.

       Obiciunt etiam quod omnis forma corporis   740
mixti causatur ex elementis; unde si intellectus
esset forma corporis humani, non esset ab
extrinseco, sed esset ex elementis causatus.

       Obiciunt etiam ulterius circa hoc, quod seque-
retur quod etiam uegetatiuum et sensitiuum   745
essent ab extrinseco: quod est contra Aristotilem;
precipue si esset una substantia anime cuius
potentie essent uegetatiuum, sensitiuum et intellectiuum; cum intellectus sit ab extrinseco,
secundum Aristotilem.   750

(43) Given this, therefore, it is clear that there are no necessary arguments for the opposed position. For it is essential to the soul that it be united to body, and this is accidentally impeded, not on its part but on the part of the body that corrupts. In the same way, it pertains as such to what is light that it be above. "This is the essence of what is light that it be above," as Aristotle says in book 8 of the *Physics,* "but it can come about through some impediment that it is not above."[11]

The response to the second argument is clear from this. Although there is a specific difference between that whose nature it is to be above and that whose nature it is not to be above, yet the thing whose nature it is to be above—although it sometimes is and sometimes is not, due to an impediment—is specifically and numerically the same nature. In much the same way, a form whose nature it is to be united to body is specifically different from one whose nature it is not to be united to body, yet a form specifically and numerically the same can be such that its nature is to be united to body, although sometimes it actually is and sometimes it is not because of an impediment.

(44) They seek yet another basis for this error in what Aristotle says in the book *On the Generation of Animals,* namely, "intellect comes only from without and it alone is divine."[12] But no form that is the act of matter comes to it from without but rather is educed from the potency of matter. Therefore, the intellect is not the form of body.

They object, too, that every form of a mixed body is caused by the elements; hence, if the intellect were the form of the human body, it would not be caused by something else but would be caused by the elements.

They further object on this score that it would follow that the vegetative and sensitive, too, would be from something else, which is contrary to Aristotle. This would be especially true when there is a soul, one in substance, whose powers are vegetative, sensitive, and intellective. But, according to Aristotle, the intellective is from without.

---

11 *Physics,* 8.8.255b15–16 and 19–20.
12 *On the Generation of Animals,* 2.3.736b27–28.

(45)   Horum autem solutio in promptu apparet
secundum premissa. Cum enim dicitur quod omnis
forma educitur de potentia materie, considerandum uidetur quid sit formam de potentia materie
educi. Si enim hoc nichil aliud sit quam materiam   755
preexistere in potentia ad formam, nichil prohibet
sic dicere materiam corporalem preexstitisse in
potentia ad animam intellectiuam; unde Aristotiles
dicit in libro De generatione animalium "Primum
quidem omnia uisa sunt uiuere talia, scilicet   760
separata fetuum, plante uita; consequenter autem
palam quia et de sensitiua dicendum anima
et de actiua et de intellectiua: omnes enim
necessarium potentia prius habere quam actu".

(46)   Sed quia potentia dicitur ad actum, necesse   765
est ut unumquodque secundum eam rationem
sit in potentia, secundum quam rationem conuenit
sibi esse actu. Iam autem ostensum est quod
aliis formis, que non habent operationem absque
communicatione materie, conuenit sic esse actu   770
ut magis ipse sint quibus composita sunt, et
quodammodo compositis coexistentes, quam quod
ipse suum esse habeant; unde sicut totum esse
earum est in concretione ad materiam, ita totaliter
educi dicuntur de potentia materie. Anima autem   775
intellectiua, cum habeat operationem sine corpore,
non est esse suum solum in concretione ad
materiam; unde non potest dici quod educatur
de materia, sed magis quod est a principio
extrinseco. Et hoc ex uerbis Aristotilis apparet   780
"Relinquitur autem intellectum solum deforis
aduenire et diuinum esse solum"; et causam
assignat subdens "Nichil enim ipsius operationi
communicat corporalis operatio".

(45) The solution of these difficulties readily appears from the foregoing, for when it is said that every form is educed from the potency of matter, it seems that what this means ought to be understood. For if this is only matter's preexisting in potency to the form, nothing prevents our saying that corporeal matter preexists in potency to the intellective soul. Hence, Aristotle says in the book *On the Generation of Animals,* "For at first all such embryos seem to live the life of a plant. And it is clear that we must be guided by this in speaking of the active and sensitive and rational soul. For all three kinds of soul must be possessed potentially before they are possessed actually."[13]

(46) Because potency is a correlative of act, a thing must be in potency in the same respect that being actual belongs to it. It has already been shown that other forms which have no activities that do not involve matter are such that composites exist through them, and they themselves, as it were, coexist with composites rather than have their own existence. Hence, just as their whole existence is in conjunction with matter, so they are said to be wholly educed from the potency of matter. The intellective soul, however, since it has an operation without body, does not exist solely in conjunction with matter; hence, it cannot be said to be educed from matter, but it is rather from an extrinsic principle. And this is obvious from Aristotle's words: "It remains, then, for reason alone so to enter and alone to be divine," and he gives the explanation when he adds, "for no bodily activity has any connection with its activity."[14]

---

13 *On the Generation of Animals,* 2.3.736b12–15.
14 *On the Generation of Animals,* 2.3.736b27–29.

(47) Miror autem unde secunda obiectio processerit,   785
quod si intellectiua anima esset forma corporis
mixti, quod causaretur ex commixtione elementorum, cum nulla anima ex commixtione
elementorum causetur. Dicit enim Aristotiles
immediate post uerba premissa "Omnis quidem   790
igitur anime uirtus altero corpore uisa est
participare et diuiniore uocatis elementis: ut
autem differunt honorabilitate anime et uilitate
inuicem, sic et talis differt natura; omnium
quidem enim in spermate existit quod facit   795
genitiua esse spermata, uocatum calidum. Hoc
autem non ignis neque talis uirtus est, sed
interceptus in spermate et in spumoso spiritus
aliquis et in spiritu natura, proportionalis existens
astrorum ordinationi". Ergo ex mixtione elemen-   800
torum nedum intellectus, sed nec anima uegetabilis
producitur.

(48) Quod uero tertio obicitur, quod sequeretur
sensitiuum et uegetatiuum esse ab extrinseco,
non est ad propositum. Iam enim patet ex uerbis   805
Aristotilis quod ipse hoc indeterminatum reliquit,
utrum intellectus differat ab aliis partibus anime
subiecto et loco, ut Plato dixit, uel ratione
tantum. Si uero detur quod sint idem subiecto,
sicut uerius est, nec adhuc inconueniens sequitur.   810
Dicit enim Aristotiles in II De anima, quod
"similiter se habent ei quod de figuris et que
secundum animam sunt: semper enim in eo
quod est consequenter, est potentia quod prius est,
in figuris et in animatis; ut in tetragono quidem   815
trigonum est, in sensitiuo autem uegetatiuum".

(47) I wonder whence comes this second objection, namely, that if the intellective soul were the form of a mixed body, it would be caused by the mingling of the elements. Yet no soul is caused by the mingling of elements. Right after the words just quoted, we read: "Now it is true that the faculty of all kinds of soul seems to have a connection with a matter different from and more divine than the so-called elements; but as one soul differs from another in high or low regard, so the nature of the corresponding matter also differs. All have in their semen that which causes it to be productive; I mean what is called a vital heat. This is not fire nor any such force, but it is a sort of breath included in the semen and the foamlike and the natural principle in the breath, being analogous to the arrangement of the stars."[15] Therefore, not even the vegetative soul, let alone intellect, is produced from the mingling of elements.

(48) The third objection, that it would follow that the sensitive and vegetative also would be from an extrinsic principle, is not relevant. For it is already evident from the words of Aristotle that he leaves indeterminate whether intellect differs from the other parts of the soul in subject and place, as Plato said, or in definition alone. Even if it were given that they are the same in subject, as is truer, still nothing absurd would follow. For Aristotle says in book 2 of *On the Soul,* "The cases of figure and soul are exactly parallel; for the particulars subsumed under the common name in both cases—figures and living things—constitute a series, each successive term of which potentially contains its predecessor, e.g., the square the triangle, the sensory power the self-nutritive" (414b28–32).

---

15 *On the Generation of Animals,* 736b29–737a1.

(49)   Si autem idem subiecto est etiam intellectiuum,
quod ipse sub dubio relinquit, similiter dicendum
esset quod uegetatiuum et sensitiuum sint in
intellectiuo ut trigonum et tetragonum in penta-   820
gono. Est autem tetragonum quidem a trigono
simpliciter alia figura specie, non autem a trigono
quod est potentia in ipso; sicut nec quaternarius
a ternario qui est pars ipsius, sed a ternario qui
est seorsum existens. Et si contingeret diuersas   825
figuras a diuersis agentibus produci, trigonum
quidem seorsum a tetragono existens haberet
aliam causam producentem quam tetragonum,
sicut et habet aliam speciem; sed trigonum
quod inest tetragono haberet eandem causam   830
producentem. Sic igitur uegetatiuum quidem
seorsum a sensitiuo existens alia species anime
est, et aliam causam productiuam habet; eadem
tamen causa productiua est sensitiui, et uegetatiui
quod inest sensitiuo. Si ergo sic dicatur quod   835
uegetatiuum et sensitiuum quod inest intellectiuo,
est a causa extrinseca a qua est intellectiuum,
nullum inconueniens sequitur: non enim inconueniens est effectum superioris agentis habere
uirtutem quam habet effectus inferioris agentis,   840
et adhuc amplius; unde et anima intellectiua,
quamuis sit ab exteriori agente, habet tamen
uirtutes quas habent anima uegetatiua et sensitiua,
que sunt ab inferioribus agentibus.

(50)   Sic igitur, diligenter consideratis fere omnibus   845
uerbis Aristotilis que de intellectu humano dixit,
apparet eum huius fuisse sententie quod anima
humana sit actus corporis, et quod eius pars siue
potentia sit intellectus possibilis.

(49) If, however, the intellective, too, is in the same subject, which he leaves in doubt, it would similarly have to be said that the vegetative and sensitive are in the intellective as triangle and square are in the pentagon. For the square is indeed a figure specifically different from the triangle, but not from the triangle potentially in it, no more than four is from the three which is its part, but only from the three existing apart. And if it should happen that different shapes are produced by different agents, the triangle considered as apart and differing from the square would have a different cause from the square, just as it has another species, but the triangle that is in the square has the same producing cause. Similarly, the vegetative existing apart from the sensitive is another species of soul and has a different productive cause, but there is the same productive cause of the sensitive and of the vegetative within the sensitive. If, then, it is said of the vegetative and sensitive, which are in the intellective, that they are from the extrinsic cause which produces the intellective, nothing irreconcilable follows. For there is nothing absurd about the effect of a higher agent having the power that the effect of a lesser agent has, even more so. Hence, the intellective soul, although it is from an external agent, nonetheless has the powers had by the vegetative and sensitive souls, which are produced by inferior agents.

(50) So it is that those who carefully consider everything that Aristotle has to say of the human intellect see clearly that his teaching was that the human soul is the act of the body and that its part or faculty is the possible intellect.

| Capitvlvm II

(51)   Nunc autem considerare oportet quid alii
Peripatetici de hoc ipso senserunt. Et accipiamus
primo uerba Themistii in Commento de anima,
ubi sic dicit "Intellectus iste quem dicimus in
potentia magis est anime connaturalis", scilicet   5
quam agens; "dico autem non omni anime, sed
solum humane. Et sicut lumen potentia uisui
et potentia coloribus adueniens actu quidem
uisum fecit et actu colores, ita et intellectus
iste qui actu non solum ipsum actu intellectum   10
fecit, sed et potentia intelligibilia actu intelligibilia
ipse instituit". Et post pauca concludit "Quam
igitur rationem habet ars ad materiam, hanc et
intellectus factiuus ad eum qui in potentia.
Propter quod et in nobis est intelligere quando   15
uolumus. Non enim est ars materie exterioris,
sed inuestitur toti potentia intellectui qui factiuus;
ac si utique edificator lignis et erarius eri non
ab extrinseco existeret, per totum autem ipsum
penetrare potens erit. Sic enim et qui secundum   20
actum intellectus intellectui potentia superueniens
unum fit cum ipso".

| Chapter II

(51) Now we should consider what the other Peripatetics had to say about all this. We will first take up the words of Themistius in his *Commentary On the Soul.* When he says: "This intellect that we say is in potency is more connatural to the soul"—he means, than the agent intellect—"I don't mean to every soul, however, but only to the human. And just as light coming to potential seeing and to colors in potency makes them actual, so when this intellect is in act, it not only makes intellect to be in act but also constitutes potential intelligibles as actual intelligibles."[16] And a little later [he says]: "As art is to matter, so is the factive intellect to that which is in potency. That is why we understand when we wish to. For it is not an art exterior to matter but rather a power invested in the whole intellect that is making; just as, if the builder did not exist exterior to the wood or the brazier to the bronze, they would be able to penetrate through and through. Thus it is that the intellect in act supervenes on intellect in potency, becoming one with it."[17]

---

[16] Themistius, *Commentaire sur le Traité de l'âme d'Aristote,* ed. Gerald Verbeke, trans. Guillaume de Moerbeke (Leiden: E. J. Brill, 1973), 225.2–8, commenting on 430a14–17.

[17] Ibid., 16–24.

(52)   Et post pauca concludit "Nos igitur sumus
aut qui potentia intellectus, aut qui actu. Siquidem
igitur in compositis omnibus ex eo quod potentia   25
et ex eo quod actu, aliud est hoc et aliud est esse
huic, aliud utique erit ego et michi esse. Et ego
quidem est compositus intellectus ex potentia et
actu, michi autem esse ex eo quod actu est.
Quare et que meditor et que scribo, scribit   30
quidem intellectus compositus ex potentia et
actu, scribit autem non qua potentia sed qua
actu; operari enim inde sibi deriuatur". Et post
pauca adhuc manifestius "Sicut igitur aliud est
animal et aliud animali esse, animali autem esse   35
est ab anima animalis, sic et aliud quidem ego,
aliud autem michi esse. Esse igitur michi ab
anima et hac non omni; non enim a sensitiua,
materia enim erat fantasie; neque rursum a
fantastica, materia enim erat potentia intellectus;   40
neque eius qui potentia intellectus, materia enim
est factiui. A solo igitur factiuo est michi esse".
Et post pauca subdit "Et usque ad hunc progressa
natura cessauit, tamquam nichil habens alterum
honoratius cui faceret ipsum subiectum. Nos   45
itaque sumus actiuus intellectus".

(53)   Et postea reprobans quorundam opinionem
dicit "Cum predixisset, scilicet Aristotiles, in
omni natura hoc quidem materiam esse, hoc
autem quod materiam mouet aut perficit, necesse   50
ait et in anima existere has differentias, et esse
aliquem hunc talem intellectum in omnia fieri,
hunc talem in omnia facere. In anima enim ait
esse talem intellectum et anime humane uelut
quandam partem honoratissimam". Et post pauca   55
dicit "Ex eadem etiam littera hoc contingit
confirmare, quod putat, scilicet Aristotiles, aut
nostri aliquid esse actiuum intellectum, aut nos".
      Patet igitur ex premissis uerbis Themistii, quod
non solum intellectum possibilem, sed etiam   60
agentem partem anime humane esse dicit, et
Aristotilem ait hoc sensisse; et iterum quod homo
est id quod est, non ex anima sensitiua ut quidam
mentiuntur, sed ex parte intellectiua et princi-
paliori.   65

(52) And, a little later, he concludes, "Therefore we are either the intellect in potency or the intellect in act. And if in everything composed of what is in potency and what is in act, *it* is one thing and its existence another, then I, too, and my existence differ. I am an intellect composed of potency and act, but what it is for me to be comes from that which is in act. Wherefore what I think and write, an intellect composed of potency and act writes, but it writes not as in potency but as in act; from it derives its activity."[18] And a little further on yet more clearly [he says]: "Just as animal and what it is for animal to exist differ, the latter being due to the animal's soul, so, too, I and what it is for me to exist differ. What it is for me to exist comes from soul, but not from every part, not from the sensitive, which is matter to the imaginative, nor indeed from the imaginative, for it is matter to possible intellect; nor from that which is intellect potentially, for it is as matter to the agent intellect. From agent intellect alone, therefore, comes what it is for me to be."[19] And he adds a little later, "And having progressed to this, nature stops, there being nothing more honorable that could serve as subject to it. We are, therefore, the agent intellect."[20]

(53) And after rejecting the opinion of some others, he says, "Since Aristotle said that in every nature there is that which is matter and that which moves and perfects matter, he says that these differences must also exist in the soul, and that there must be an intellect that becomes all things and another that makes it all things. For he says there is in the soul such an intellect, and it is the most noble part of the human intellect";[21] a bit afterwards adding, "This same text confirms that he, Aristotle, thinks that either we are the agent intellect or it is a part of us."[22]

From the foregoing words of Themistius, it is clear that he not only holds that the possible intellect is a part of the human soul but the agent as well, and he says that Aristotle taught this; and further that man is what he is, not because of the sensitive soul, as some falsely said, but from the principal part, the intellective.

---

18 Ibid., 228–29.68–75.
19 Ibid., 79–85.
20 Ibid., 89–91.
21 Ibid., 233–34.73–79.
22 Ibid., 88–90.

(54)   Et Theophrasti quidem libros non uidi, sed
eius uerba introducit Themistius in Commento
que sunt talia, sic dicens "Melius est autem et
dicta Theophrasti proponere de intellectu potentia
et de eo qui actu. De eo igitur qui potentia hec   70
ait: Intellectus autem qualiter a foris existens
et tamquam superpositus, tamen connaturalis?
Et que natura ipsius? Hoc quidem enim nichil
esse secundum actum, potentia autem omnia
bene, sicut et sensus. Non enim sic accipiendum   75
est ut neque sit ipse, litigiosum est enim, sed
ut subiectam quandam potentiam sicut et in
materialibus. Sed hoc a foris igitur, non ut
adiectum, sed ut in prima generatione compre-
hendens ponendum".   80

(55)   Sic igitur Theophrastus, cum quesisset duo:
primo quidem quomodo intellectus possibilis sit
ab extrinseco, et tamen nobis connaturalis; et
secundo que sit natura intellectus possibilis:
respondit primo ad secundum quod est in   85
potentia omnia, non quidem sicut nichil existens
sed sicut sensus ad sensibilia. Et ex hoc concludit
responsionem prime questionis, quod non intelligitur sic esse ab extrinseco quasi aliquid adiectum
accidentaliter uel tempore procedente, sed a prima   90
generatione, sicut continens et comprehendens
naturam humanam.

(56)   Quod autem Alexander intellectum possibilem
posuerit esse formam corporis, etiam ipse
Auerroys confitetur; quamuis, ut arbitror,   95
peruerse uerba Alexandri acceperit, sicut et
uerba Themistii preter eius intellectum assumit.
Nam quod dicit, Alexandrum dixisse intellectum
possibilem non esse aliud quam preparationem
que est in natura humana ad intellectum agentem   100
et ad intelligibilia: hanc preparationem nichil
aliud intellexit quam potentiam intellectiuam
que est in anima ad intelligibilia. Et ideo dixit
eam non esse uirtutem in corpore quia talis
potentia non habet organum corporale, et non   105
ex ea ratione, ut Auerroys impugnat, secundum
quod nulla preparatio est uirtus in corpore.

(54) I have not seen the books of Theophrastus, but Themistius cites him in his commentary, writing, "However, it is better to set forth the sayings of Theophrastus concerning the intellect that is in potency and that which is in act. Of that which is in potency he asks: How could intellect exist from outside and as imposed and yet be connatural? And what is its nature? For it is actually nothing, yet everything potentially, just like sense. Nor should this be taken to mean that it itself is not, which is carping, but it is as a kind of potential subject, as is found in material things. But this ought not be said to be from without, therefore, or something conjoined, but is included from the first coming into being."[23]

(55) So Theophrastus asks two things: first, how the possible intellect is from an extrinsic principle yet connatural to us; and second, what the nature of the possible intellect is. He answers the second question first, saying that it is potentially all things, not indeed existing as nothing, but in the way sense is related to sensibles. His answer to the first question follows from this, that it ought not be so understood to be from outside, as if it were something accidentally conjoined or temporally prior, but is there in the first coming into being, as containing and comprehending human nature.

(56) That Alexander held the possible intellect to be the form of the body, Averroes himself admits, although, as I think, he perversely understands Alexander's words just as he uses the words of Themistius beyond the meaning intended. For he claims that Alexander said that the possible intellect was precisely the preparation in human nature for agent intellect and intelligibles; he understands this preparation to be nothing other than the soul's intellective potency to intelligible things. Therefore, he said that it is not a power in body because such a power does not have a bodily organ, and not for the reason Averroes attributes to him, [namely,] that no preparation is a power in body.

---

23 Ibid., 242.54–62.

(57)   Et ut a Grecis ad Arabes transeamus, primo
manifestum est quod Auicenna posuit intellectum
uirtutem anime que est forma corporis. Dicit   110
enim sic in suo libro De anima "Intellectus
actiuus, id est practicus, eget corpore et uirtutibus
corporalibus ad omnes actiones suas; contempla-
tiuus autem intellectus eget corpore et uirtutibus
eius, sed nec semper nec omnino: sifficit enim   115
ipse sibi per se ipsum. Nichil autem horum est
anima humana, sed anima est id quod habet has
uirtutes et, sicut postea declarabimus, est substantia solitaria, id est per se, que habet aptitudinem
ad actiones, quarum quedam sunt que non   120
perficiuntur nisi per instrumenta et per usum
eorum ullo modo; quedam uero sunt quibus non
sunt necessaria instrumenta aliquo modo".
        Item, in prima parte dicit quod "anima humana
est perfectio prima corporis naturalis instrumen-   125
talis, secundum quod attribuitur ei agere actiones
electione deliberationis, et adinuenire meditando,
et secundum hoc quod apprehendit uniuersalia".
Sed uerum est quod postea dicit et probat quod
anima humana, secundum id quod est sibi   130
proprium, id est secundum uim intellectiuam,
"non sic se habet ad corpus ut forma, nec eget
ut sibi preparetur organum".

(58)   Deinde subiungenda sunt uerba Algazelis sic
dicentis "Cum commixtio elementorum fuerit   135
pulcrioris et perfectioris equalitatis, qua nichil
possit inueniri subtilius et pulcrius, tunc fiet
apta ad recipiendum a datore formarum formam
pulcriorem formis aliis, que est anima hominis.
Huius uero anime humane due sunt uirtutes: 140
una operans et altera sciens", quam uocat
intellectum, ut ex consequentibus patet. Et
tamen postea multis argumentis probat, quod
operatio intellectus non fit per organum corporale.

(57) To turn from the Greeks to the Arabs, it is clear first of all that Avicenna held intellect to be a power of soul, which is the form of body. For he says in his book *On the Soul,* "The active—that is, practical intellect—needs the body and bodily powers for its own actions, but the contemplative intellect does not always and completely need the body and its powers: for it is sufficient unto itself. None of these is the human soul, but the soul is what has these powers and, as we shall maintain later, is a solitary substance, that is, is in itself, and has aptitude for activities, some of which are perfected only through instruments and some use of them, while others do not need instruments in any way.[24]

Again, in the first part, he says that "the human soul is the first perfection of a natural body with organs insofar as the ability to perform acts of deliberate choice, to discover by inquiry, and to grasp universals are attributed to it."[25] But it is true that later he says and proves that the human soul, because of that which is proper to it, that is, according to its intellective power, "is not related to body as form nor does it require that an organ be supplied it."[26]

(58) Next, these words of Algazel should be added: "When the mingling of the elements will have been of a most beautiful and perfect equality, than which nothing more subtle and beautiful can be found, then it will become apt to receive from the giver of forms a form more beautiful than other forms, which are the soul of man. There are two powers of this human soul: one operative, the other knowing,"[27] which, as is clear from what follows, means intellect. Afterwards he proves with many arguments that the operation of the intellect does not take place through a bodily organ.

---

24 Avicenna, *De anima,* ed. Van Riet, 80.54–63.
25 Ibid., 80.12–16.
26 Ibid., 113.44–45.
27 Cf. *Algazel's Metaphysics,* ed. J. T. Muckle (Toronto: St. Michael's College, 1933), 172.

(59) Hec autem premisimus, non quasi uolentes ex   145
philosophorum auctoritatibus reprobare supra-
positum errorem; sed ut ostendamus quod non
soli Latini, quorum uerba quibusdam non sapiunt,
sed etiam Greci et Arabes hoc senserunt, quod
intellectus sit pars uel potentia seu uirtus anime   150
que est corporis forma. Vnde miror ex quibus
Peripateticis hunc errorem se assumpsisse glo-
rientur, nisi forte quia minus uolunt cum ceteris
Peripateticis recte sapere, quam cum Auerroys
oberrare, qui non tam fuit Peripateticus quam   155
philosophie peripatetice deprauator.

▮ Capitvlvm III

(60) Ostenso igitur ex uerbis Aristotilis et aliorum
sequentium ipsum quod intellectus est potentia
anime que est corporis forma, licet ipsa potentia
que est intellectus non sit alicuius organi actus,
"quia nichil ipsius operationi communicat corpo-   5
ralis operatio", ut Aristotiles dicit; inquirendum
est per rationes quid circa hoc sentire sit necesse.
Et quia, secundum doctrinam Aristotilis, oportet
ex actibus principia actuum considerare, ex ipso
actu proprio intellectus qui est intelligere primo   10
hoc considerandum uidetur.

(61) In quo nullamfirmiorem
rationem habere possumus ea quam
Aristotiles ponit, et sic argumentatur: 'Anima
est primum quo uiuimus et intelligimus, ergo
est ratio quedam et species' corporis cuiusdam.   15
Et adeo huic rationi innititur, quod eam dicit
esse demonstrationem, nam in principio capituli
sic dicit "Non solum quod quid est oportet
diffinitiuam rationem ostendere, sicut plures ter-
minorum dicunt, sed et causam inesse et demons-   20
trare"; et ponit exemplum: sicut demonstratur
quid est tetragonismus, id est quadratum, per
inuentionem medie linee proportionalis.

(59) We have set forth these things, not wishing to refute the above-mentioned error by the authority of philosophers, but in order to show that not only Latin writers—whose language some do not savor—but also Greeks and Arabs thought that intellect is a part or power or faculty of the soul, which is the form of body. So I wonder from what Peripatetics they boast to have derived this error, unless perhaps they have less desire to think correctly with other Peripatetics than to err with Averroes, who was not a Peripatetic but the perverter of Peripatetic philosophy.

I Chapter III

(60) Having shown from the words of Aristotle and those who followed him that the intellect is a potency of the soul, which is the form of the body—although that potency which is intellect is not the act of any organ "because its operation is not shared by any bodily operation,"[28] as Aristotle says—we must now inquire by way of arguments what ought to be made of all this. And since, according to the teaching of Aristotle, it is from acts that their principles are known, our consideration must begin with the proper act of intellect, namely, understanding.

(61) Concerning this, there is no stronger argument than that given by Aristotle when he argues thus: "The soul is that whereby we first live and understand; therefore it is a certain form and species" of some body (414a12–14). He relies on this argument, therefore, characterizing it as a demonstration, for in the beginning of the chapter he says, "For it is not enough for a definitive formula to express, as most now do, the mere fact; it must include and exhibit the ground also" (413a13–20). By way of example, he says that what a component of a tetragon or square is, is demonstrated through the discovery of the proportional mean.

---

28 *On the Generation of Animals,* 2.3.736b28–29.

(62)   Virtus autem huius demonstrationis et insolu-
bilitas apparet, quia quicumque ab hac uia   25
diuertere uoluerint, necesse habent inconueniens
dicere. Manifestum est enim quod hic homo
singularis intelligit: numquam enim de intellectu
quereremus nisi intelligeremus; nec cum querimus
de intellectu, de alio principio querimus quam   30
de eo quo nos intelligimus. Vnde et Aristotiles
dicit "Dico autem intellectum quo intelligit
anima". Concludit autem sic Aristotiles quod si
aliquid est primum principium quo intelligimus,
oportet illud esse formam corporis; quia ipse   35
prius manifestauit quod illud quo primo aliquid
operatur est forma. Et patet hoc per rationem,
quia unumquodque agit in quantum est actu;
est autem unumquodque actu per formam: unde
oportet illud quo primo aliquid agit esse formam.   40

(63)   Si autem dicas quod principium huius actus
qui est intelligere, quod nominamus intellectum,
non sit forma, oportet te inuenire modum quo
actio illius principii sit actio huius hominis.
Quod diuersimode quidam conati sunt dicere.   45
Quorum unus Auerroys, ponens huiusmodi princi-
pium intelligendi quod dicitur intellectus possibilis
non esse animam nec partem anime nisi equiuoce,
sed potius quod sit substantia quedam separata,
dixit quod intelligere illius substantie separate   50
est intelligere mei uel illius, in quantum intellectus
ille possibilis copulatur michi uel tibi per fantasmata que sunt in me et in te. Quod sic fieri
dicebat: species enim intelligibilis que fit unum
cum intellectu possibili, cum sit forma et actus   55
eius, habet duo subiecta, unum ipsa fantasmata,
aliud intellectum possibilem. Sic ergo intellectus
possibilis continuatur nobiscum per formam
suam mediantibus fantasmatibus; et sic dum
intellectus possibilis intelligit, hic homo intelligit.   60

(62) The power and irrefutability of this demonstration is clear from the fact that whoever wishes to differ with it necessarily says what is absurd. That this singular man understands is manifest, for we would never ask about intellect unless we understood; nor when we ask about intellect are we asking about anything other than that whereby we understand. Thus, Aristotle says, "I mean the intellect whereby the soul understands" (429a23), and concludes accordingly that if something is the first principle whereby we understand, it must be the form of the body because he earlier showed that that whereby we first do anything is the form. And this is clear from argument: anything acts insofar as it is in act; anything is in act through its form; therefore, that through which something first acts must be form.

(63) If, however, you should say that the first principle of the act which is understanding—what we call intellect—is not form, then you must find a way in which the act of this principle can be an action of this man. There are those who have tried in various ways to do this. One of them, Averroes, held that the principle of understanding which is called the possible intellect is not a soul or a part of the soul, except equivocally; rather, it is a separated substance. He said that the separate substance's understanding is mine or yours insofar as possible intellect is joined to me or you through the phantasms that are in me and you. He says that comes about in this way: the intelligible species that becomes one with the possible intellect as its form and act has two subjects: the one, those phantasms; the other the possible intellect. Therefore the possible intellect is continuous with us through its form by way of phantasms, and thus when the possible intellect understands, this man understands.

(64)   Quod autem hoc nichil sit, patet tripliciter.
Primo quidem quia sic continuatio intellectus
ad hominem non esset secundum primam eius
generationem, ut Theophrastus dicit et Aristotiles
innuit in II Phisicorum, ubi dicit quod terminus   65
naturalis considerationis de formis est ad formam
secundum quam homo generatur ab homine et
a sole. Manifestum est autem quod terminus
considerationis naturalis est in intellectu; secun-
dum autem dictum Auerroys, intellectus non   70
continuaretur homini secundum suam genera-
tionem, sed secundum operationem sensus, in
quantum est sentiens in actu: fantasia enim est
"motus a sensu secundum actum", ut dicitur
in libro De anima.   75

(65)   Secundo uero, quia ista coniunctio non esset
secundum aliquid unum, sed secundum diuersa.
Manifestum est enim quod species intelligibilis
secundum quod est in fantasmatibus, est intellecta
in potentia; in intellectu autem possibili est   80
secundum quod est intellecta in actu, abstracta
a fantasmatibus. Si ergo species intelligibilis non
est forma intellectus possibilis nisi secundum
quod est abstracta a fantasmatibus, sequitur
quod per speciem intelligibilem non continuatur   85
fantasmatibus, sed magis ab eis est separatus.
Nisi forte dicatur quod intellectus possibilis
continuatur fantasmatibus sicut speculum continuatur homini cuius species resultat in speculo;
talis autem continuatio manifestum est quod   90
non sufficit ad continuationem actus. Manifestum
est enim quod actio speculi, que est representare,
non propter hoc potest attribui homini: unde
nec actio intellectus possibilis propter predictam
copulationem posset attribui huic homini qui est   95
Sortes, ut hic homo intelligeret.

(64) There are three ways of showing that this amounts to nothing. First, because the union of intellect and man would not then come into being when he does, as Theophrastus maintains and Aristotle indicates in book 2 of the *Physics,* where he says that the goal of the naturalist's consideration of forms is the form according to which man is generated by man and the sun.[29] Intellect is obviously the goal of the naturalist's consideration; yet, according to what Averroes says, intellect is not united with man from his generation but through the operation of sense insofar as he is actually sensing: imagination is "a movement resulting from an actual exercise of a power of sense," as is said in *On the Soul* (429a1–2).

(65) Second, because this union would have not one, but rather diverse causes. For clearly the intelligible species as it exists in the phantasm is understood only potentially; but abstracted from phantasms in the possible intellect it is actually understood. If, then, the intelligible species is the form of possible intellect only insofar as it is abstracted from phantasms, it follows that [possible intellect] is not united with phantasms through the intelligible species but rather is separated from them. Unless, perhaps, it is said that the possible intellect is one with phantasms in the way in which the mirror is one with the man whose image is reflected in the mirror; but such a union manifestly does not suffice for the union of the act. For it is obvious that the act of the mirror, which is to represent, is not on this account attributed to the man. No more could the action of possible intellect on the basis of the foregoing conjunction be attributed to this man, Socrates, in order that this man might understand.

---

29 *Physics,* 2.4.194b9–13.

(66)   Tertio, quia dato quod una et eadem species
numero esset forma intellectus possibilis et esset
simul in fantasmatibus: nec adhuc talis copulatio
sufficeret ad hoc quod hic homo intelligeret.   100
Manifestum est enim quod per speciem intelli-
gibilem aliquid intelligitur, sed per potentiam
intellectiuam aliquid intelligit; sicut etiam per
speciem sensibilem aliquid sentitur, per potentiam
autem sensitiuam aliquid sentit. Vnde paries in   105
quo est color, cuius species sensibilis in actu
est in uisu, uidetur, non uidet; animal autem
habens potentiam uisiuam, in qua est talis species,
uidet. Talis autem est predicta copulatio intellectus
possibilis ad hominem, in quo sunt fantasmata   110
quorum species sunt in intellectu possibili, qualis
est copulatio parietis in quo est color ad uisum
in quo est species sui coloris. Sicut igitur paries
non uidet, sed uidetur eius color, ita sequeretur
quod homo non intelligeret, sed quod eius   115
fantasmata intelligerentur ab intellectu possibili.
Impossibile est ergo saluari quod hic homo
intelligat, secundum positionem Auerroys.

(67)   Quidam uero uidentes quod secundum uiam
Auerroys sustineri non potest quod hic homo   120
intelligat, in aliam diuerterunt uiam, et dicunt
quod intellectus unitur corpori ut motor; et sic,
in quantum ex corpore et intellectu fit unum ut
ex mouente et moto, intellectus est pars huius
hominis: et ideo operatio intellectus attribuitur   125
huic homini, sicut operatio oculi que est uidere
attribuitur huic homini. Querendum est autem
ab eo qui hoc ponit, primo quid sit hoc singulare
quod est Sortes: utrum Sortes sit solus intellectus
qui est motor; aut sit motum ab ipso, quod est   130
corpus animatum anima uegetatiua et sensitiua;
aut sit compositum ex utroque. Et quantum ex
sua positione uidetur, hoc tertium accipiet quod
Sortes sit aliquid compositum ex utroque.

(66) Third, even granted that numerically one and the same species were the form of the possible intellect and at the same time in phantasms, such a conjunction would not suffice to explain that this man understands. For it is obvious that just as something is sensed through a sensible species, but one senses something through the sensitive power, so something is understood through the intelligible species, but one understands something through the intellective power. Hence, the wall in which the color is, whose sensible species is actually in sight, is seen and does not see; it is the animal having the power of sight, in which such a species is, that sees. The aforesaid union of the possible intellect with man—in whom exist the phantasms whose species are in the possible intellect—is like the union of the wall, in which the color is, with sight, in which the species of its color is. The wall does not see, but its color is seen; thus, it would follow that man does not understand, but his phantasms are understood by the possible intellect. It is impossible, therefore, on the basis of Averroes's position, to show that this man understands.

(67) Some, seeing that on Averroes's position it cannot be sustained that this man understands, take another path and say that intellect is united to body as its mover, and thus, insofar as body and intellect become one as mover and moved, the intellect is part of this man; therefore, the operation of intellect is attributed to this man in the same way that the operation of the eye, seeing, is attributed to this man. He who says this must be asked, first, what this singular thing Socrates is. Is he only intellect, which is a mover? Or is he what is moved by it—a body animated by vegetative and sensitive soul? Or is he composed of both? So far as his position can be discerned, it appears that he adopts the third possibility, namely, that Socrates is composed of both.

(68)   Procedamus ergo contra eos per rationem   135
Aristotilis in VIII Methaphisice "Quid est igitur
quod facit unum hominem". "Omnium enim
que plures partes habent et non sunt quasi
coaceruatio totum, sed est aliquod totum preter
partes, est aliqua causa unum essendi: sicut in   140
quibusdam tactus, in quibusdam uiscositas, aut
aliquid aliud huiusmodi. . . . Palam autem quia si sic
transformant, ut consueuerunt diffinire et dicere,
non contingit reddere et soluere dubitationem.
Si autem est ut dicimus: hoc quidem materia   145
illud uero forma, et hoc quidem potestate illud
uero actu, non adhuc dubitatio uidebitur esse".

(69)   Sed si tu dicas quod Sortes non est unum
quid simpliciter, sed unum quid aggregatione
motoris et moti, sequntur multa inconuenientia.   150
Primo quidem quia, cum unumquodque sit
similiter unum et ens, sequitur quod Sortes non
sit aliquid ens, et quod non sit in specie nec
in genere; et ulterius quod non habeat aliquam
actionem, quia actio non est nisi entis. Vnde   155
non dicimus quod intelligere naute sit intelligere
huius totius quod est nauta et nauis, sed naute
tantum; et similiter intelligere non erit actus
Sortis, sed intellectus tantum utentis corpore
Sortis: in solo enim toto quod est aliquid unum   160
et ens, actio partis est actio totius. Et si quis
aliter loquatur, improprie loquitur.

(70)   Et si tu dicas
quod hoc modo celum intelligit per motorem
suum, est assumptio difficilioris: per intellectum
enim humanum oportet nos deuenire ad cognos-   165
cendum intellectus superiores, et non e conuerso.
    Si uero dicatur quod hoc indiuiduum quod
est Sortes, est corpus animatum anima uegetatiua
et sensitiua, ut uidetur sequi secundum eos qui
ponunt quod hic homo non constituitur in specie   170
per intellectum, sed per animam sensitiuam
nobilitatam ex aliqua illustratione seu copulatione
intellectus possibilis: tunc intellectus non se
habet ad Sortem nisi sicut mouens ad motum.
Sed secundum hoc actio intellectus que est   175
intelligere, nullo modo poterit attribui Sorti: quod
multipliciter apparet.

(68) Let us then proceed against them, making use of Aristotle's argument in book 8 of the *Metaphysics,* "What then is it that makes man one?" (1045a14). "In the case of all things which have several parts and in which the whole is not, as it were, a mere heap, but the totality is something besides the parts, there is a cause of unity; for as regards material things, contact is the cause in some cases, and in others viscosity or some other such quality" (1045a8–12). "Clearly, then, if people proceed thus in their usual manner of definition and speech, they cannot explain and solve the difficulty. But if, as we say, one element is matter and another is form, and one potentially and the other actually, the question will no longer be thought a difficulty" (1045a20–25).

(69) But if you should say that Socrates is not some one thing absolutely, but one by the coming together of mover and moved, many incoherencies follow. First, indeed, that since anything is one in the manner in which it exists, it would follow that Socrates is not a being and does not belong in a species or genus; and further, that he would have no action, since only beings act. Hence, we do not say that the understanding of the sailor is the grasp of the whole made up of sailor and boat, but of sailor alone; similarly, understanding would not be Socrates' activity but rather only that of the intellect using the body of Socrates. The action of a part is the action of the whole only when the whole is one being. Anyone who says otherwise speaks improperly.

(70) And if you should say that in this way the heaven understands through its motor, this is to appeal to the more difficult case. We must go by way of the human intellect to grasp the higher intellects, not vice versa.

If it be said that this individual, Socrates, is a body animated by the vegetative and sensitive soul—which seems to follow for those who hold that this man is not placed in a species because of intellect but because of the sensitive soul ennobled by an illumination or conjunction with possible intellect—then intellect relates to Socrates only as mover to moved. But then the action of intellect, which is understanding, can in no wise be attributed to Socrates. There are many ways in which this consequence is seen to be obvious.

(71)   Primo quidem per hoc quod dicit Philosophus in
IX Methaphisice, quod "quorum diuersum aliquid
erit preter usum quod fit, horum actus in facto   180
est, ut edificatio in edificato et contextio in
contexto; similiter autem et in aliis, et totaliter
motus in moto. Quorum uero non est aliud
aliquod opus preter actionem, in eis existit actio,
ut uisio in uidente et speculatio in speculante".   185
Sic ergo, etsi intellectus ponatur uniri Sorti ut
mouens, nichil proficit ad hoc quod intelligere
sit in Sorte, nedum quod Sortes intelligat: quia
intelligere est actio que est in intellectu tantum.
Ex quo etiam patet falsum esse quod dicunt,   190
quod intellectus non est actus corporis, sed
ipsum intelligere; non enim potest esse alicuius
actus intelligere, cuius non sit actus intellectus,
quia intelligere non est nisi in intellectu, sicut
nec uisio nisi in uisu: unde nec uisio potest   195
esse alicuius, nisi illius cuius actus est uisus.

(72)   Secundo, quia actio mouentis propria non
attribuitur instrumento aut moto, sed magis e
conuerso actio instrumenti attribuitur principali
mouenti: non enim potest dici quod serra   200
disponat de artificio, potest tamen dici quod
artifex secat, quod est opus serre. Propria autem
operatio ipsius intellectus est intelligere; unde
dato etiam quod intelligere esset actio transiens
in alterum sicut mouere, non sequitur quod   205
intelligere conueniret Sorti si intellectus uniatur
ei solum ut motor.

(73)   Tertio, quia in hiis quorum actiones in alterum
transeunt, opposito modo attribuuntur actiones
mouentibus et motis: secundum edificationem   210
enim edificator dicitur edificare, edificium uero
edificari. Si ergo intelligere esset actio in alterum
transiens sicut mouere, adhuc non esset dicendum
quod Sortes intelligeret ad hoc quod intellectus
uniretur ei ut motor, sed magis quod intellectus   215
intelligeret et Sortes intelligeretur; aut forte
quod intellectus intelligendo moueret Sortem, et
Sortes moueretur.

(71) First, because of what the Philosopher says in book 9 of the *Metaphysics:* "Where, then, the result is something apart from the exercise, the actuality is in the thing that is being made, e.g., the act of building is in the thing that is being built and that of weaving in the thing that is being woven, and similarly in all other cases, and in general the movement is in the thing that is being moved; but when there is no product apart from the actuality, the actuality is in the agents, e.g., the act of seeing is in the seeing subject and that of theorizing in the theorizing subject" (1050a30–36). So, then, although intellect is said to be united with Socrates as mover, this is of no help in locating understanding in Socrates nor in grounding the claim that Socrates understands, for understanding is an action that is in intellect alone. From this, too, it is clear that they speak falsely who say that understanding itself, not intellect, is the act of body: there can be no act of understanding that is not the act of intellect because understanding is in intellect alone, just as seeing is in sight alone. Seeing can only belong to that whose act is sight.

(72) Second, because the proper act of the mover is attributed neither to the instrument nor to the moved. On the contrary, the action of the instrument is attributed to the principal mover. It cannot be said that the saw makes the artifact, although the artisan can be said to saw, which is the work of the saw. Understanding is the proper activity of intellect; hence, even granting that understanding is an action passing over to another like moving, it does not follow that understanding belongs to Socrates if intellect is united to him only as a mover.

(73) Third, because in those things whose activities are transitive, passing over into other things, actions are attributed in opposite ways to movers and moved. Thanks to building, the builder is said to build and the building to be built. If, then, understanding were a transitive action like motion, it still ought not be said that Socrates understands because intellect is united to him as a mover, but rather that intellect understands and Socrates is understood. Or perhaps that intellect, by understanding, moves Socrates, and Socrates is moved.

(74)   Contingit tamen quandoque quod actio mo-
uentis traducitur in rem motam, puta cum ipsum   220
motum mouet ex eo quod mouetur, et calefactum
calefacit. Posset ergo aliquis sic dicere quod
motum ab intellectu, qui intelligendo mouet, ex
hoc ipso quod mouetur intelligit. Huic autem
dicto Aristotiles resistit in II De anima, unde   225
principium huius rationis assumpsimus. Cum
enim dixisset quod id quo primo scimus et
sanamur est forma, scilicet scientia et sanitas,
subiungit "Videtur enim in patienti et disposito
actiuorum inesse actus". Quod exponens   230
Themistius dicit "Nam et si ab aliis aliquando
scientia et sanitas est, puta a docente et medico,
tamen in patiente et disposito facientium inexistere
actus ostendimus prius, in hiis que De natura".
Est ergo intentio Aristotilis, et euidenter est   235
uerum, quod quando motum mouet et habet
actionem mouentis, oportet quod insit ei actus
aliquis a mouente quo huiusmodi actionem
habeat, et hoc est primum quo agit, et est actus
et forma eius; sicut si aliquid est calefactum,   240
calefacit per calorem qui inest ei a calefaciente.

(75)   Detur ergo quod intellectus moueat animam
Sortis, uel illustrando uel quocumque modo:
hoc quod est relictum ab impressione intellectus
in Sorte est primum quo Sortes intelligit. Id   245
autem quo primo Sortes intelligit, sicut sensu
sentit, Aristotiles probauit esse in potentia omnia,
et per hoc non habere naturam determinatam
nisi hanc quod sit possibilis; et per consequens
quod non misceatur corpori, sed sit separatus.   250
Dato ergo quod sit aliquis intellectus separatus
mouens Sortem, tamen adhuc oportet quod iste
intellectus possibilis de quo Aristotiles loquitur,
sit in anima Sortis, sicut et sensus qui est in
potentia ad omnia sensibilia, quo Sortes sentit.   255

(74) Sometimes it happens that the action of the mover passes into the thing moved, as when that which is moved moves because it is moved, e.g., when the heated heats. In this way, someone might say that that which is moved by the intellect, which in understanding moves, understands by the very fact that it is moved. Aristotle, from whom we take the principle of this argument, resists this claim in book 2 of *On the Soul*. For when he said that that whereby we first know or are healed is a form—namely, science and health—he adds, "For the activity of that which is capable of originating change seems to take place in that which is changed or altered" (414a11–12). In explaining this, Themistius says, "Although knowledge or health are sometimes from others, as from a teacher or a physician, nonetheless we have shown that, in things that are from nature, the activity of that which is capable of originating change is in what is changed or altered."[30] It is Aristotle's meaning, therefore, and evidently true as well, that when the moved moves and has the action of a mover, there must be in it some act from the mover whereby it performs an action of this kind; it is thanks to this that it primarily acts, and this is its act and form, for example, when something heated heats from the heat that is in it from the heater.

(75) Given that the intellect moves Socrates, whether by illumining or in some other way, then the impression made on Socrates by the intellect is that whereby Socrates primarily understands. However, Aristotle has proved (429a9–b5) that that whereby Socrates primarily understands, as he senses by sense, is potentially all things and for this reason has no determinate nature other than to be possible. Consequently, it is not mixed with body but separate. Granted, then, that there is some separate intellect moving Socrates, it would still be necessary that the possible intellect of which Aristotle speaks is in the soul of Socrates, just as sense, which is that whereby Socrates senses and is potentially all sensible things, is.

---

30 Themistius, 109.68–71.

(76)   Si autem dicatur quod hoc indiuiduum quod
est Sortes neque est aliquid compositum ex
intellectu et corpore animato, neque est corpus
animatum tantum, sed est solum intellectus: hec
iam erit opinio Platonis, qui, ut Gregorius   260
Nissenus refert, "propter hanc difficultatem non
uult hominem ex anima et corpore esse,
sed animam corpore utentem et uelut indutam
corpus". Sed et Plotinus, ut Macrobius refert,
ipsam animam hominem esse testatur, sic dicens   265
"Ergo qui uidetur non ipse uerus homo est,
sed ille a quo regitur qui uidetur. Sic, cum
morte animalis discedit animatio, cadit corpus a
regente uiduatum, et hoc est quod uidetur in
homine mortale. Anima uero, qui uerus homo   270
est, ab omni mortalitatis condicione aliena est".
Qui quidem Plotinus unus de magnis ponitur
inter commentatores Aristotilis, ut Simplicius
refert in Commento Predicamentorum.

(77)   Hec autemsententia nec
a uerbis Aristotilis multum aliena   275
uidetur: dicit enim in IX Ethicorum quod "boni
hominis est bonum elaborare et sui ipsius gratia;
intellectiui enim gratia quod unusquisque esse
uidetur". Quod quidem non dicit propter hoc
quod homo sit solus intellectus, sed quia id quod   280
est in homine principalius est intellectus; unde
in consequentibus dicit quod "quemadmodum
ciuitas principalissimum maxime esse uidetur, et
omnis alia constitutio, sic et homo": unde
subiungit quod "unusquisque homo uel est hoc,   285
scilicet intellectus, uel maxime". Et per hunc
modum arbitror et Themistium in uerbis supra
positis, et Plotinum in uerbis nunc inductis,
dixisse quod homo est anima uel intellectus.

(76) Should it be said, however, that this individual, Socrates, is neither composed of intellect and an animated body nor an animated body alone, but only intellect—well, this was the view of Plato, who, as Gregory of Nyssa says, "because of this difficulty did not want man to be composed of body and soul, but to be a soul using and as it were clothed with a body."[31] But Plotinus, as Macrobius reports, claimed that the soul itself is man, saying, "Therefore the true man is not what is seen but rather that which rules what is seen. Thus, when at death animation departs from the animal, the body falls widowed from the ruler; and it is this which is seen in man and is mortal. Every mark of mortality is alien to the soul, which is truly man."[32] Yet Simplicius, in his commentary on the *Categories*,[33] includes Plotinus among the greatest commentators on Aristotle.

(77) This opinion does not seem far distant from the words of Aristotle, who says in book 9 of the *Nicomachean Ethics:* "For it is characteristic of the good man to exert himself for the good, and he does so for his own sake, that is, for the sake of the intellectual element in him, which each person seems to be."[34] Of course, he says this not because man is intellect alone but because intellect is the chief thing in man. Hence, in the sequel he says that "just as the state and every other organized whole seems to be that which is the chief thing in it, so, too, man";[35] and he adds that "any man either is this, namely, intellect, or it especially."[36] It is in this sense that I appraise Themistius's words quoted earlier[37] and Plotinus's now when they say that man is soul or intellect.

---

31 Nemesius, *De natura hominis,* Migne Patrologia Graeca, vol. 40, 593B.

32 Macrobius, *Commentarium in somnium Scipionis,* ed. F. Eyssenhardt (Leipzig: Teubner, 1893), 2.12.

33 Simplicius, *In Aristotelis Categorias commentarium,* prooemium, ed. C. Kalbfleisch, vol. 8 of *Commentaria in Aristotelem Graeca* (Berlin: G. Reimer, 1907), 2.3.

34 *Nicomachean Ethics,* 9.4.1166a15–17.

35 Ibid., 1168a31–33.

36 Ibid., 1168a2.

37 Cf. no. 74 above.

(78)   Quod enim homo non sit intellectus tantum   290
uel anima tantum, multipliciter probatur. Primo
quidem ab ipso Gregorio Nisseno, qui inducta
opinione Platonis subdit "Habet autem hic
sermo difficile uel indissolubile quid: qualiter
enim unum esse potest cum indumento anima?   295
Non enim unum est tunica cum induto". Secundo,
quia Aristotiles in VII Methaphisice probat quod
"homo et equs et similia" non sunt solum forma,
"sed totum quoddam ex materia et forma ut
uniuersaliter; singulare uero ex ultima materia,   300
ut Socrates iam est, et in aliis similiter". Et hoc
probauit per hoc quod nulla pars corporis potest
diffiniri sine parte aliqua anime; et recedente
anima, nec oculus nec caro dicitur nisi equiuoce:
quod non esset, si homo aut Sortes esset tantum   305
intellectus aut anima. Tertio, sequeretur quod,
cum intellectus non moueat nisi per uoluntatem,
ut probatur in III De anima, hoc esset de rebus
subiectis uoluntati, quod retineret corpus homo
cum uellet, et abiceret cum uellet: quod manifeste   310
patet esse falsum.

(79)   Sic igitur patet quod intellectus non unitur
Sorti solum ut motor; et quod, etiam si hoc
esset, nichil proficeret ad hoc quod Sortes
intelligeret. Qui ergo hanc positionem defendere   315
uolunt, aut confiteantur se nichil intelligere et
indignos esse cum quibus aliqui disputent, aut
confiteantur quod Aristotiles concludit: quod id
quo primo intelligimus est species et forma.

(78) That man is not intellect alone nor soul alone is proved in many ways. The first is from Gregory of Nyssa, who, having mentioned Plato's view, adds, "This saying is puzzling and difficult: how can the soul be one with its garment? For a tunic and its wearer are not one thing."[38] Second, because Aristotle in book 7 of the *Metaphysics* proves that "man and horse and the like" are not form alone, "but terms that are thus applied to individuals, but universally, are not substance but something composed of this particular formula and this particular matter treated as universal; but when we come to the individual, Socrates is composed of ultimate individual matter; and similarly in all other cases."[39] The proof of this is that no part of the body can be defined independently of some part of soul; and, the soul being gone, flesh and eye are such only equivocally, which would not be the case if man or Socrates were intellect or soul alone. Third, it would follow that, since intellect moves only through the will, as is proved in book 3 of *On the Soul* (433a22), this would be among the things subject to will that man could keep his body or shuffle it off when he wished, which is manifestly false.

(79) It is therefore evident that the intellect is not joined to Socrates just as a mover; but, even if it were, it would not advance the claim that Socrates understands. Those who wish to defend this position, therefore, must either admit that they themselves understand nothing and are unworthy participants in the debate, or admit what Aristotle concludes: that that with which we first understand is species and form.

---

38 Nemesius, *De natura hominis,* 593B.
39 *Metaphysics,* 7.10.1035b27–31.

(80)   Potest etiam hoc concludi ex hoc quod hic   320
homo in aliqua specie collocatur. Speciem autem
sortitur unumquodque ex forma: id igitur per
quod hic homo speciem sortitur forma est.
Vnumquodque autem ab eo speciem sortitur,
quod est principium proprie operationis speciei;   325
propria autem operatio hominis, in quantum est
homo, est intelligere: per hoc enim differt ab
aliis animalibus, et ideo in hac operatione
Aristotiles felicitatem ultimam constituit. Principium autem quo intelligimus est intellectus, ut   330
Aristotiles dicit; oportet igitur ipsum uniri
corpori ut formam, non quidem ita quod ipsa
intellectiua potentia sit alicuius organi actus, sed
quia est uirtus anime que est actus corporis
phisici organici.   335

(81)   Adhuc, secundum istorum positionem destru-
untur moralis philosophie principia: subtrahitur
enim quod est in nobis. Non enim est aliquid
in nobis nisi per uoluntatem; unde et hoc ipsum
uoluntarium dicitur, quod in nobis est. Voluntas   340
autem in intellectu est, ut patet per dictum
Aristotilis in III De anima, et per hoc quod in
substantiis separatis est intellectus et uoluntas;
et per hoc etiam quod contingit per uoluntatem
aliquid in uniuersali amare uel odire, sicut odimus   345
latronum genus, ut Aristotiles dicit in sua
Rhetorica.

(82)   Si igitur intellectus non est aliquid
huius hominis ut sit uere unum cum eo, sed
unitur ei solum per fantasmata uel sicut motor,
non erit in hoc homine uoluntas, sed in intellectu   350
separato. Et ita hic homo non erit dominus sui
actus, nec aliquis eius actus erit laudabilis uel
uituperabilis: quod est diuellere principia moralis
philosophie. Quod cum sit absurdum et uite
humane contrarium, non enim esset necesse   355
consiliari nec leges ferre, sequitur quod intellectus
sic uniatur nobis ut uere ex eo et nobis fiat
unum; quod uere non potest esse nisi eo modo
quo dictum est, ut sit scilicet potentia anime que
unitur nobis ut forma. Relinquitur igitur hoc   360
absque omni dubitatione tenendum, non propter
reuelationem fidei, ut dicunt, sed quia hoc
subtrahere est niti contra manifeste apparentia.

(80) This can also be concluded from the fact that this man is placed in some species. The species is derived from form; therefore, that through which this man has a species is form. But each thing has its species from that which is the principle of the proper activity of the species; the proper operation of man as man is understanding; it is in this that he differs from the other animals, and that is why Aristotle locates ultimate happiness in this activity. But the principle thanks to which we understand is the intellect, as Aristotle says; therefore, it must be united to the body as form, not indeed in such a way that the intellective power is the act of some organ, but because it is a power of the soul, which is the act of a physically organized body.

(81) Moreover, the position under discussion would destroy the principles of moral philosophy, for it would take away what is in our power. Something is in our power thanks to will, which is why the voluntary is defined as that which is in our power. But will is in intellect, as is evident from Aristotle in book 3 of *On the Soul* (432b5) and from the fact that intellect and will are found in separate substances as well as from the fact that something is loved or hated universally. We hate the genus of robbers, as Aristotle says in the *Rhetoric*.[40]

(82) If, then, intellect is not something of this man such that it is truly one with him but is united to him only through phantasms or as a mover, will would not be in man but in the separated intellect. And thus a man would not have dominion over his acts, nor could anyone be praised or blamed for his acts, which would destroy the principles of moral philosophy. And since that is absurd and out of keeping with human life—it would be unnecessary to take counsel or to pass laws—it follows that intellect is united to us in such a way that we are truly one with it, which can only be in the way suggested, namely, that it be a power of the soul, which is united to us as our form. It follows, then, that this must be held without any doubt, not because of the revelation of faith, as our opponents say, but because to deny it is to go against things manifestly obvious.

---

40 *Rhetoric,* 2.4.1382a6.

(83)   Rationes uero quas in contrarium adducunt
non difficile est soluere. Dicunt enim quod ex   365
hac positione sequitur quod intellectus sit forma
materialis, et non sit denudata ab omnibus
naturis rerum sensibilium; et quod per consequens
quicquid recipitur in intellectu, recipietur sicut
in materia indiuidualiter et non uniuersaliter. Et   370
ulterius quod si est forma materialis, quod non
est intellecta in actu, et ita intellectus non poterit
se intelligere: quod est manifeste falsum. Nulla
enim forma materialis est intellecta in actu, sed
in potentia tantum: fit autem intellecta in actu   375
per abstractionem.
      Horum autem solutio apparet ex hiis que
premissa sunt. Non enim dicimus animam humanam esse formam corporis secundum intellectiuam
potentiam, que secundum doctrinam Aristotilis   380
nullius organi actus est: unde remanet quod
anima, quantum ad intellectiuam potentiam, sit
immaterialis et immaterialiter recipiens et se
ipsam intelligens. Vnde et Aristotiles signanter
dicit quod anima est locus specierum "non tota"   385
sed intellectus".

(84)   Si autem contra hoc obiciatur quod potentia
anime non potest esse immaterialior aut simplicior
quam eius essentia: optime quidem procederet
ratio, si essentia humane anime sic esset forma   390
materie, quod non per esse suum esset sed per
esse compositi, sicut est de aliis formis, que
secundum se nec esse nec operationem habent
preter communicationem materie, que propter
hoc materie immerse dicuntur. Anima autem   395
humana, quia secundum suum esse est, cui
aliqualiter communicat materia non totaliter comprehendens ipsam, eo quod maior est dignitas
huius forme quam capacitas materie: nichil
prohibet quin habeat aliquam operationem uel   400
uirtutem ad quam materia non attingit.

(83) It is an easy matter to refute the arguments put forward on behalf of the opposite view. For they say that it follows from their position that intellect is a material form and is not free of every sensible nature, with the consequence that whatever is received in intellect is received as in matter, individually and not universally. And further, if it is a material form, that it is not understood in act, and thus intellect is incapable of understanding itself, which is manifestly false. No material form is understood in act but only in potency; it becomes understood in act through abstraction.

The answer is obvious from what has been said earlier. For we do not say that the human soul is the form of body according to the intellective power, which, according to Aristotle's teaching, is not the act of any organ (429a27–28). The soul, with respect to the intellective power, is immaterial and receives immaterially and understands itself. Hence, Aristotle significantly says that soul is the place of forms, "not the whole soul, but the intellect" (429a28–29).

(84) If one objects to this that a power of the soul cannot be more immaterial or simpler than its essence—well, that would be a good argument if the essence of the human soul were the form of matter in such a way that it did not exist of itself but only in dependence on the existence of the composite, as is the case with other forms that have no existence or operations of themselves without a sharing in matter, and are therefore said to be immersed in matter. The human soul exists in its own right and is to a degree united with a matter that does not wholly capture it—this form is greater in dignity than to be a capacity of matter. Nothing prevents its having some operation or power to which matter does not attain.

(85)   Consideret autem qui hoc dicit, quod si hoc
intellectiuum principium quo nos intelligimus,
esset secundum esse separatum et distinctum ab
anima que est corporis nostri forma, esset   405
secundum se intelligens et intellectum, et non
quandoque intelligeret, quandoque non; neque
etiam indigeret ut se ipsum cognosceret per
intelligibilia et per actus, sed per essentiam suam
sicut alie substantie separate. Neque etiam esset   410
conueniens quod ad intelligendum indigeret fan-
tasmatibus nostris: non enim inuenitur in
rerum ordine quod superiores substantie ad suas
principales perfectiones indigeant inferioribus substantiis; sicut nec corpora celestia formantur   415
aut perficiuntur ad suas operationes ex corporibus
inferioribus. Magnam igitur improbabilitatem
continet sermo dicentis quod intellectus sit
quoddam principium secundum substantiam sepa-
ratum, et tamen quod per species a fantasmatibus   420
acceptas perficiatur et fiat actu intelligens.

(85) Let him who says this consider that if this intellective principle whereby we understand existed separate and distinct from the soul, which is the form of our body, it would be of itself understanding and understood—and not sometimes understanding, sometimes not. Nor would it need to understand itself by way of intelligibles and acts but would do so through its own essence, like other separated substances, and it would not be fitting that it need our phantasms in order to understand. The order of things is not such that higher substances require lower substances for their own principal perfection, no more than celestial bodies are formed or perfected in their operations by lower bodies.

The claim that the intellect is some principle separated in substance and yet is perfected and comes actually to understand through species taken from phantasms is, therefore, improbable in the extreme.

▍ Capitvlvm IV

(86) Hiis igitur consideratis quantum ad id quod
ponunt intellectum non esse animam que est
nostri corporis forma, neque partem ipsius,
sed aliquid secundum substantiam separatum:
considerandum restat de hoc quod dicunt intel-   5
lectum possibilem esse unum in omnibus. Forte
enim de agente hoc dicere aliquam rationem
haberet, et multi philosophi hoc posuerunt:
nichil enim uidetur inconueniens sequi, si ab
uno agente multa perficiantur, quemadmodum   10
ab uno sole perficiuntur omnes potentie uisiue
animalium ad uidendum. Quamuis etiam hoc
non sit secundum intentionem Aristotilis, qui
posuit intellectum agentem esse aliquid in anima,
unde comparauit ipsum lumini; Plato autem   15
ponens intellectum unum separatum, comparauit
ipsum soli, ut Themistius dicit: est enim unus
sol, sed plura lumina diffusa a sole ad uidendum.
Sed quicquid sit de intellectu agente, dicere
intellectum possibilem esse unum omnium homi-   20
num, multipliciter impossibile apparet.

▌ Chapter IV

(86) So much for the contention that intellect is not the soul, which is the form of our body, nor a part of it, but some kind of separate substance. There remains to discuss the claim that there is one possible intellect for everybody.[41] There would perhaps be some reason for saying this of agent intellect, and many philosophers do say it, for nothing absurd seems to follow from several things being perfected by one agent, as by one sun the visual powers of all animals are able to see. Although this is not Aristotle's intention—he holds that the agent intellect is in the soul—he nonetheless compares it to a light, and Plato, holding that the intellect is one separate thing, likened it to the sun, as Themistius tells us; for there is one sun but many lights diffused from it for the sake of seeing.[42] But, however it be with the agent intellect, to say that the possible intellect is one for all men appears impossible in many ways.

---

41 Siger of Brabant, *In III De anima,* q. 11, lines 4–5; and q. 9, lines 55–56: "Intellect is one and is not multiplied with the multiplication of individual men."

42 Themistius, 235.10–11.

(87)   Primo quidem, quia si intellectus possibilis est
quo intelligimus, necesse est dicere quod homo
singularis intelligens uel sit ipse intellectus, uel
intellectus formaliter ei inhereat: non quidem   25
ita quod sit forma corporis, sed quia est uirtus
anime que est forma corporis. Si quis autem
dicat quod homo singularis est ipse intellectus,
consequens est quod hic homo singularis non
sit alius ab illo homine singulari, et quod omnes   30
homines sint unus homo, non quidem partici-
patione speciei, sed secundum unum indiuiduum.
Si uero intellectus inest nobis formaliter, sicut iam
dictum est, sequitur quod diuersorum corporum
sint diuerse anime. Sicuti enim homo est ex   35
corpore et anima, ita hic homo, ut Callias aut
Sortes, ex hoc corpore et ex hac anima. Si autem
anime sunt diuerse, et intellectus possibilis est
uirtus anime qua anima intelligit, oportet quod
differat numero; quia nec fingere possibile est   40
quod diuersarum rerum sit una numero uirtus.
Si quis autem dicat quod homo intelligit per
intellectum possibilem sicut per aliquid sui,
quod tamen est pars eius non ut forma sed sicut
motor: iam ostensum est supra quod hac positione   45
facta, nullo modo potest dici quod Sortes
intelligat.

(87) First, because if the possible intellect is that whereby we understand, it must be said of an individual man who understands either that he is intellect itself or that intellect formally inheres in him, not indeed in such a way that it be the form of the body but rather a power of the soul, which is the form of the body. Should anyone say that the singular man is intellect itself, it would follow that this singular man would not differ from another singular man and that all men are one man, not by sharing in the same species, but as one individual. But if intellect is in us formally, it would follow, as has already been said, that there are different forms of different bodies. For just as man is composed of body and soul, so this man, Callias or Socrates, is composed of this body and this soul. If souls differ, however, and the possible intellect is the power of the soul whereby the soul understands, they must differ numerically, for it is impossible to imagine numerically one power of different things. Should someone say that man understands through possible intellect as by something of his own that, however, is not a part of him as a form but rather as a mover, it has already been shown above [79] that on this view it can in no wise be said that Socrates understands.

(88) Sed demus quod Sortes intelligat per hoc quod
intellectus intelligit, licet intellectus sit solum
motor, sicut homo uidet per hoc quod oculus   50
uidet; et ut similitudinem sequamur, ponatur
quod omnium hominum sit unus oculus numero:
inquirendum restat utrum omnes homines sint
unus uidens uel multi uidentes. Ad cuius ueritatis
inquisitionem considerare oportet quod aliter se   55
habet de primo mouente, et aliter de instrumento.
Si enim multi homines utantur uno et eodem
instrumento numero, dicentur multi operantes:
puta, cum multi utuntur una machina ad lapidis
proiectionem uel eleuationem. Si uero principale   60
agens sit unum quod utatur multis ut instrumentis,
nichilominus operans est unum, sed forte operationes diuerse propter diuersa instrumenta;
aliquando autem et operatio una, etsi ad eam
multa instrumenta requirantur. Sic igitur unitas   65
operantis attenditur non secundum instrumenta,
sed secundum principale quod utitur instrumentis.
    Predicta ergo positione facta, si oculus esset
principale in homine, qui uteretur omnibus
potentiis anime et partibus corporis quasi instru-   70
mentis, multi habentes unum oculum essent unus
uidens; si uero oculus non sit principale hominis,
sed aliquid sit eo principalius quod utitur oculo,
quod diuersificaretur in diuersis, essent quidem
multi uidentes sed uno oculo.   75

(88) But let us grant that Socrates understands because the intellect understands although intellect is only a mover, as a man sees because the eye sees. And, to keep to the analogy, let us posit that there is numerically one eye for all men. Now we ask whether all men are one seeing entity or many. To discover the truth of the matter, it should be noted that the first mover differs from the instrument, for if many men use numerically one instrument, we say there are many agents—for example, when many use one machine for the throwing of stones or for elevation. If, however, the chief agent is one but uses many instruments, there is nonetheless one agent, even though many instruments are needed for it, though perhaps a diversity of operations because of the diversity of instruments. Sometimes, however, there is one operation, although many instruments are required for it. The unity of the one acting is read, not from the instruments, but from the chief agent who uses the instruments.

Thus, on the position described earlier, if the eye were what is principal in a man and it would use all powers of the soul and parts of the body as instruments, many having one eye would be one seeing thing. But if the eye were not what is principal in man, but something higher that uses the eye and is diversified in diverse men, there would indeed be many seeing, but with one eye.

(89)   Manifestum est autem quod intellectus est id
quod est principale in homine, et quod utitur
omnibus potentiis anime et membris corporis
tamquam organis; et propter hoc Aristotiles
subtiliter dixit quod homo est intellectus "uel   80
maxime". Si igitur sit unus intellectus omnium,
ex necessitate sequitur quod sit unus intelligens,
et per consequens unus uolens et unus utens pro
sue uoluntatis arbitrio omnibus illis secundum
que homines diuersificantur ad inuicem. Et ex   85
hoc ulterius sequitur quod nulla differentia sit
inter homines quantum ad liberam uoluntatis
electionem, sed eadem sit omnium, si intellectus,
apud quem solum residet principalitas et domi-
nium utendi omnibus aliis, est unus et indiuisus   90
in omnibus. Quod est manifeste falsum et
impossibile: repugnat enim hiis que apparent,
et destruit totam scientiam moralem et omnia
que pertinent ad conuersationem ciuilem, que est
hominibus naturalis, ut Aristotiles dicit.   95

(89) But obviously it is intellect that is principal in man and uses all the powers of the soul and bodily members as organs. Hence Aristotle's careful remark that man is intellect "or especially it."[43] If, then, there were one intellect for all, it would necessarily follow that there is only one who understands and consequently only one who wills and of his own free will uses all those things thanks to which men are diverse from one another. From this it follows further that there would be no difference between men as to the free choice of will, but it would be the same for all if, indeed, intellect, in which resides the principality and dominion of using all the others, is one and undivided in all. But this is clearly false, impossible, and repugnant to what is obvious: it destroys the whole of moral science and all those things that pertain to civil interchange, which is natural to man, as Aristotle says.[44]

---

43 *Nicomachean Ethics,* 9.9.1169a2.
44 *Politics,* 1.1.1253a2–3.

(90)   Adhuc, si omnes homines intelligunt uno
intellectu, qualitercumque eis uniatur, siue ut
forma siue ut motor, de necessitate sequitur
quod omnium hominum sit unum numero ipsum
intelligere quod est simul et respectu unius   100
intelligibilis: puta, si ego intelligo lapidem et
tu similiter, oportebit quod una et eadem sit
intellectualis operatio et mei et tui. Non enim
potest esse eiusdem actiui principii, siue sit
forma siue sit motor, respectu eiusdem obiecti   105
nisi una numero operatio eiusdem speciei in
eodem tempore: quod manifestum est ex hiis
que Philosophus declarat in V Phisicorum. Vnde
si essent multi homines habentes unum oculum,
omnium uisio non esset nisi una respectu eiusdem   110
obiecti in eodem tempore.

(91)   Similiter ergo, si
intellectus sit unus omnium, sequitur quod
omnium hominum idem intelligentium eodem
tempore sit una actio intellectualis tantum;
et precipue cum nichil eorum secundum que   115
ponuntur homines differre ab inuicem, commu-
nicet in operatione intellectuali. Fantasmata enim
preambula sunt actioni intellectus, sicut colores
actioni uisus: unde per eorum diuersitatem non
diuersificaretur actio intellectus, maxime respectu   120
unius intelligibilis; secundum que tamen ponunt
diuersificari scientiam huius a scientia alterius,
in quantum hic intelligit ea quorum fantasmata
habet et ille alia quorum fantasmata habet. Sed
in duobus qui idem sciunt et intelligunt, ipsa   125
operatio intellectualis per diuersitatem fantas-
matum nullatenus diuersificari potest.

(90) Again, if all men understand by one intellect—however it be united to them, whether as form or as mover—it necessarily follows that of all men there would be numerically one act of understanding, which is both simultaneous and of one intelligible object. For example, if I understand stone and you do likewise, it would be necessary that my intellectual activity and yours be one and the same. The operation of the same active principle, be it form or mover, with respect to the same object at the same time must be numerically one, as is clear from what the Philosopher says in book 5 of the *Physics*.[45] So, if there were many men having one eye, the seeing of all with respect to the same object at the same time could only be one.

(91) So, too, if there were one intellect for all, it would follow that there is but one intellectual operation of all men understanding the same thing at the same time, especially since nothing in terms of which men differ from one another would share in the intellectual operation. For phantasms are preambles to the action of intellect, as colors are to the act of vision, hence the action of intellect would not be diversified because of their differences, especially with regard to one intelligible. They distinguish the knowledge of this one from the knowledge of that one because the one understands those things of which he has phantasms, and the other those of which he has phantasms. But when two know and understand the same thing, intellectual activity itself can in no way be diversified by the diversity of phantasms.

---

44 *Physics,* 5.6.227b21–228a3.

(92)   Adhuc autem ostendendum est quod hec positio
manifeste repugnat dictis Aristotilis. Cum enim
dixisset de intellectu possibili quod est separatus   130
et quod est in potentia omnia, subiungit quod
"cum sic singula fiat, scilicet in actu, ut sciens
dicitur qui secundum actum", id est hoc modo
sicut scientia est actus, et sicut sciens dicitur esse
in actu in quantum habet habitum; unde subdit   135
"hoc autem confestim accidit cum possit operari
per se ipsum. Est quidem igitur et tunc potentia
quodammodo, non tamen similiter ante addiscere
aut inuenire". Et postea, cum quesiuisset "si
intellectus simplex est et impassibile et nulli   140
nichil habet commune, sicut dixit Anaxagoras,
quomodo intelliget si intelligere pati aliquid
est?"; et ad hoc soluendum respondet dicens
quod "potentia quodammodo est intelligibilia
intellectus, sed actu nichil antequam intelligat.   145
Oportet autem sic sicut in tabula nichil est actu
scriptum: quod quidem accidit in intellectu".
Est ergo sententia Aristotilis quod intellectus
possibilis ante addiscere aut inuenire est in
potentia, sicut tabula in qua nichil est actu   150
scriptum; sed post addiscere et inuenire est
actu secundum habitum scientie, quo potest per
se ipsum operari, quamuis et tunc sit in potentia
ad considerare in actu.

(92) Further, it should be pointed out that this position manifestly conflicts with the teaching of Aristotle. For when he says of
possible intellect that it is separate and potentially all things, he
adds that "when thought has become each thing in the way in which
a man who actually knows is said to do so"—that is, in the way that
knowledge is an act and the knower is said to be in act insofar as he
has the habit—he adds, "this happens when he is now able to exercise the power on his own initiative; its condition is still one of potentiality, but in a different sense from the potentiality that preceded
the acquisition of knowledge by learning or discovery" (429b5–9).
Later, he asks, "If intellect is simple and impassible and has nothing
in common with anything else, as Anaxagoras says, how can it come
to think at all if thinking involves a kind of passivity?" (429b23–25).
And in reply, he says, "intellect is in a sense potentially whatever is
thinkable, though actually it is nothing until it has thought. What it
thinks must be in it, just as characters are said to be on a writing-
tablet on which as yet nothing actually stands written: this is exactly what happens with intellect" (429b30–430a2). It is the
teaching of Aristotle, therefore, that the possible intellect is in potency prior to learning or discovery, like a tablet on which nothing is
yet written, but after learning and discovery it is in act by the habit
of science, thanks to which it can actuate itself, even though it is
then in potency to actually considering.

(93)   Vbi tria notanda sunt. Primum, quod habitus   155
scientie est actus primus ipsius intellectus possibilis, qui secundum hunc fit actu et potest per
se ipsum operari. Non autem scientia est solum
secundum fantasmata illustrata, ut quidam dicunt,
uel quedam facultas que nobis acquiritur ex   160
frequenti meditatione et exercitio, ut continuemur
cum intellectu possibili per nostra fantasmata.
Secundo, notandum est quod ante nostrum
addiscere et inuenire, ipse intellectus possibilis
est in potentia sicut tabula in qua nichil est   165
scriptum. Tertio, quod per nostrum addiscere seu
inuenire ipse intellectus possibilis fit actu.

(94)   Hec
autem nullo modo possunt stare, si sit unus
intellectus possibilis omnium qui sunt et erunt
et fuerunt.   170
     Manifestum est enim quod species conseruantur
in intellectu, est enim locus specierum, ut supra
Philosophus dixerat; et iterum scientia est habitus
permanens. Si ergo per aliquem precedentium
hominum factus est in actu secundum aliquas   175
species intelligibiles, et perfectus secundum habitum scientie, ille habitus et ille species in
eo remanent. Cum autem omne recipiens sit
denudatum ab eo quod recipit, impossibile erit
quod per meum addiscere aut inuenire ille species   180
acquirantur in intellectu possibili. Etsi enim
aliquis dicat quod per meum inuenire intellectus
possibilis secundum aliquid fiat in actu de nouo,
puta si ego aliquid intelligibilium inuenio quod
a nullo precedentium est inuentum: tamen in   185
addiscendo hoc contingere non potest, non enim
possum addiscere nisi quod docens sciuit. Frustra
ergo dixit quod ante addiscere aut inuenire
intellectus erat in potentia.

(93) Three things should be noted here. First, that the habit of science is the first act of the possible intellect, which, thanks to it, comes to be in act and can operate on its own. Science is not only according to illumined phantasms, as some say, or a faculty that we acquire by frequent meditation and exercise in order that we might be linked with possible intellect by way of our phantasms. Second, it should be noted that before we learn or discover, the possible intellect itself is in potency as a tablet on which nothing is written. Third, that through our learning or discovering the possible intellect becomes actual.

(94) None of these things could be if there were only one possible intellect for all who are, were, or will be.

It is obvious that species are conserved in the intellect, for it is the place of forms, as the Philosopher said above (*On the Soul,* 3.4291a27–28); moreover, science is a permanent habit. If, then, one of the foregoing men becomes actual with respect to some intelligible species and is perfected by the habit of science, that habit and those species remain in him. Since any recipient does not have what it receives, it will be impossible that, through my learning or discovering, those species be acquired by the possible intellect. For although someone might say that through my discovery the possible intellect can newly come to be in act with respect to something—for example, if I should discover some knowable thing never before discovered— yet this could not come about through learning, for I can learn only what the teacher knew. It would therefore be pointless to say that the intellect was in potency prior to learning or discovering.

(95)   Sed et si quis addat homines semper fuisse   190
secundum opinionem Aristotilis, sequetur quod
non fuerit primus homo intelligens; et sic
per fantasmata nullius species intelligibiles sunt
acquisite in intellectu possibili, sed sunt species
intelligibiles intellectus possibilis eterne. Frustra   195
ergo Aristotiles posuit intellectum agentem, qui
faceret intelligibilia in potentia intelligibilia in
actu; frustra etiam posuit quod fantasmata se
habent ad intellectum possibilem sicut colores
ad uisum, si intellectus possibilis nichil a fantasma-   200
tibus accipit. Quamuis et hoc ipsum irrationabile
uideatur, quod substantia separata a fantasmatibus
nostris accipiat, et quod non possit se intelligere
nisi post nostrum addiscere aut intelligere; quia
Aristotiles post uerba premissa subiungit "et ipse   205
se ipsum tunc potest intelligere", scilicet post
addiscere aut inuenire. Substantia enim separata
secundum se ipsam est intelligibilis: unde per
suam essentiam se intelligeret intellectus possibilis,
si esset substantia separata; nec indigeret ad hoc   210
speciebus intelligibilibus ei superuenientibus per
nostrum intelligere aut inuenire.

(96)   Si autem hec inconuenientia uelint euadere,
dicendo quod omnia predicta Aristotiles dicit de
intellectu possibili secundum quod continuatur   215
nobis, et non secundum quod in se est: primo
quidem dicendum est quod uerba Aristotilis hoc
non sapiunt, immo de ipso intellectu possibili
loquitur secundum id quod est proprium sibi,
et secundum quod distinguitur ab agente. Deinde   220
si non fiat uis de uerbis Aristotilis, ponamus,
ut dicunt, quod intellectus possibilis ab eterno
habuerit species intelligibiles, per quas continuetur
nobiscum secundum fantasmata que sunt in nobis.

(95) Were someone to add that, according to the opinion of Aristotle, there have always been men, it would follow that there was never a first man who understood; and thus, intelligible species are acquired by possible intellect through no one's phantasms but are intelligible species of an eternal possible intellect. In vain, therefore, did Aristotle posit an agent intellect to make potentially intelligible things actually intelligible; in vain, too, did he posit that phantasms are to the possible intellect as colors are to sight, if the possible intellect receives nothing from phantasms. For this, too, seems irrational that a separated substance should receive from our phantasms and that it cannot understand itself save through our learning or understanding. But Aristotle added to the foregoing, "and it can then understand itself" (429b9), namely, after learning or discovering. Separate substance is intelligible in itself, and thus the possible intellect would understand itself through its essence, as if it were a separate substance; nor in order to do this would it need intelligible species coming to it because of our understanding and discovery.

(96) Should they wish to evade these absurdities by claiming that Aristotle says all those things about the possible intellect insofar as it is made one with us and not as it is in itself, it must first be said that Aristotle's words do not mean that. Indeed, he speaks of the possible intellect in terms of what is proper to it and insofar as it is distinguished from the agent. Then, if no help is forthcoming from Aristotle's words, let us posit, as they say, that the possible intellect eternally has intelligible species through which it is made one with us according to the phantasms which are in us.

(97)   Oportet enim quod species intelligibiles que   225
sunt in intellectu possibili, et fantasmata que
sunt in nobis, aliquo horum trium modorum
se habeant: quorum unus est, quod species
intelligibiles que sunt in intellectu possibili sint
accepte a fantasmatibus que sunt in nobis, ut   230
sonant uerba Aristotilis; quod non potest esse
secundum predictam positionem, ut ostensum
est. Secundus autem modus est ut ille species non
sint accepte a fantasmatibus, sed sint irradiantes
supra fantasmata nostra; puta, si species alique   235
essent in oculo irradiantes supra colores qui sunt
in pariete. Tertius autem modus est ut neque
species intelligibiles que sunt in intellectu possibili
sint recepte a fantasmatibus, neque imprimant
aliquid supra fantasmata.   240

(98)   Si autem ponatur secundum, scilicet quod
species intelligibiles illustrent fantasmata et secundum hoc intelligantur: primo quidem sequetur
quod fantasmata fiunt intelligibilia actu, non
per intellectum agentem, sed per intellectum   245
possibilem secundum suas species. Secundo, quod
talis irradiatio fantasmatum non poterit facere
quod fantasmata sint intelligibilia actu: non
enim fiunt fantasmata intelligibilia actu nisi per
abstractionem; hoc autem magis erit receptio   250
quam abstractio. Et iterum, cum omnis receptio
sit secundum naturam recepti, irradiatio specierum
intelligibilium que sunt in intellectu possibili
non erit in fantasmatibus que sunt in nobis
intelligibiliter, sed sensibiliter et materialiter; et   255
sic nos non poterimus intelligere uniuersale per
huiusmodi irradiationem. Si autem species intelligibiles intellectus possibilis neque accipiuntur a
fantasmatibus, neque irradiant super ea, erunt
omnino disparate et nichil proportionale habentes,   260
nec fantasmata aliquid facient ad intelligendum:
quod manifestis repugnat. Sic igitur omnibus
modis impossibile est quod intellectus possibilis
sit unus tantum omnium hominum.

(97) It is necessary that the intelligible species which are in the possible intellect and the phantasms that are in us be related in one of three ways. The first is that the intelligible species which are in the possible intellect are taken from the phantasms that are in us, as Aristotle's words suggest. That this is ruled out by the position under consideration has been shown. The second way is that the species are not taken from phantasms, but are shining upon our phantasms—for example, if there were species in the eye shining on the colors that are in the wall. The third way is that the intelligible species neither are received in the possible intellect from the phantasms nor imprint something on the phantasms.

(98) If the second way is taken, namely, that the intelligible species illumine the phantasms and in this way are understood, it would follow, first, that the phantasms come to be intelligible in act, not through the agent intellect but through the possible intellect and its species. Second, that such an illumination of phantasms could not make phantasms intelligible in act: phantasms do not become intelligible in act except through abstraction; but this would be more like a receiving than an abstracting. Again, since any reception is according to the nature of the receiver, the illumining of the intelligible species that are in the possible intellect will not be of phantasms that are in us in an intelligible mode, but sensibly and materially. Thus, we could not understand the universal thanks to this kind of illumination. But if the intelligible species of the possible intellect neither are taken from phantasms nor shine upon them, they will be wholly disparate, having no similarity, and phantasms would have nothing to do with understanding, which flies in the face of the obvious. Thus there is no possible way in which the possible intellect could be one and the same for all men.

| Capitvlvm V

(99)   Restat autem nunc soluere ea quibus plurali-
tatem intellectus possibilis nituntur excludere.
Quorum primum est, quia omne quod multiplicatur secundum diuisionem materie est forma
materialis: unde substantie separate a materia   5
non sunt plures in una specie. Si ergo plures
intellectus essent in pluribus hominibus qui
diuiduntur ad inuicem numero per diuisionem
materie, sequeretur ex necessitate quod intellectus
esset forma materialis: quod est contra uerba   10
Aristotilis et probationem ipsius qua probat quod
intellectus est separatus. Si ergo est separatus et
non est forma materialis, nullo modo multiplicatur
secundum multiplicationem corporum.

(100) Huic autem rationi tantum innituntur, quod   15
dicunt quod Deus non posset facere plures
intellectus unius speciei in diuersis hominibus:
dicunt enim quod hoc implicaret contradictionem,
quia habere naturam ut numeraliter multiplicetur
est aliud a natura forme separate. Procedunt   20
autem ulterius, ex hoc concludere uolentes quod
nulla forma separata est una numero nec aliquid
indiuiduatum. Quod dicunt ex ipso uocabulo
apparere, quia non est unum numero nisi quod
est unum de numero; forma autem liberata a   25
materia non est unum de numero, quia non habet
in se causam numeri, eo quod causa numeri est
a materia.

| Chapter V

(99) Arguments intended to exclude a plurality of possible intellects remain to be dealt with. The first is this: Whatever is multiplied by a division of matter is a material form, which is why substances separate from matter cannot be many members of the same species. If, then, there were a plurality of intellects in many men who are numerically distinguished from one another by the division of matter, it would necessarily follow that intellect is a material form. But that goes against the words of Aristotle and the argument in which he proves that the intellect is separate. If, then, it is separate, it is not a material form and can in no way be multiplied according to the multiplication of bodies.

(100) So attached are they to this argument that they say that God could not make many intellects of the same species in diverse men because, they say, this would imply a contradiction: to have a nature that can be numerically multiplied is other than the nature of separated form. They go beyond this, however, and want to conclude from this that no separate form is numerically one nor an individuated thing. They say that this is apparent from the word itself, for only that is numerically one which is one of a number of things, but form freed from matter is not one of a number because it does not have within it the cause of number, which is taken from matter.

(101) Sed ut a posterioribus incipiamus, uidentur
uocem propriam ignorare in hoc quod ultimo   30
dictum est. Dicit enim Aristotiles in IV Methaphisice quod "cuiusque substantia unum est
non secundum accidens", et quod "nichil est
aliud unum preter ens". Substantia ergo separata
si est ens, secundum suam substantiam est una;   35
precipue cum Aristotiles dicat in VIII Metha-
phisice quod ea que non habent materiam, non
habent causam ut sint unum et ens. Vnum
autem in V Methaphisice dicitur quadrupliciter,
scilicet numero, specie, genere, proportione. Nec   40
est dicendum quod aliqua substantia separata sit
unum tantum specie uel genere, quia hoc non
est esse simpliciter unum: relinquitur quod
quelibet substantia separata sit unum numero.
Nec dicitur aliquid unum numero quia sit unum   45
de numero—non enim numerus est causa
unius sed e conuerso—, sed quia in numerando
non diuiditur; unum enim est id quod non
diuiditur.

(102) Nec iterum hoc uerum est, quod omnis   50
numerus causetur ex materia: frustra enim
Aristotiles quesiuisset numerum substantiarum
separatarum. Ponit etiam Aristotiles in V Methaphisice quod multum dicitur non solum numero,
sed specie et genere. Nec etiam hoc uerum est,   55
quod substantia separata non sit singularis et
indiuiduum aliquid; alioquin non haberet aliquam
operationem, cum actus sint solum singularium,
ut Philosophus dicit; unde contra Platonem
argumentatur in VII Methaphisice quod si ydee   60
sunt separate, non predicabitur de multis ydea,
nec poterit diffiniri, sicut nec alia indiuidua que
sunt unica in sua specie, ut sol et luna. Non
enim materia est principium indiuiduationis in
rebus materialibus, nisi in quantum materia non   65
est participabilis a pluribus, cum sit primum
subiectum non existens in alio; unde et de ydea
Aristotiles dicit quod, si ydea esset separata
"esset quedam, id est indiuidua, quam impossibile
esset predicari de multis".   70

(101) To begin at the end, they seem not to understand their own words in what was just said. For Aristotle, in book 4 of the *Metaphysics,* says that "the essence of each thing is one in no merely accidental way" and that "similarly it is from its very nature something that *is.*"[46] If separated substance is a being, therefore, it must be one substance, especially since Aristotle says in book 8 of the *Metaphysics* that things which have no matter have no cause of their being or of their being one.[47] In book 5 of the *Metaphysics,*[48] four kinds of unity are distinguished, namely, numeric, specific, generic, and proportional. It cannot be said that any separate substance is one only specifically or generically, since this is not to be one simply speaking. There remains that any separate substance is numerically one. Nor is it said to be numerically one because it is one among numbers—number is not the cause of the one but vice versa—but because in numbering it is not divided: one is that which is undivided.

(102) Nor is it true to say that every number is caused by matter, for then Aristotle would have inquired in vain after the number of separated substances.[49] For Aristotle says in book 5 of the *Metaphysics* that "many" is said not only numerically but specifically and generically.[50] Nor is it true that separate substance is not singular and individuated; otherwise it would have no operation, since acts belong only to singulars, as the Philosopher says;[51] hence, he argues against Plato in book 7 of the *Metaphysics* that if the Idea is separate, it will not be predicated of many, nor will it be definable any more than other individuals that are unique in their species, such as the sun and moon.[52] Matter is the principle of individuation in material things insofar as matter is not shareable by many, since it is the first subject not existing in another. Hence, Aristotle says that if the Idea were separate, "it would be something, that is, an individual, which it would be impossible to predicate of many."

---

46 *Metaphysics,* 4.2.1003b31–32.
47 Ibid., 8.5.1045a35–b6.
48 Ibid., 5.6.1016b31–35.
49 See *Metaphysics,* 12.10.1073b17–1074b14.
50 *Metaphysics,* 5.8.1017a2–6.
51 Ibid., 1.1.981a16–17.
52 Ibid.,7.15.1040a25–30.

(103) Indiuidue ergo sunt substantie separate et
singulares; non autem indiuiduantur ex materia,
sed ex hoc ipso quod non sunt nate in alio esse,
et per consequens nec participari a multis. Ex
quo sequitur quod si aliqua forma nata est   75
participari ab aliquo, ita quod sit actus alicuius
materie, illa potest indiuiduari et multiplicari per
comparationem ad materiam. Iam autem supra
ostensum est quod intellectus est uirtus anime
que est actus corporis; in multis igitur corporibus   80
sunt multe anime, et in multis animabus sunt
multe uirtutes intellectuales que uocantur intellectus: nec propter hoc sequitur quod intellectus
sit uirtus materialis, ut supra ostensum est.

(104) Si quis autem obiciat quod, si multiplicantur   85
secundum corpora, sequitur quod destructis corporibus non remaneant multe anime: patet
solutio per ea que supra dicta sunt. Vnumquodque
enim sic est ens sicut unum, ut dicitur in
IV Methaphisice; sicut igitur esse anime est   90
quidem in corpore in quantum est forma corporis,
nec est ante corpus, tamen destructo corpore
adhuc remanet in suo esse: ita unaqueque anima
remanet in sua unitate, et per consequens multe
anime in sua multitudine.   95

(103) Separate substances, therefore, are individual and singular, but they are individuated not by matter but by the fact that it is not their nature to exist in another and consequently to be participated in by many. From which it follows that if any form is of a nature to be participated in by something, such that it be the act of some matter, it can be individuated and multiplied by comparison with matter. It has already been shown above that the intellect is a power of the soul, which is the act of the body. Therefore, in many bodies, there are many souls; and in many souls, there are many intellectual powers, that is, intellects. Nor does it follow from this that the intellect is a material power, as has been shown.

(104) Should anyone object that if the many souls are multiplied according to bodies, it follows that they will not remain when the bodies have been destroyed, the response is obvious from what has already been said. A thing is one in the way it is a being, as is said in book 4 of the *Metaphysics;*[53] therefore, for the soul to be is to be in the body as its form, nor is it prior to body, nonetheless it remains in existence after the body is destroyed; thus each soul remains in its unity, and consequently many souls in their manyness.

---

53 *Metaphysics*, 4.2.1003b30–34.

(105) Valde autem ruditer argumentantur ad ostendendum quod hoc Deus facere non possit quod
sint multi intellectus, credentes hoc includere
contradictionem. Dato enim quod non esset
de natura intellectus quod multiplicaretur, non   100
propter hoc oporteret quod intellectum multi-
plicari includeret contradictionem. Nichil enim
prohibet aliquid non habere in sua natura causam
alicuius, quod tamen habet illud ex alia causa:
sicut graue non habet ex sua natura quod sit   105
sursum, tamen graue esse sursum non includit
contradictionem; sed graue esse sursum secundum
suam naturam contradictionem includeret. Sic
ergo si intellectus naturaliter esset unus omnium
quia non haberet naturalem causam multipli-   110
cationis, posset tamen sortiri multiplicationem
ex supernaturali causa, nec esset implicatio
contradictionis. Quod dicimus non propter propositum, sed magis ne hec argumentandi forma
ad alia extendatur; sic enim possent concludere   115
quod Deus non posset facere quod mortui
resurgant, et quod ceci ad uisum reparentur.

(106) Adhuc autem ad munimentum sui erroris
aliam rationem inducunt. Querunt enim utrum
intellectum in me et in te est unum penitus,   120
aut duo in numero et unum in specie. Si unum
intellectum, tunc erit unus intellectus; si duo
in numero et unum in specie, sequitur quod
intellecta habebunt rem intellectam: quecumque
enim sunt duo in numero et unum in specie   125
sunt unum intellectum, quia est una quiditas per
quam intelligitur; et sic procedetur in infinitum,
quod est impossibile. Ergo impossibile est quod
sint duo intellecta in numero in me et in te;
est ergo unum tantum, et unus intellectus numero   130
tantum in omnibus.

(105) They argue most crudely to show that God cannot bring it about that there should be many intellects, believing this to involve a contradiction. For, even granted that it is not of the nature of intellect that it be multiplied, it does not follow from this that the multiplying of intellect involves a contradiction. Nothing prevents a thing's getting from another something that it is not of its nature to have: it is not of the nature of the heavy to be above, yet for the heavy to be above does not involve a contradiction, although for the heavy to be above by its very nature would involve a contradiction. Thus, if the intellect were naturally one for all because it had no natural cause of multiplication, multiplication could nonetheless come about through a supernatural cause without involving any contradiction. We say this not because of the present question but lest this form of arguing be extended to other cases, for in this way one could conclude that God cannot bring it about that the dead should rise and the blind have their sight restored to them.

(106) To bolster their error, they bring forth another argument. They ask whether what is understood in me and in you is in all respects one, or numerically two but specifically one. If what is understood is one, there will be one intellect. If numerically two but specifically one, it follows that they will have as things understood the thing understood. Wherever there are numerically two but specifically one, there is one thing understood because there is one quiddity through which understanding takes place, and so on to infinity, which is impossible. Therefore, it is impossible that there be numerically two things understood in me and you. There is one alone, then, and numerically only one intellect in all.

(107) Querendum est autem ab hiis qui tam subtiliter
se argumentari putant, utrum quod sint duo
intellecta in numero et unum in specie, sit contra
rationem intellecti in quantum est intellectum,   135
aut in quantum est intellectum ab homine. Et
manifestum est secundum rationem quam ponunt,
quod hoc est contra rationem intellecti in quantum
est intellectum; de ratione enim intellecti, in
quantum huiusmodi, est quod non indigeat   140
quod ab eo aliquid abstrahatur ad hoc quod sit
intellectum. Ergo secundum eorum rationem
simpliciter concludere possumus quod sit unum
intellectum tantum, et non solum unum intellec-
tum ab omnibus hominibus. Et si est unum   145
intellectum tantum, secundum eorum rationem
sequitur quod sit unus intellectus tantum in toto
mundo, et non solum in hominibus. Ergo
intellectus noster non solum est substantia sepa-
rata, sed etiam est ipse Deus; et uniuersaliter   150
tollitur pluralitas substantiarum separatarum.

(108) Si quis autem uellet respondere quod intellectum
ab una substantia separata et intellectum ab alia
non est unum specie, quia intellectus differunt
specie, se ipsum deciperet; quia id quod intelli-   155
gitur comparatur ad intelligere et ad intellectum
sicut obiectum ad actum et potentiam. Obiectum
autem non recipit speciem ab actu neque a
potentia, sed magis e conuerso: est ergo
simpliciter concedendum quod intellectum unius   160
rei, puta lapidis, est unum tantum non solum
in omnibus hominibus, sed etiam in omnibus
intelligentibus.

(107) It ought to be asked by those who consider themselves to argue so subtly whether for things understood to be numerically two but specifically one is contrary to the notion of the understood insofar as it is understood, or insofar as it is understood by man. It is clear from the argument they formulate that it is contrary to the notion of the thing understood. For it is of the notion of the thing understood as such that nothing need be abstracted from it in order that it be understood. Therefore, on the basis of their argument, we can conclude not just that there is only one thing understood by all men but that there is simply one thing understood. And if there is but one thing understood, according to their reasoning it follows that there is only one intellect in the whole world, not only for men. Therefore, not only is our intellect a separate substance, it is also God Himself, and the plurality of separated substances is wholly swept away.

(108) Anyone who sought to respond that the thing understood by one separate substance and that understood by another are not specifically one because the intellects differ specifically would deceive himself, because that which is understood is related to understanding and to intellect as an object to act and potency. The object does not take its species from either the act or the power but rather the other way around. Therefore it must simply be conceded that the understanding of one thing—say a stone—is one alone, not only in all men but also in all intelligences.

(109) Sed inquirendum restat quid sit ipsum intellectum. Si enim dicant quod intellectum est una   165
species immaterialis existens in intellectu, latet
ipsos quod quodammodo transeunt in dogma
Platonis, qui posuit quod de rebus sensibilibus
nulla scientia potest haberi, sed omnis scientia
habetur de forma una separata. Nichil enim   170
refert ad propositum, utrum aliquis dicat quod
scientia que habetur de lapide habetur de una
forma lapidis separata, an de una forma lapidis
que est in intellectu: utrobique enim sequitur
quod scientie non sunt de rebus que sunt hic,   175
sed de rebus separatis solum. Sed quia Plato
posuit huiusmodi formas immateriales per se
subsistentes, poterat etiam cum hoc ponere
plures intellectus participantes ab una forma
separata unius ueritatis cognitionem. Isti autem   180
quia ponunt huiusmodi formas immateriales—
quas dicunt esse intellecta—in intellectu,
necesse habent ponere quod sit unus intellectus
tantum, non solum omnium hominum, sed etiam
simpliciter.   185

(110) Est ergo dicendum secundum sententiam
Aristotilis quod intellectum quod est unum est
ipsa natura uel quiditas rei; de rebus enim est
scientia naturalis et alie scientie, non de speciebus
intellectis. Si enim intellectum esset non ipsa   190
natura lapidis que est in rebus, sed species que
est in intellectu, sequeretur quod ego non
intelligerem rem que est lapis, sed solum intentionem que est abstracta a lapide. Sed uerum
est quod natura lapidis prout est in singularibus,   195
est intellecta in potentia; sed fit intellecta in
actu per hoc quod species a rebus sensibilibus,
mediantibus sensibus, usque ad fantasiam perue-
niunt, et per uirtutem intellectus agentis species
intelligibiles abstrahuntur, que sunt in intellectu   200
possibili. Hee autem species non se habent ad
intellectum possibilem ut intellecta, sed sicut
species quibus intellectus intelligit, sicut et species
que sunt in uisu non sunt ipsa uisa, sed ea quibus
uisus uidet: nisi in quantum intellectus reflectitur   205
supra se ipsum, quod in sensu accidere non potest.

(109) But it remains to ask what is the understood itself. For if they say that the thing understood is one immaterial species existing in the intellect, in a way they unwittingly slide into the teaching of Plato, who taught that there can be no science of sensible things, but that every science is of one separated form.[54] It is not relevant to the point at issue whether someone says that the knowledge of a rock is of one separated form of rock or of one form of rock that is in the intellect. In either case, it follows that sciences are not of the things that are here but only of separated things. Because Plato taught that immaterial forms of this kind are of themselves subsistent, he could maintain along with this that many intellects derive, from one separate form, knowledge of one truth. But those who posit in the intellect immaterial forms of this kind—which they call the things understood—they have to say that there is only one intellect, not only for all men but absolutely speaking.

(110) In keeping with the teaching of Aristotle, therefore, it ought to be said that the understood thing, which is one, is the very nature or quiddity of the thing; natural science and the other sciences are of things, not of understood species. For if the thing understood were not rock's very nature, which is in things, but the species, which is in the intellect, it would follow that I do not understand the thing that is a stone but only the intention that is abstracted from the stone. It is true that the nature of stone, as it is in singulars, is only potentially understood, but it comes to be actually understood because the species come from sensible things, through the mediation of the senses, to the imagination; from which the intelligible species, which are in the possible intellect, are abstracted by the power of the agent intellect. These species, however, do not relate to possible intellect as what is understood but as species by means of which the intellect understands, just as the species that are in sight are not the things seen but that whereby sight sees, save insofar as the intellect reflects upon itself, which cannot happen in the case of sense.

---

54 See *Metaphysics,* 1.10.987a30 ff.

(111) Si autem intelligere esset actio transiens in
exteriorem materiam, sicut comburere et mouere,
sequeretur quod intelligere esset secundum
modum quo natura rerum habet esse in singu-   210
laribus, sicut combustio ignis est secundum
modum combustibilis. Sed quia intelligere est
actio in ipso intelligente manens, ut Aristotiles
dicit in IX Methaphisice, sequitur quod intelligere
sit secundum modum intelligentis, id est secundum   215
exigentiam speciei qua intelligens intelligit. Hec
autem, cum sit abstracta a principiis indiuidualibus, non representat rem secundum condiciones
indiuiduales, sed secundum naturam uniuersalem
tantum. Nichil enim prohibet, si aliqua duo   220
coniunguntur in re, quin unum eorum representari
possit etiam in sensu sine altero: unde color
mellis uel pomi uidetur a uisu sine eius sapore.
Sic igitur intellectus intelligit naturam uniuersalem
per abstractionem ab indiuidualibus principiis.   225

(112) Est ergo unum quod intelligitur et a me et
a te, sed alio intelligitur a me et alio a te, id
est alia specie intelligibili; et aliud est intelligere
meum et aliud tuum; et alius est intellectus
meus et alius tuus. Vnde et Aristotiles in   230
Predicamentis dicit aliquam scientiam esse singularem quantum ad subiectum, "ut quedam
grammatica in subiecto quidem est anima, de
subiecto uero nullo dicitur". Vnde et intellectus
meus quando intelligit se intelligere, intelligit   235
quendam singularem actum; quando autem
intelligit intelligere simpliciter, intelligit aliquid
uniuersale. Non enim singularitas repugnat intel-
ligibilitati, sed materialitas: unde, cum sint
aliqua singularia immaterialia, sicut de substantiis   240
separatis supra dictum est, nichil prohibet huiusmodi singularia intelligi.

(111) If, however, understanding were a transitive action passing into exterior matter, like burning and moving, it would follow that understanding exists in the way that the nature of things exists in singulars, just as the combustion of fire exists according to the manner of the combustible. But because understanding is an action that remains in the person understanding, as Aristotle says in book 9 of the *Metaphysics*,[55] it follows that understanding is according to the mode of the one understanding, that is, according to the demands of the species whereby the understander understands. But this, since it is abstracted from individual principles, does not represent the thing in its individual conditions but only according to the universal nature. If two things are conjoined in a thing, nothing prevents one of them being represented in sense without the other; hence, the color of honey or of an apple is seen by sight without its taste. Just so the intellect understands the universal nature by abstraction from individual principles.

(112) Therefore, there is one thing that is understood by me and you, but it is understood by means of one thing by me and by means of another by you, that is, by different intelligible species, and my understanding differs from yours and my intellect differs from yours. Hence, Aristotle in the *Categories* says that knowledge is singular with respect to its subject: "the individual knowledge of grammar is in a subject, the soul, but is not said of any subject."[56] Hence, when my intellect understands itself to understand, it understands some singular activity; when, however, it understands understanding simply, it understands something universal. It is not singularity that is repugnant to intelligibility, but materiality; thus, since they are immaterial singulars, as was said of separate substances above, nothing prevents such singulars from being understood.

---

55 *Metaphysics,* 9.8.1050a34–36.
56 *Categories,*chap. 2.1a25–27.

(113) Ex hoc autem apparet quomodo sit eadem
scientia in discipulo et doctore. Est enim eadem
quantum ad rem scitam, non tamen quantum   245
ad species intelligibiles quibus uterque intelligit;
quantum enim ad hoc, indiuiduatur scientia in
me et in illo. Nec oportet quod scientia que est
in discipulo causetur a scientia que est in magistro,
sicut calor aque a calore ignis; sed sicut sanitas   250
que est in materia a sanitate que est in anima
medici. Sicut enim in infirmo est principium
naturale sanitatis, cui medicus auxilia subministrat
ad sanitatem perficiendam, ita in discipulo est
principium naturale scientie, scilicet intellectus   255
agens et prima principia per se nota; doctor autem
subministrat quedam amminicula, deducendo
conclusiones ex principiis per se notis. Vnde et
medicus nititur eo modo sanare quo natura
sanaret, scilicet calefaciendo et infrigidando; et   260
magister eodem modo inducit ad scientiam quo
inueniens per se ipsum scientiam acquireret,
procedendo scilicet de notis ad ignota. Et sicut
sanitas in infirmo fit non secundum potestatem
medici, sed secundum facultatem nature: ita   265
et scientia causatur in discipulo non secundum
uirtutem magistri, sed secundum facultatem addis-
centis.

(114) Quod autem ulterius obiciunt, quod si rema-
nerent plures substantie intellectuales, destructis   270
corporibus, sequeretur quod essent ociose, sicut
Aristotiles in XI Methaphisice argumentatur
quod, si essent substantie separate non mouentes
corpus, essent ociose: si bene litteram Aristotilis
considerassent, de facili possent dissoluere. Nam   275
Aristotiles, antequam hanc rationem inducat,
premittit "Quare et substantias et principia
immobilia tot rationabile suscipere; necessarium
enim dimittatur fortioribus dicere". Ex quo
patet quod ipse probabilitatem quandam sequitur,   280
non necessitatem inducit.

(113) Thus, it is clear how there can be the same science in the learner and teacher. For it is the same with respect to the thing known, but not with respect to the intelligible species whereby each knows—in that respect, science is individuated in me and you. Nor is it necessary that the knowledge that is in the learner be caused by the knowledge that is in the teacher, as the heat of water is by the heat of fire, but rather as the health in matter is caused by the health that is in the mind of the physician. Just as in the patient there is a natural principle of health to which the physician supplies aids in order that health might be perfected, so in the learner there is a natural principle of knowledge, namely, the agent intellect and the first self-evident principles. The teacher supplies certain aids, deducing conclusions from principles known in themselves. Thus, the physician strives to heal in the way nature would heal, namely, by heating and chilling; similarly, the master leads to science in the way in which one discovering it for oneself would acquire it, proceeding, that is, from the known to the unknown. And just as health in the sick person does not come about by the power of the physician but by the capacity of nature, so, too, knowledge is not caused in the learner by the power of the master but rather by the capacity of the learner.

(114) As to the further objection—that if, their bodies having been destroyed, many intellectual substances should remain—it would follow that they are otiose, since Aristotle in book 11 of the *Metaphysics*[57] argued that if there were separate substances that did not move bodies, they would be futile. But if one carefully considers the text of Aristotle, the difficulty is easily solved. For Aristotle, before giving this argument, says, "the unmovable substances and principles may reasonably be taken to be just so many; the assertion of *necessity* must be left to more powerful thinkers."[58] It is clear from this that he is pursuing a kind of probability and not claiming necessity.

---

57 Actually *Metaphysics,* 12.10.1074a18–22.
58 Ibid., 1074a15–17.

(115) Deinde, cum ociosum sit quod non pertingit
ad finem ad quem est, non potest dici etiam
probabiliter quod substantie separate essent ociose,
si non mouerent corpora; nisi forte dicant quod   285
motiones corporum sint fines substantiarum sepa-
ratarum: quod est omnino impossibile, cum
finis sit potior hiis que sunt ad finem. Vnde nec
Aristotiles hoc inducit quod essent ociose si
non mouerent corpora, sed quod "omnem   290
substantiam impassibilem secundum se optimum
sortitam finem esse oportet existimare". Est
enim perfectissimum uniuscuiusque rei ut non
solum sit in se bonum, sed ut bonitatem in aliis
causet. Non erat autem manifestum qualiter   295
substantie separate causarent bonitatem in inferio-
ribus, nisi per motum aliquorum corporum; unde
ex hoc Aristotiles quandam probabilem rationem
assumit, ad ostendendum quod non sunt alique
substantie separate nisi que per motus celestium   300
corporum manifestantur: quamuis hoc necessi-
tatem non habeat, ut ipsemet dicit.

(116) Concedimus autem quod anima humana a
corpore separata non habet ultimam perfectionem
sue nature, cum sit pars nature humane; nulla   305
enim pars habet omnimodam perfectionem si a
toto separetur. Non autem propter hoc frustra
est; non enim est humane anime finis mouere
corpus, sed intelligere, in quo est sua felicitas,
ut Aristotiles probat in X Ethicorum.   310

(115) Since that thing is futile which does not attain the end for which it is designed, these objections cannot say even with probability that the separate substances are futile if they do not move bodies, unless perhaps they mean that the motions of bodies are the ends of separate substances, which is completely impossible, since the end is higher than the things that are for the sake of the end. Nor does Aristotle here conclude that they would be otiose if they did not move bodies, but that "every being and every substance that is immune from change and in virtue of itself has attained to the best must be considered an end."[59] It is the most perfect state of any thing that it not only is good in itself but also causes goodness in others. But it was not clear how separate substances would cause goodness in inferior bodies save by the motion of some bodies; hence, Aristotle derived from this a probable argument to show that there are as many separate substances as are manifested by the heavenly bodies, although, as he himself says, this has no claim to necessity.

(116) We concede that the human soul separated from body does not have the ultimate perfection of its nature, since it is a part of human nature: no part has complete perfection if it is separated from its whole. But it is not for this reason frustrated, for the end of the human soul is not to move the body but to understand—in which its happiness consists, as Aristotle proves in book 10 of the *Ethics*.[60]

---

59 *Metaphysics,* 12.10.1074a19–20.
60 *Nicomachean Ethics,* 10.10.1177a13–17.

(117) Obiciunt etiam ad sui erroris assertionem, quia
si intellectus essent plures plurium hominum,
cum intellectus sit incorruptibilis, sequeretur
quod essent actu infiniti intellectus secundum
positionem Aristotilis, qui posuit mundum   315
eternum et homines semper fuisse. Ad hanc
autem obiectionem sic respondet Algazel in sua
Methaphisica: dicit enim quod "in quocumque
fuerit unum istorum sine alio", id est quantitas uel
multitudo sine ordine, "infinitas non remouebitur   320
ab eo, sicut a motu celi". Et postea subdit
"Similiter et animas humanas, que sunt separabiles
a corporibus per mortem, concedimus esse infinitas
numero, quamuis habeant esse simul, quoniam
non est inter eas ordinatio naturalis, qua remota   325
desinant esse anime: eo quod nulle earum sunt
cause aliis, sed simul sunt sine prius et posterius
natura et situ. Non enim intelligitur in eis prius
et posterius secundum naturam nisi secundum
tempus creationis sue. In essentiis autem earum,   330
secundum quod sunt essentie, non est ordinatio
ullo modo, sed sunt equales in esse; e contrario
spatiis et corporibus et causa et causato".

(118) Quomodo autem Aristotiles hoc solueret, a
nobis sciri non potest, quia illam partem Metha-   335
phisice non habemus quam fecit de substantiis
separatis. Dicit enim Philosophus in II Phisicorum
quod de formis "que sunt separate, in materia
autem", in quantum sunt separabiles considerare
"est opus philosophie prime". Quicquid autem   340
circa hoc dicatur, manifestum est quod ex hoc
nullam angustiam Catholici patiuntur, qui ponunt
mundum incepisse.

(119) Patet autem falsum esse quod dicunt hoc
fuisse principium apud omnes philosophantes,   345
et Arabes et Peripateticos, quod intellectus non
multiplicetur numeraliter, licet apud Latinos non.
Algazel enim Latinus non fuit, sed Arabs.
Auicenna etiam, qui Arabs fuit, in suo libro
De anima sic dicit "Prudentia et stultitia et   350
opinio et alia huiusmodi similia, non sunt nisi
in essentia anime. Ergo anima non est una sed
est multe numero, et eius species una est".

(117) In advancing their error they also say that if there were many intellects for many men, since intellect is incorruptible, it would follow according to Aristotle, since he held the world to be eternal and men to have always existed, that there would be an actual infinity of intellects. Algazel responded to this in his *Metaphysics,* saying that "in anything where there is one of these without the other"—that is, quantity or a multitude without order—"infinity will not be taken from it, as in the case of the movement of the heaven." And later he adds, "Similarly we grant that human souls, which are separable from the body at death, are infinite in number, although they exist at the same time, since there is no natural ordering among them by the removal of which souls would cease to exist; none of them is the cause of the others, but in nature and position they are simultaneously without prior and posterior. There is no prior and posterior in them according to nature save according to the time of their creation. In their essences, insofar as they are essences, there is no ordering in any way, but they are equal in existence, unlike spaces and bodies and cause and effect."[61]

(118) We cannot know what Aristotle's solution to this might have been because we do not possess that part of the *Metaphysics* in which he deals with separate substances. In book 2 of the *Physics,* the Philosopher says that about the forms "the mode of existence of the separable" insofar as they are separable, "it is the business of first philosophy to define."[62] But it is obvious that whatever he says about this would cause no distress to Catholics, who hold that the world began.

(119) They speak falsehood who say that it was a principle with all those who philosophize, both Arabs and Peripatetics, if not for the Latins, that the intellect is not multiplied numerically. Algazel was an Arab, not a Latin. And Avicenna too, who was an Arab, speaks thus in his book *On the Soul:* "Prudence, stupidity, opinion, and other attributes of that sort can only inhere in the essence of the soul. Therefore the soul is not numerically one but many, though of one species."[63]

---

61 *Algazel's Metaphysics,* 40.23–25; 41.1–10.
62 *Physics,* 2.4.194b13–15.
63 Avicenna, *De anima,* 111.16–20.

(120) Et ut Grecos non omittamus, ponenda sunt
circa hoc uerba Themistii in Commento. Cum   355
enim quesisset de intellectu agente utrum sit
unus aut plures, subiungit soluens "Aut primus
quidem illustrans est unus, illustrati autem et
illustrantes sunt plures. Sol quidem enim est
unus, lumen autem dices modo aliquo partiri   360
ad uisus. Propter hoc enim non solem in
comparatione proposuit, scilicet Aristotiles, sed
lumen; Plato autem solem". Ergo patet per
uerba Themistii quod nec intellectus agens, de
quo Aristotiles loquitur, est unus qui est illustrans,   365
nec etiam possibilis qui est illustratus; sed uerum
est quod principium illustrationis est unum,
scilicet aliqua substantia separata: uel Deus
secundum Catholicos, uel intelligentia ultima
secundum Auicennam. Vnitatem autem huius   370
separati principii probat. Themistius per hoc
quod docens et addiscens idem intelligit, quod
non esset nisi esset idem principium illustrans.
Sed uerum est quod postea dicit, quosdam
dubitasse de intellectu possibili utrum sit unus.   375

(121) Nec circa hoc plus loquitur, quia non erat intentio
eius tangere diuersas opiniones philosophorum,
sed exponere sententias Aristotilis, Platonis et
Theophrasti; unde in fine concludit "Sed quod
quidem dixi pronuntiare quidem de eo quod   380
uidetur philosophis, singularis est studii et solli-
citudinis. Quod autem maxime aliquis utique ex
uerbis que collegimus accipiat de hiis sententiam
Aristotilis et Theophrasti, magis autem et ipsius
Platonis, hoc promptum est propalare".   385
    Ergo patet quod Aristotiles et Theophrastus
et Themistius et ipse Plato non habuerunt pro
principio, quod intellectus possibilis sit unus in
omnibus. Patet etiam quod Auerroys peruerse
refert sententiam Themistii et Theophrasti de   390
intellectu possibili et agente; unde merito supra
diximus eum philosophie peripatetice peruerso-
rem. Vnde mirum est quomodo aliqui, solum
commentum Auerroys uidentes, pronuntiare pre-
sumunt, quod ipse dicit hoc sensisse omnes   395
philosophos Grecos et Arabes, preter Latinos.

(120) And lest we omit the Greeks, we should cite the words of Themistius in his commentary. For when he asked concerning the agent intellect whether it was one or many, he answered: "Or the first illuminator is one but the illumined and illumining many: for the sun is one, but you will say that light is in some way imparted to the senses of sight. For this reason Aristotle proposes light rather than the sun in the comparison, but Plato proposes the sun."[64] It is clear from these words of Themistius that neither the agent intellect, of which Aristotle speaks, is the one who is illuminator, nor the possible that which is illumined. There is indeed one principle of illumination, namely, a certain separate substance that is either God, according to Catholics, or the ultimate intelligence, according to Avicenna.[65] Themistius proves the unity of this separate principle by the fact that the teacher and learner understand the same thing, which would not be the case if there were not the same illuminating principle. What he says later—that some doubt whether the possible intellect is one—is certainly true.

(121) But he says no more of this because his intention was not to discuss the diverse opinions of philosophers but rather to explicate the teachings of Aristotle, Plato, and Theophrastus. Hence, at the end he concludes, "What I said to express what seemed to philosophers to be the case is of singular difficulty and concern. From the excerpts that we have assembled concerning the opinion of Aristotle and of Theophrastus, and most of all of Plato himself, what one can principally gather is laid open to view."[66]

It is evident, therefore, that Aristotle, Theophrastus, Themistius, and Plato himself did not hold as a principle that the possible intellect is one for all. Averroes, it is clear, distorts in reporting it the thought of Themistius and Theophrastus concerning possible and agent intellects; so we rightly said above that he is the perverter of Peripatetic philosophy. How amazing, then, that some, consulting only the commentary of Averroes, presume to pronounce that what he says is the common view of all philosophers, Greek and Arab, if not the Latins.

---

64 Themistius, 430a25, 235.7–11.
65 See Avicenna, *Metaphysics,* 9.3 (Venice, 1508. Reprint. Louvain: Edition de la bibliothèque S.J., 1961), 104 rb F.
66 Themistius, 242.2–6.

(122) Est etiam maiori ammiratione uel etiam indi-
gnatione dignum, quod aliquis Christianum se
profitens tam irreuerenter de christiana fide loqui
presumpserit: sicut cum dicit quod "Latini pro   400
principiis hoc non recipiunt", scilicet quod sit
unus intellectus tantum, "quia forte lex eorum
est in contrarium". Vbi duo sunt mala: primo,
quia dubitat an hoc sit contra fidem; secundo,
quia alienum se innuit esse ab hac lege. Et quod   405
postmodum dicit "Hec est ratio per quam
Catholici uidentur habere suam positionem", ubi
sententiam fidei positionem nominat. Nec minoris
presumptionis est quod postmodum asserere
audet, Deum non posse facere quod sint multi   410
intellectus, quia implicat contradictionem.

(123) Adhuc autem grauius est quod postmodum
dicit "Per rationem concludo de necessitate quod
intellectus est unus numero, firmiter tamen teneo
oppositum per fidem". Ergo sentit quod fides   415
sit de aliquibus quorum contraria de necessitate
concludi possunt; cum autem de necessitate
concludi non possit nisi uerum necessarium,
cuius oppositum est falsum impossibile, sequitur
secundum eius dictum quod fides sit de falso   420
impossibili, quod etiam Deus facere non potest:
quod fidelium aures ferre non possunt. Non caret
etiam magna temeritate, quod de hiis que ad
philosophiam non pertinent, sed sunt pure fidei,
disputare presumit, sicut quod anima patiatur   425
ab igne inferni, et dicere sententias doctorum de
hoc esse reprobandas; pari enim ratione posset
disputare de Trinitate, de Incarnatione et aliis
huiusmodi, de quibus nonnisi cecutiens loque-
retur.   430

(122) It is yet more amazing, indeed worthy of indignation, that anyone professing himself to be a Christian should presume to speak so irreverently of the Christian faith as to say that "the Latins do not accept this as a principle," namely, that there is only one intellect, "perhaps because their law is contrary to it." There are two evils in this: first, to doubt whether this is against the faith; second, to give the nod to what is alien to this law. Afterward, he said, "This is the reason why Catholics seem to hold their position," where the judgment of the faith is called a position! Nor is there less presumption in what he dares later to assert, namely, that God cannot bring it about that there are many intellects because this implies a contradiction.

(123) Even more serious is this subsequent remark: "Through reason I conclude necessarily that intellect is numerically one, but I firmly hold the opposite by faith." Therefore, he thinks that faith is of things whose contrary can be necessarily concluded; since the only thing that can be necessarily concluded is a necessary truth whose opposite is false and impossible, it follows from this statement that faith is of the false and impossible, which not even God can bring about and the ears of the faithful cannot bear. He does not lack the high temerity to presume to discuss what does not pertain to philosophy but is purely of faith, such that the soul suffers from the fire of hell, and to say that the teaching of the doctors concerning these things should be reprobated. By equal right, one could dispute concerning the Trinity, the Incarnation, and the like, concerning which he speaks only out of blindness.

(124) Hec igitur sunt que in destructionem predicti
erroris conscripsimus, non per documenta fidei,
sed per ipsorum philosophorum rationes et dicta.
Si quis autem gloriabundus de falsi nominis
scientia uelit contra hec que scripsimus aliquid   435
dicere, non loquatur in angulis nec coram pueris
qui nesciunt de tam arduis iudicare, sed contra
hoc scriptum rescribat, si audet; et inueniet non
solum me, qui aliorum sum minimus, sed multos
alios ueritatis zelatores, per quos eius errori   440
resistetur, uel ignorantie consuletur.

(124) This, then, is what we have written to destroy the error mentioned, using the arguments and teachings of the philosophers themselves, not the documents of faith. If anyone glorying in what is falsely named a science wishes to say anything in reply to what we have written, let him not speak in corners nor to boys who cannot judge of such arduous matters, but reply to this in writing, if he dares. He will find that not only I, who am the least of men, but many others zealous for the truth, will resist his error and correct his ignorance.

| **Analysis**

The claim that the intellect is a substance existing apart from the body is in conflict not only with Christian faith but also with philosophy. Thomas will not argue here that the claim is incompatible with Christian faith, although he says that this argument can be easily made. Rather, he sets forth the philosophical untenability of the claim in two ways. First, by appeal to authority, Thomas shows that it was not taught by the philosophers, most notably not by Aristotle, whom Thomas's opponents invoked. Second, Thomas fashions philosophical arguments to prove that the intellect is the substantial form of body and that the intellect is not one for all people, after which he answers objections to this truth.

| Chapter I
| (numbers 1–50; lines 1–849)

This is the longest chapter of the work. In it Thomas argues that Aristotle did not teach that the intellect is a substance existing separatcly from thc body. Thc argument relies throughout on textual interpretation. Thomas seeks to show that what his opponents attribute to Aristotle cannot be reconciled with the text of *On the Soul*.

The chapter can be divided into three parts:
1. Analysis of the text of *On the Soul;*
2. Analysis of a text from the *Physics;*
3. Answers to objections.

1. Analysis of *On the Soul* (numbers 3–25; lines 39–468).

   a. Aristotle's definition of soul applies to intellectual soul (nos. 3–11; lines 39–227). The definition of soul given at the outset of book 2 of *On the Soul,* "the first act of a physically organized body" (412b5), applies to all souls, as is clear from 412b8–12 (no. 3), including the intellective part (413a4–7; no. 4). Those who wish to exempt the intellectual soul from the common definition need to distinguish between the soul being the act of a body and *a part* of the soul being the act of a body. Thomas promises to establish this distinction later. (The promise is kept in no. 27; lines 469–87.)

That the body is no longer alive when the soul is separated from it may seem proof enough that the soul is the act of the body, but Aristotle invites the doubt that the soul is a mover rather than a form (413a8–10; no. 5). Because this doubt is unresolved, Aristotle describes his account thus far as "in outline" (413a11–13). He will solve this doubt by approaching the soul through vital activities, these being more easily grasped by us; the animate differs from the inanimate by living, by vital operations (413a21–25). These operations are intellect, sense, and local motion. The soul is the principle of all these and thus has parts: vegetative, sensitive, locomotive, and intellective (413b11–13; no. 6). Is each of these a soul or are they parts of one soul? The vegetative and sensitive present no problem (413b13–26). But of intellect and the contemplative faculty nothing yet has been shown (413b24–25). When Aristotle says that "some present a difficulty" (413b16), he means that it is not yet clear whether intellect is a soul or a *part* of the soul; and if it is a part, whether it is separate in place or in definition only (no. 7).

But does not Aristotle say that the intellect seems to be another kind of soul (413b25–26)? Averroes perversely takes this to mean that intellect is called soul equivocally. Against this, Thomas cites 413b26–27: If intellect is called perpetual, this is to contrast it with other parts of the soul, which are corruptible. Intellect is separate from the other powers of the soul, not from the body (no. 8). This is explicit in 413b27–28, as in the sequel (413b29–30), where to have an opinion and to sense are said to differ in account or definition. The powers of the soul differ in the way they are understood but are not separable in place (no. 9). The soul is to body as form is to matter, not as a sailor to a boat.

That through which a thing first operates is the act of the one operating. We can be said to know either thanks to the soul or thanks to science, but science is that through which we first know. So, too, if being healed is attributed to both the body and health, it is primarily attributed to health. Science is as form or act is to the soul, and health is as form or act is to the body in these examples (no. 10). But the soul is that whereby we first live (vegetative power), sense (sensitive power), move (locomotive power), and understand (intellective power). The soul therefore is as species or form, not matter or subject (414a12–14). Soul is the first act of a physical body; and intellect, as that whereby we understand, is the form of a physical body. (Thomas invokes book 3, 429a23: "I call intellect that whereby the soul thinks and understands" [no. 11].)

b. Intellect a power of soul that is form of body (nos. 12–16; lines 228–306). In book 2, having defined soul in general, Aristotle distinguishes its powers: the vegetative, sensitive, appetitive, locomotive, and intellective (414a31–32). That intellective means the intellect is clear from 414b18 (no. 12). The analogy of soul and figure (414b19–22) confirms that intellect is a part of the soul and that the definition of the soul is common to all the parts distinguished.

c. Comparison of intellect and sense (nos. 17–26; lines 307–468). Sense is (1) in potency to the sensible, and (2) affected by it, i.e., passible. Intellect is in potency to intelligibles, but impassible; it is not destroyed by a too intelligible object. But intellect is in some way affected by its object; it is receptive of species. Sense has a limited range, while intellect is potentially all things. Intellect does not have a determinate nature; it is potency to all. Intellect has no bodily organ of which it is the act. That is why it is called separate. (This section is a commentary on *On the Soul,* 3.4.429a10–b5, and is a parallel to lectio 7 of the *Sentencia.*)

2. Confirmation from the *Physics* (numbers 27–30; lines 469–534). How can the soul, which is the form of a body, have a power that is not a power of the body? Comparison with forms of inanimate things can shed some light on this. Not every power of a physical body is reducible to its elements. Some powers of the soul are acts of organs, but intellect is not. The *Physics* (2.4) elucidates Aristotle's view that the soul is midway between corporeal forms and separate substances.

3. Reply to objections (numbers 31–50; lines 535–849).

a. How can incorruptible intellect be part of the soul, which is the form of a corruptible body? (nos. 31–43; lines 535–732). The human soul, thanks to its intellective part, can survive death. Why is this because of the intellective part and not because of the others? Intellect is not the act of a bodily organ. Aristotle said at the beginning of *On the Soul* (403a10–12) that if there is an activity proper to the soul and not to the composite, the soul would be separable. A form that has such a proper act exists of itself and not simply thanks to the composite.

How can the soul think apart from images? Aristotle did not keep his promise to discuss this in the *Metaphysics*.

b. Three more objections (nos. 44–50; lines 733–849).

> **i.** *Objection:* No form that is the act of matter comes from without but rather is educed from the potency of matter. *Response:* Matter is in potency to the human soul, but potency is relative to act, and thinking is not an act that communicates with matter. That is why Aristotle says that the intellectual soul must come from without (*On the Generation of Animals,* 736b27–29).

> **ii.** *Objection:* The form of a body formed from elements is caused by those elements. *Response:* No soul is caused by the elements (736b29–737a1).

> **iii.** *Objection:* The soul is one; if one of its powers comes from without, why not all? *Response:* The analogy of the soul and figure settles this (414b28–32).

Chapter II
(numbers 51–59; lines 1–156)

This is the shortest chapter of the work. In it, Thomas deprives his opponents of the support of other Peripatetics—first the Greeks, then the Arabs.

1. Greek Peripatetics do not support the Averroists (numbers 51–56; lines 1–107). Themistius, Theophrastus, and Alexander of Aphrodisias hold intellect to be a faculty of the soul.

2. Arab Peripatetics do not support the Averroists (numbers 57–59; lines 108–56). Thomas cites Avicenna and Algazel.

Chapter III
(numbers 60–85; lines 1–421)

Having argued from the authority of Aristotle and some Greek and Arab Aristotelians that views espoused by his opponents cannot be attributed to Aristotle or his followers, Thomas now formulates three philosophical arguments showing that the intellect is a power of the soul, which is the form of a body. We ask about intellect and understanding because we know that we engage in the latter, and the former is that thanks to which we do it. That whereby we primarily perform such vital acts is the soul. This is an account of the soul that is used to "demonstrate" the first account—the soul is the first act or substantial form of an organic body. How else can one account for the undeniable fact of our thinking?

1. "This man understands" (numbers 60–79; lines 1–311).

   a. Assuming the soul is form (nos. 61–66; lines 11–118). Averroes explains thinking by appealing to a separate intellect that makes use of my phantasms and allows me to say that I think. The intelligible species or concepts thus have two subjects, the separated intellect and the phantasms.

   The first thing wrong with this view is that it deprives one of intellect as a constituent of being; in this view, one is not born with intellect but rather becomes associated with it episodically.

   Further, the intelligible species as it is in the phantasms is potential only. It is actual as abstracted from the phantasms. Nor would it help to say that it is reflected or represented in us as a mirror reflects a person. Then we would not be able to say that the person thinks any more than we can say the mirror smiles.

   Again, even granting that the numerically same intelligible species is in the possible intellect and in phantasms, this would not enable us to say that this, i.e., a particular, person understands. Something is understood through the species, and the intellect is that through which one understands. The color of the wall is seen thanks to the sense image. The species in the phantasm is like the color in the wall; it is what is known, not that which knows or through which one knows. Averroes is unable to say that this person understands.

   b. The soul as mover rather than form (nos. 67–75; lines 120–255). Some seek to avoid these difficulties by making the soul a mover rather than a form. Thomas relies on Aristotle's discussion in the *Metaphysics* of what constitutes a human. If the human is not just a pile, then it is a compound of which one component is potency and the other is act, which results in a substantial unit. But maybe the human is one in the same way that the mover and moved are one.

   This will not do because a thing is one in the way that it is a being. If the human being is one only as mover and moved, it is not a substantial unity. If one says that Socrates is a certain individual because he is an animated body thanks to a soul that is vegetative and sensitive, then thinking can in no way be attributed to him. Thomas draws these consequences of the view he is criticizing:

   First, the act of understanding is not a transitive act but rather exists in the one engaged in it. Thus it is the separate intellect that thinks, not this person.

Second, even if it were a transitive act, it does not follow that it would be the person's act, any more than the saw makes the artifact.

Third, in transitive action, the action is attributed in different ways to mover and moved: The builder builds but the building is built. If intellect were a mover, the human would be what is understood, not the one who understands. Sometimes the moved also moves because of what it receives from the mover, but humans cannot be said to understand in this way, unless they have their own intellect with which to think.

c. The human being as identical with intellect (nos. 76–79; lines 256–311). Despairing of accounting for the soul as either form or mover, one might seek to escape the problem by saying that a person simply is intellect. This sounds like the Aristotelian tenet that we are chiefly mind; taken literally, it is false and can be disproved in three ways.

2. The human being is a member of a species (number 80; lines 312–35). If the human being is distinguished from other animals by mind and thus specified and defined in that way, intellect must be its form.

3. Moral argument (numbers 81–82; lines 336–63). If intellect is not in us, neither is will, and thus we do not have dominion over our acts. This conclusion makes a mockery of the moral order, law, praise, blame, etc.

4. Objections refuted (numbers 83–85; lines 364–421). The dodge that intellect is a material form will not work, since, *inter alia,* it could not then understand itself.

    That the human soul can be the form of the body and yet have a power whose activity does not involve matter is no puzzle when it is recognized that the human soul has an existence of itself and not simply as the form of a composite.

▌ Chapter IV
▌ (numbers 86–98; lines 1–264)

Thomas turns again to the claim that there is one intellect for all people and argues, first, that it leads to absurdities; second, that it is incompatible with Aristotle's doctrine; and third, that none of the efforts to relate intellect to our phantasms makes sense as an explanation of human knowledge.

1. Absurd consequences of saying there is only one intellect (numbers 86–91; lines 1–127). If a person understands, he or she must

either be intellect, or intellect must be formally in him or her. If any individual person were identical with intellect (e.g., Socrates = intellect), he is identical with other people, who are also identical with intellect. On the contrary, intellects are multiplied with individuals.

2. Averroes runs afoul of Aristotle's teaching (numbers 92–96; lines 128–224). The possible intellect is in potency to all things, a slate on which nothing is written. When one learns, the knowledge is in that person and can be used. By learning, the possible intellect comes to be in act. Thomas shows in many ways that a single separate possible intellect is not compatible with Aristotelian doctrine.

3. Role of phantasms in understanding (numbers 97–98; lines 225–64). Of the three ways in which intelligible species can be related to phantasms—be abstracted from them, shine upon them, or neither—the Averroist may take the second (it having been just shown that the first is closed to him), and the difficulties of this way are developed. To take the third would be to give up the argument.

❙ Chapter V
(numbers 99–124; lines 1–441)

Thomas defends the claim that there is a plurality of possible intellects—one for each person—against six objections, and ends by observing how particularly outrageous it is for a Christian to fall into the error addressed by the opusculum.

1. *Objection:* Intellect as an immaterial form cannot be multiplied by the multiplication of bodies (numbers 99–103; lines 1–84). *Response:* Not all individuation is by way of matter; one separated substance differs from another. A form that can be shared in by many is individuated by matter. The intellect is the power of a form that is the act of the body.

2. *Objection:* Even if the intellect were multiplied, it would be one after the demise of the bodies (numbers 104–5; lines 85–117). *Response:* A thing is one in the way in which it exists. Thomas has already shown that the soul is not educed from the potency of matter. He dismisses as crude the claim that God cannot do something because it could not naturally come about.

3. *Objection:* What is understood is one; therefore intellects are one (numbers 106–13; lines 118–268). *Response:* My singular act of understanding and yours have a content that is specifically the

same. I do not understand my concept of rock but rather the nature of rock.

4. *Objection:* If many intellects survived their bodies, what would they do? (numbers 114–16; lines 269–310). *Response:* Separated substances have a cosmic function as movers. What would all the separated souls do? That which attains its end is not idle. Besides, Aristotle characterizes his linking of separate substances and movements of heavenly bodies as only probable. A human soul separated from its body does not have the ultimate perfection of its nature, but it does not follow that it is idle.

5. *Objection:* There would be an infinity of intellects (numbers 117–18; lines 311–43). *Response:* Insofar as this difficulty is predicated on the eternity of the world, it cannot distress the Catholic.

6. *Objection:* All philosophers except the Latins have asserted that there is only one intellect (numbers 119–21; lines 344–96). *Response:* Thomas shows that this is historically false.

7. *Conclusion:* That a Christian should maintain the position that has now been refuted is particularly rash (numbers122–24; lines 397–441). The claim that one can know for sure the opposite of what is believed implies that faith bears on the necessarily false. No believer should play fast and loose with the faith.

| **Interpretive Essays**

| Faith and Reason

As the text of this polemical opusculum makes clear, while Thomas is outraged that fellow Christians should take the position he attacks to be compatible with their faith, his chief concern is to discuss the status of the human soul on a terrain that the believer can share with the nonbeliever, the mere philosopher. The whole of the first and longest chapter turns on the text of Aristotle: What precisely is Aristotle's teaching? Is Aristotle's teaching true?

The text in question is Aristotle's *On the Soul.* We saw in the Introduction that Thomas composed a commentary on that work—perhaps the first of his dozen Aristotelian commentaries—most likely prior to returning to Paris and entering into the fray of Latin Averroism or heterodox Aristotelianism. Moreover, he produced a *Disputed Question on Spiritual Creatures* at roughly this same time. The *Disputed Question* is an overtly theological work, the product of one of the principal tasks of a *magister regens.* Of course, Thomas did not wait until the end of his career to discuss the soul. For important discussions of it, we can go to the commentary on the *Sentences* or the *Summa contra gentiles,* to the *Summa theologiae,* as well as to dozens of other places in his vast literary production. The highly relevant questions 79–119 of the first part of the *Summa* are thought to have been written between the end of 1267 and the end of 1268. The *Disputed Question on the Soul* may also date from just before Thomas's return to Paris in 1269. Our concern in this section is to underscore one of the great divisions within that literature, that between the theological and the philosophical writings.

How Do Theology and Philosophy Differ?

The vast majority of Thomas's writings are theological—commentaries on Scripture, the commentary on the *Sentences* of Peter Lombard, the disputed and quodlibetal questions, the summaries of Christian doctrine. Indeed, this is so much the case that it is sometimes overlooked that, unlike most other theological masters—except, of course, his teacher Albert the Great—Thomas also produced a significant number of philosophical works.

There are some logical works attributed to Thomas. There is *The Principles of Nature,* a succinct presentation of Aristotle's teaching on the constitution of things that come to be as the result of a change. *On Being and Essence,* a metaphysical treatise of brevity and depth, can be read as a companion to book 7 of the *Metaphysics.* Thomas's commentary on Boethius's *De hebdomadibus* is arguably a philosophical work. He also wrote a commentary on *The Book of Causes,* a précis derived from Proclus. And, remarkable achievement, there are a dozen commentaries, not all of them finished, on Aristotelian treatises.

It may seem that a sufficient workaday difference between writings that we would recognize as philosophical and those that we would call theological is that the latter make reference in a more than passing way to Christian doctrine, whereas the former do not. Thomas once put it thus:

> With respect to creatures, the philosopher and the believer are concerned with different things, since the philosopher considers what belongs to them given their proper natures, for example, that fire leaps up. The believer however considers only those things in creatures which belong to them insofar as they are related to God, for example, that they are created by God, are subject to God, and the like.[1]

That is true enough, roughly, but Thomas would insist on a more formal statement of their difference.

It is best to begin with the notion of an argument. If you seek to persuade another of the truth of a certain claim, one way to do so would be to show that it is closely tied to other things your interlocutor already knows to be true. Your effort then consists in linking what you are proposing to what your addressee already knows so that the only way that one can reject your proposal is to abandon what one already knows to be true, something that you are confident one will not choose to do. This is particularly the case because, with a recalcitrant interlocutor, you would try to take matters back to things so obvious that to deny them would be Pickwickian at best, irrational at worst.

Thomas learned from Aristotle this technique of looking for principles or starting points that we hold in common and that function as grounds for other statements. By and large, these principles are latent in our thought and language, and there can be a shock of discovery when we first articulate them and make explicit that which in some sense we knew implicitly all along.

Sometimes, of course, when you are assuring another of the truth of something or other, what you say turns on a truth or fact that you know but your addressee cannot be expected to know. Say you are making assertions about Salta, Argentina, which you have visited and the other has not. If the other accepts what you say as true, it will be on your say-so; he or she relies on your veracity and takes your authority for it. It would be a tough call to say whether the bulk of our convictions are of this latter sort or of the former sort, where we are expected to have equal access with its formulator to the principles of the argument.

Aristotle held both that there is a fund of common principles that every human being can in principle know and that are in some way latent in whatever a person thinks and says, *and* that disagreement among people is rampant; discussions seldom end in one person's being reasonably persuaded by another. Historically, there arose at the same time as the philosopher another figure, who came to be called the sophist. The sophist sees inquiry and argument as instruments of power, advancement, and practical success rather than as the pursuit of truth, as the desire to know what is the case or what ought to be done. Plato saw sophistry as principally a moral fault, whereas Aristotle concentrated on the bogus logic it employed in his *On Sophistical Refutations*. The seeming arguments of the sophist are based on fallacies that we must be armed against by isolating and analyzing them.

If some arguments gain our agreement because their conclusions are tied inexorably to what we already know and ultimately to what everyone in some way knows to be true, and if sophistic arguments gain our assent on the basis of fallacies, there are many kinds of discourse in between. Sometimes we take a person's word for a truth. Sometimes, more often than not, the link between the premises and the conclusion is less than tight, ranging from high to low probability. Sometimes the engagement of our emotions is part of the force of the argument. Add to these the notion of poetic argument, ranging from metaphor to the way in which a sequence of events is so arranged that a certain outcome seems inevitable, as in the plot of a tragedy, and you have a sense of the range of natural reasoning in Thomas Aquinas.[2]

It is necessary to mention these things lest we think that the conception of philosophical discourse that Thomas took from Aristotle is hopelessly naive, as if he thought that agreement can always easily be achieved simply by the construction of a few syllogisms. Nonetheless, this conception of philosophy rests on the robust confidence that truth is not the privilege of the few, that sophisticated claims can be commended only to the degree that they can be linked with principles that are in the public domain, and that the unwillingness or inability to establish such linkage counts against the philosopher, not against the receptive layperson. However difficult philosophical inquiry may be, however scandalous the radical differences among sophisticated philosophical theories appear, the Aristotelian view is that communication and agreement are in principle possible because the discussants are human beings with common cognitive equipment and a common fund of experience.[3]

In short, a philosophical position or argument must always be analyzable into truths that are in the public domain. By contrast, theological discourse depends essentially on truths that are held to be such on the basis of faith, a gift, a deliverance of divine grace, not an achievement. It is not simply that mention is made of Christian doctrine and Scripture, the assumed truth of whose teachings specifies the discourse. A specifically theological argument is one that is analyzable into revealed truths, what God has revealed to us in the Bible, in his Son, and which, as Boethius observes, is guarded and taught by the Catholic Church.[4]

If we left the matter here, however, we would seem to have two bodies of discourse that overlap in no way whatsoever. But that is as unlikely as that Scripture could proceed without referring to food, water, rest, shelter, fishing, and a great many other things that are in the public domain. The ordinary human world, we might say, is present in the Scriptural vision of human life, but that is not what is distinctive of Scripture. Ordinary human activities—taking food together, washing and anointing, on and on—are elevated to a higher use and significance that do not, of course, destroy their natural meanings.

Analogously, theological discourse incorporates philosophical discourse, at least as Thomas understood theology. The very first question of the *Summa theologiae* asks why we have need of any science other than the philosophical ones. Does not philosophy cover the whole terrain of being, and what else is there? Thomas clearly assumes that his reader has already studied philosophy. The structure of medieval education makes that assumption inevitable. One entered upon the study of theology only after having completed the arts course, and the liberal arts had to accommodate the philosophical sciences newly available in the Latin translations from the Greek and Arabic.

The governing principles of theology are the truths revealed by God and accepted by faith. Faith is a sine qua non of theology. But theology is discursive as faith is not. Theology is a reflection on beliefs with an eye to dispelling as much as possible their obscurity, clarifying them, drawing out their implications, defending them against attack. The reader of Thomas's theological writings is struck by the amount of sheer philosophy in them, borrowings from philosophical texts but also ad hoc philosophizing required for the theological task at hand. Thus, in discussing the Trinity and explaining that there are three divine persons in one divine nature, Thomas must clarify what is meant by person, by nature, by one, by three, and he is helped in doing this by earlier efforts, among them philosophical ones. Is what he has to say about person theological? Clearly one could accept or reject what he says about person without any reference to the truth of Christian teaching. Sometimes we find short treatises on philosophical issues preceding the specifically theological discussion, and these are not always simply summaries of received doctrine or of matters established elsewhere. For example, when Thomas asks whether God has speculative or practical knowledge of creatures, he first provides us with a succinct statement of the criteria of practical thought and of its possible degrees.[5] But within the theological work, such a discussion is always at the service of clarifying the dogma.

| The Case of the Soul

But let us narrow the focus to the discussion of soul. In the introduction to question 75 of the first part of the *Summa theologiae,* Thomas tells us that with respect to humans the theologian's interest is primarily the soul; the body is of interest only with reference to the soul. This means that he concentrates on the ultimate and supernatural destiny of the human soul, which is union with God, to see Him even as we are seen. The body is the instrument of the soul's career in earthly life; our status in the next life is determined by our free response to the promptings of divine grace in this life.

This being the case, we should not be surprised to find Thomas begin by asking whether the soul is a thing in itself, subsistent, a substance. This is an astonishing beginning, or at least it would be if we took it to be the absolute beginning of Thomas's discourse about the soul. If, in quest of Thomas's views on humanity, readers go first to his theological writings, they may get the impression that he is far closer to Platonic dualism than to the Aristotle who insists that soul and body are one as the seal and the wax are one. For the philosopher interested in the soul, the task is to inquire whether the soul is separable from the body, and the question cannot even be adequately framed until a great many other things have been established. Far from being a given, the opposite seems compelling. Thus a complicated and difficult argument—the argument which is at the heart of the controversy that interests us—must be fashioned to establish that the soul, the substantial form of the body, can exist apart from its body after death. This seems to contradict the very notion of a substantial form. Establishing the immortality of the soul, which is one way to describe the issue, is by any account one of the most difficult of philosophical tasks. Nonetheless, as theologian, Thomas proceeds as if that truth were established. And why not? He can take it as an implication of his faith—if death is not the end, and the body corrupts and turns to dust, it must be the soul that survives and enjoys continued existence apart from the body. It is at the heart of Thomas's Christian faith, anchored on the great Easter event, that the dead will rise, souls will be united with bodies, and our eternal bliss will be fully human, involving body and soul. Does this mean that Thomas took the separability of soul from body to be a revealed truth, dependent for its acceptance on grace and faith?

Yes, in the sense that he takes it to be revealed and would not suggest that most believers have, or that any need to have, any other basis for their confidence that this life is not the full story of our existence than the grace of faith. Similarly, believers accept the existence of God, the fact that there is only one God, that He is intelligent and powerful and one on whom all else depends in order to be, in much the same way that they accept the Trinity and Incarnation and forgiveness of sins. Nonetheless, Thomas found it important to distinguish two groupings within the things that are revealed and believed; the one includes what he called the *mysteries of faith,* and the other includes what he called *preambles of faith.*

Mysteries of faith are taken to be true solely on the basis of revelation; there is no other basis possible for them in this life. For example, I cannot *prove* that there is a Trinity of persons in one divine nature, I cannot *prove* that Christ is one person with two natures, one human, one divine. I can, of course, argue for these on the basis of passages in Scripture and the long tradition of Christian belief as exhibited in its worship and prayer, but such arguments presuppose that Scripture and tradition are taken to be authoritative. Scripture is authoritative only for believers. The discourse of the theologian thus seems to move within the circle of faith. Indeed, if things were left like this, it might seem that there is no relation between the language and discourse of theologians and that which by contrast would be called ordinary human discourse—discourse, that is, which does not invoke special and terminal authorities.

The *preambles of faith* cover those truths which, while they are included in revelation, can be seen to be true apart from that setting. The phrase is introduced to cover truths about God that can be known on the basis of arguments which appeal only to what all people can know thanks to their experience of the world and themselves. Thomas is guided here by what he finds in the philosophers. Aristotle had things to say about God—notably that there is one— which are substantially the same as some revealed truths. When Thomas, early in the *Summa,* indicates five ways in which God's existence can be known, he says of the subjects of each of the conclusions—prime mover, first efficient cause, necessary being, most perfect, final cause, *quam omnes Deum nominant,* or *et hoc dicimus Deum*—this is what we, or all, call God. The conclusion is unavoidable. Some of the things that God has revealed to us about Himself are knowable apart from revelation. This implies either that the arguments fashioned by the philosophers are sound and cogent, or that arguments of the philosophical kind can be fashioned. Thomas's interest in Aristotle can scarcely be understood apart from this subdivision of revealed truths into mysteries and preambles.

How does this apply to the case of the soul? The theologian is interested primarily in the soul because it is thanks to the soul that humans have a destiny beyond this life. As Paul pointed out, Christians would be the most miserable of creatures, living as they do, if the assumptions of their lives were false. *If Christ has not risen, our faith is in vain.* It is embedded in the rich context of resurrection and eternal bliss, won for us by Christ, that the separability of the soul is part of Christian belief. That we are accountable for what we do in this life, our future condition being dependent on our terrestrial behavior, is another way in which it can be said that the survivability of the soul, its ability to exist separated from the body, is part of Christian faith. The believer's unshakable confidence in the whole package of revelation affects his/her reaction to the question whether the soul is something that can exist in its own right. Of course it is!

The theologian begins from this rich store of believed truths, and it is of no small significance that, as Thomas observed, some of these truths turn up in the writings of philosophers. There is an overlap of philosophy and revelation in the area of that which, from a believer's perspective, he calls preambles of faith. In the case of the human soul, Thomas finds it to be of enormous significance that philosophers have argued for the separability of the soul, deriving this from other truths that ultimately demanded nothing more for their acceptance than the common experience and ordinary cognitive equipment all people can be presumed to have. A truth held on the basis of revelation can be known to be true on the basis of an argument whose premises are in the public domain.

Does this mean that one who accepts the philosophical argument is required to accept the rich context in which for the believer the truth proved is embedded? No. Does this mean that the believer has inaugurated an activity whose logical goal is to reduce all believed truths to known truths? Emphatically not. The set of truths that Thomas calls preambles of faith is minuscule in comparison with the totality of revealed truths. But could that which was previously thought to be a mystery of faith turn out to be a preamble and thus susceptible of proof? On this, Thomas is guided by tradition, the nonoccurrence of certain claims in philosophical discourse, and the claim that truths such as the Trinity can be shown not to have possible premises in ordinary experience.

As for the soul itself, we can better appreciate now the distinction with which Thomas begins the *De unitate intellectus*. It would be an easy matter, he observes, to show that the position under discussion is in conflict with Christian faith:

> Take away from men the diversity of intellect, which alone among the parts of soul is seen to be incorruptible and immortal, it would follow that after death nothing of the souls of men would remain save that unique intellectual substance. Thus would be swept away all reward of prize and pain, and the difference between them.

This is, for the believer, a *reductio ad absurdum*. If the Averroistic claim is true, Christianity is false. But it is not Thomas's task now to dwell on that. Rather he intends to show that the view put forward is in conflict not just with the teachings of the faith but with philosophical principles as well. And when he speaks of what philosophers teach, he means chiefly Aristotle, *the* philosopher.

▌NOTES

1. "Et propter hoc etiam alia circa creaturas et Philosophus et Fidelis considerat. Philosophus namque considerat illa quae eis secundum naturam propriam conveniunt: sicut igni ferri sursum. Fidelis autem ea solum considerat circa creaturas quae eis conveniunt secundum quod sunt a Deo creata, quod sunt Deo subiecta, et huiusmodi" (*Summa contra gentiles*, vol. 15 of *Sancti Thomae Opera omnia* [Rome: Commissio Leonina, 1930], 2.4). This whole brief chapter is relevant to our present discussion.

2. See, for example, Thomas's proem to his commentary on Aristotle's *On Interpretation*, where the different kinds of argument are linked with the works of the Organon (*In Perihermeneias*, prooemium, ed. R. M. Spiazzi [Turin: Marietti, 1955], nos. 5–6).

3. See *In XII libros Metaphysicorum Aristotelis expositio,* ed. M. Cathala and R. Spiazzi (Turin: Marietti, 1950), book 2, lectio 1, where Thomas discusses the notion that the grasp of truth is in some ways easy, in some ways difficult; and lectio 5, where he discusses the influence of habit and environment on the pursuit of knowledge. Among the works of disputed authenticity attributed to Thomas, we find a short one that provides maxims for the student, the *De modo studendi.* The text of these sixteen maxims, together with a commentary on them by John Paul Nazarius, O.P. (1556–1645/6) is found in *D. Thomae Aquinatis monita et preces,* ed. Thomas Esser, O.P. (Paderborn: Ferdinand Schoeningh, 1890).

4. Boethius, *The Theological Tractates and The Consolation of Philosophy,* ed. H. H. Stewart, E. K. Rand, and S. J. Tester (Cambridge, Mass.: Harvard University Press, 1978). See 33, 53–54, and 73 for Boethius on the fundaments of the kind of discussion in which he is there engaged. For a discussion of these matters, see my *Boethius and Aquinas* (Washington, D.C.: Catholic University of America Press, 1990).

5. *Summa theologiae,* part 1, question 14, article 16 (Ia, q. 14, a. 16). Thomists, wearing their philosophical hats, regularly pillage and plunder the theological writings for such extractable loot. Sternly secular philosophers frown at references to theological works, thinking perhaps that what is cited depends for its validity on the assumptions of the discourse in which it was embedded. This is not the case, as reflection on the example I have given makes clear. Some discussions of Christian philosophy by Thomists unfortunately invite the view that such philosophical passages within theological works, because they are prompted by the theological task, can only be accepted if one accepts as true the Christian faith.

| In Pursuit of the Soul

| The Order among Aristotle's Works

If one wished to know what Aristotle taught about the soul, there is no better place to look than in his treatise called *On the Soul*.[1] The text is difficult, however, and one explanation of this is that the treatise presupposes that we already know certain things about physical or natural things. Thomas Aquinas saw the writings of Aristotle as pieces in a vast systematic whole, and he held that the pieces should be taken up in an orderly fashion if we are to grasp their meaning. Moreover, Thomas sees this ordering of discussions and treatises as preeminently characteristic of the works that make up Aristotle's natural doctrine—by far the bulk of his writings. Because this is so, and because Thomas sees *On the Soul* as one of a set of natural writings, a first way of grasping his interpretation of *On the Soul* is to sketch the main lines of his understanding of the order among Aristotle's natural writings. Confronted with the *Physics, On the Heavens,* the *Meteorology, On Generation and Corruption, The History of Animals, On Sense and the Sensed Object,* and all the other natural writings, where is one to begin? Or does it matter?

It was clear to Thomas that the *Physics* comes first among the natural writings. For one thing, it defines the domain. It addresses the initial question, What is a physical object, what is a natural thing, thus:

> When the objects of an inquiry, in any department, have principles, causes, or elements, it is through acquaintance with these that knowledge, that is to say scientific knowledge, is attained. For we do not think that we know a thing until we are acquainted with its primary causes or first principles, and have carried our analysis as far as its simplest elements. Plainly then, in the science of Nature, as in other branches of study, our first task will be to try to determine what relates to principles. (*Physics,* 1.1.184a1–16)[2]

The science of nature is unified because it has one subject, the knowledge of whose properties is attained through the causes of those properties. The path traversed by our pursuit of knowledge will begin with things more knowable and obvious to us, and in the case of natural science, these should not be confused with what is more knowable in itself: "So in the present inquiry we must follow this method and advance from what is more obscure by nature, but clearer to us, towards what is more clear and more knowable by nature" (*Physics,* 1.1.184a19–21). We begin with general, confused knowledge of things and gradually achieve clear and distinct knowledge of them. We advance from generalities to particulars. In the

Physics, we find the first and most general truths about natural things, and thus this work is presupposed by other, more particular inquiries into natural things.

Natural things depend upon matter both in order to exist and to be defined; but whatever has matter is subject to change. Therefore, natural science can be recognized as having for its subject changeable or moveable being. Natural science is concerned with those things which have within them a principle of change, namely, matter.[3]

> The other books on natural science in which types of mobile being are treated follow on this one. Thus in *On the Heavens,* that which is changeable by local motion, which is the first type of motion, is treated; in *On Generation and Corruption,* of change-toward-form and of the first changeable things or elements, as to their common changes, their special ones being considered in the *Meteorology.* The consideration of mixed inanimate bodies is to be found in *On Minerals,* but of animals in *On the Soul* and the works that follow on it. (*In I Physicorum,* lectio 1, no. 4)

In this passage, Thomas not only locates *On the Soul* in the wider panorama of Aristotelian natural writings but also says that it stands in relation to other and subsequent works in somewhat the way in which the *Physics* stands to all the natural writings that presuppose it. Thomas often elaborates on this understanding of the way in which Aristotle's works relate to one another and the way in which the works dealing with natural things form an ordered descent from the general to the particular. For our purposes, it is useful to look at one fairly extensive statement of the order among the Aristotelian works having to do with living things.

Thomas recalls the basic methodological assumption about the way human knowledge moves from the general to the specific, from the confused to the distinct. The *Physics* takes up the most common features of natural things, motion and the principle of motion, and with that in hand the naturalist goes on to study such things as concretized in more determinately described natural things, some of which are living bodies:

> Proceeding in a similar way here, he [Aristotle] subdivides this consideration into three parts. First he considers the soul in itself, in a more or less abstract way. Second, he enters into a consideration of those things true of soul in its concretion or application to body, but this in general. Third, applying all these things to the species of animal and plant, he determines which is peculiar to each species.[4]

The first consideration, he notes, is to be found in *On the Soul,* the third in the various works on plants and animals. The second, intermediate consideration is found in those books devoted to things common either to several types of living things, or even to all of them, and among these is the book *On Sense and the Sensed Object.*[5]

∎ The Structure of Physical Things

What Aristotle does in *On the Soul* presupposes what he has already done in the *Physics,* whose analysis of the natural or physical thing is meant to apply to living as well as nonliving physical things, this distinction being posterior to that analysis. According to his conception of how our knowledge naturally progresses from general to particular, Aristotle first asks what the most general, common, obvious things are that we can say of physical things. The answer will amount to the least that can be truly said of anything whatsoever that can be called a physical thing. But what is a physical or natural thing?

The adjective *naturalis, physikon*, whether in Latin or Greek, is etymologically related to being born, coming into being by way of birth, but it is used more generally to pick out those things which have come into being as the result of a change.[6] In his commentary on the *Physics,* Thomas keeps close to the text and to the slow and careful development of the doctrine that whatever comes to be is a complex of form and matter. Aristotle begins with an everyday example of change, the acquisition of a skill. *A person becomes musical.* Then, noting that this change can be expressed in various other ways—*The non-musical person becomes musical* and *The non-musical becomes musical*—Aristotle contrasts the *A becomes B* form of all these expressions with the form *From A, B comes to be.* While each of the three original expressions of the change can be turned into expressions of the latter form, we may hesitate to say, *From a person, musical comes to be.* Aristotle suggests that our reluctance is due to the connotation of *From A, B comes to be* expressions, namely, that A ceases to be when B comes to be. But a person does not cease to be as the result of acquiring a skill; rather he/she becomes the possessor of that skill and thus must survive the change. Accordingly, a distinction is made between the grammatical subject of a sentence expressing a change and the subject of the change. By subject of the change is meant that to which the change is attributed and which survives the change. And, since the subject lacked the skill it acquires as the result of the change, any change minimally involves three factors: a subject, a lack in that subject, and a new acquisition that is the contrary of the lack. Or, thanks to another example of change—the reshaping of some stuff—change is said to involve stuff or matter, shape or form, and privation. This is the terminology that becomes quasi-technical for the Aristotelian.

It would be difficult to rival the pedagogical movement of this passage in the *Physics,* and one may doubt that Thomas had any intention of doing so when he summed it up in *On the Principles of Nature,* a youthful work in which he lays out this doctrine in a swift, schematic way.

Thomas begins with a distinction that occurs only at the end of the Aristotelian analysis, that between that which can be although it is not, on the one hand; and that which already is, on the other. The first applies to what is in potency, the second to what actually is. But there are two ways in which a thing can be said to be: essentially or substantially, as when a person is, which is for the person simply to be; or in an accidental sense, as when a person is said to be white, which is for him/her to be in a secondary or derivative sense. Something can be potentially in both senses of what it is to be. Sperm may be said to be potentially a person, and a person may be said to be potentially white. Let us call matter that which potentially is, whether the being in question is substantial or accidental, but we must distinguish the matter which is in potency to substantial being—the "matter of which"—from that which is in potency to accidental being—the "matter in which." The former is prime matter; the latter is a subject that, as host of an accident such as white, makes the accident be. The only way an accident—color, shape, position, location, activity, etc.—exists is in a subject. That is why substantial form is not said to be *in* a subject. A subject does not exist simply speaking because an accidental form inheres in it; rather, for the accident to be is for it to be in a subject. A person is not said to exist simply speaking because he/she has some accidental form or other. But prime matter is said to be because of what comes to it as form: of itself it is incomplete being and does not exist in either of the senses noted. Absolutely speaking, then, form makes prime matter exist, but the accident does not make its subject exist.

Substantial form and accidental form are correlative to prime matter and subject. Thomas explains:

> Just as anything which potentially is can be called matter, so whatever makes a thing be in either way, substantially or accidentally, can be called form; as when a man is potentially white he becomes thanks to whiteness actually white, and sperm when it is potentially man actually becomes man thanks to soul. Because form makes something actually to be, form is called act, and the form which causes something actually to be a substance is called substantial form, and what makes it to be accidentally is called accidental form.[7]

The change whereby a substance—that which is in the primary sense—comes into being is called generation, and the change whereby a substance ceases to be is called corruption. The changes whereby a substance acquires accidental forms have special names: the acquisition of a quality is called alteration; of quantity, growth; of a new place, locomotion.

Thomas, in *On the Principles of Nature,* summarizes the doctrine of the first two books of the *Physics* in a number of pages equal to several lessons in the commentary. (There are thirty lessons in all in Thomas's commentary on those two books.) By any account, the opusculum is a remarkable achievement. It shows us how imbued with the teaching of Aristotle Thomas already was at an early age. The opusculum is thought to have been written for his confreres in the Convent of Saint Jacques in Paris prior to 1256. It puts before its reader with precision and brevity the heart of the Aristotelian doctrine on physical objects, their principles and causes.

As Thomas interprets this doctrine, any change, substantial or accidental, involves three factors whereby a subject can acquire a form it presently lacks: matter, form, and privation. If what comes to be previously was not, change can be described as *toward* being and *from* nonbeing.

> Generation is a kind of change from not-to-be or non-being toward to-be or being, and corruption from to-be or being to not-to-be or not being, but generation does not begin from just any non-being, but rather from the non-being which is potential being, as the statue comes from bronze which is potentially though not actually a statue.[8]

It was the recognition of the distinction between potential and actual being that enabled Aristotle to resolve Parmenides' difficulties about change as nothing becoming being. Change does not take its rise from nothing but rather from something that potentially is what it will actually be as the result of the change.

Another corollary of this teaching is that neither prime matter nor substantial form is generated or corrupted. They do not come to be as the result of a change.

> It should be noticed that neither prime matter nor form is generated or corrupted: every generation is from something to something. Matter is that from which something is generated and form what is acquired by generation. Thus, if either matter or form were generated, there would have to be a matter of matter and a form of form, and so on to infinity. Only a complex thing is generated in the proper sense of the term.[9]

It is this doctrine that is presupposed in *On the Soul.* One who reads this treatise is presumed to know that anything that comes to be as the result of a change is a compound of form and matter. That is, of course, the broadest and vaguest way to put it, but it has the merit of covering every product of change. One cannot be content with such common characteristics of physical things; this is only the first stage of the inquiry that is natural philosophy. When physical objects are divided into nonliving and living, we shall want to know what characterizes living things, that is, what is true of them over and above what is true of any physical object whatsoever. *On the Soul* stands first in the inquiry into living things.

∎ NOTES

1. This treatise does not represent Aristotle's first effort to speak about the soul. In dialogues that have been reconstructed by scholars, we find an Aristotle who, like Plato, tends to equate the soul with the human soul and seems to regard immortality or separate existence of the soul as all but self-evident. The problem becomes one of explaining how the soul got mixed up with the body.

2. Aristotle here recalls the scientific methodology laid out in the *Posterior Analytics*. Thomas, in his commentary, reminds his reader that one distinguishes theoretical sciences from one another on the basis of the different ways their subjects are defined. In his early commentary on Boethius's *De trinitate,* q. 5, Thomas gives an extended statement of this Aristotelian doctrine. Perhaps his principal source in Aristotle is *Metaphysics,* 6.1.

1. There are things that depend upon matter in order to exist and in order to be defined: this is the realm of natural or physical things.
2. There are other things that, although they can exist only in matter, are defined without it: such are mathematicals.
3. There are things that exist independently of matter and can thus be defined without matter: metaphysics is concerned with these. (See *In I Physicorum,* vol. 2 of *Sancti Thomae Opera omnia* [Rome: Commissio Leonina, 1884], lectio 1, nos. 1–3.)

Why is the mode of defining crucial for distinguishing sciences? "It should be known that, since every science is in the intellect—a thing becomes actually intelligible insofar as it is abstracted from matter—things pertain to diverse sciences insofar as they are diversely related to matter. Moreover, since any science is had by way of demonstration and the definition functions as the middle term of demonstration, sciences are diversified on the basis of diverse modes of defining" (ibid., no. 1).

3. This argument relies on things yet to be established, but in an introduction or *prooemium* to a commentary, our guide will give us the lay of the land in broad strokes. If we take his word for such matters, it is on the assumption that they will later be shown to be true. In this case, Thomas is borrowing on the very first thing to be discussed—after surveying with Aristotle what others have had to say of these things—namely, the makeup of things that come to be as a result of a change.

4. *Commentary on Sense and the Sensed Object,* lectio 1, no. 2. See A. M. Festugière, "La place du 'De anima' dans le système aristotélicien d'après St Thomas," *Archives d'histoire littéraire et doctrinal du moyen âge* 6 (1931): 25–47.

5. This much on the order to the Aristotelian works is sufficient for our purposes. Needless to say, during the heyday of the evolutionary or developmental approach to Aristotle, talk of the order of the treatises to one another, along with a search for the internal order, came under suspicion. See, for example, Werner Jaeger, *Aristotle: The History of the Fundamentals of His Development,* trans. Richard Robinson, 2d ed. (Oxford: The Clarendon Press, 1948) and the more sympathetic discussion of Auguste Mansion, *Introduction à la Physique aristotélicienne* (Louvain: Institut Supérieur de Philosophie, 1913). Now, when the question is less likely to be begged on the basis of alleged philological and/or historical discoveries, Thomas's view can be appraised on the basis on which it is offered. Does it or does it not match the explicit and implicit teachings of the texts? Whatever the fate of that discussion, it seems clear that we shall not understand Thomas's approach to *On the Soul* if we are unaware of his understanding of the quite detailed relations among the Aristotelian treatises.

6.   That there are things which are not products of change, that is, substances which do not depend upon matter in order to exist, is, as we have seen, a presupposition of metaphysics. In order for us to know that to be and to be material or changeable are not synonymous, we require proof that there are existent things which are separate from matter. It is just such a proof in *On the Soul* that is at issue in the polemical opusculum we are examining.

7.   Thomas, *De principiis naturae,* introduction and critical text by John J. Pauson (Fribourg: Société Philosophique, 1950), no. 340.

8.   "Et quia generatio est quaedam mutatio de non esse vel de non ente ad esse vel ad ens, e contrario autem corruptio debet esse de esse vel ente ad non esse vel non ens, non ex quolibet non esse fit generatio, sed ex non ente quod est ens in potentia; sicut idolum ex cupro, quod est idolum in potentia, et non in actu" (*On the Principles of Nature,* chap. 1, no. 341).

9.   "Et sciendum est quod materia prima, et etiam forma, non generatur neque corrumpitur, quia omnis generatio est ex aliquo in aliquid. Id autem ex quo est generatio, est materia; id autem ad quod est generatio, est forma. Si ergo materia et forma generarentur, materiae esset materia, et formae esset formae, et sic in infinitum. Unde generatio non est nisi compositi, proprie loquendo" (ibid., chap. 2, no. 347).

I Defining the Soul

Thomas begins his commentary on Aristotle's *On the Soul* with a methodological reminder. In any area of study, we should first inquire into what is common and then go on to the peculiarities and differences of things. So with respect to living things, we should first ask what all of them have in common and only then inquire into the various types of living being. But what all living things have in common is a soul; all animate things have an *anima*. That is why Aristotle begins his study of living things with a treatise on the soul.[1] We saw earlier how Thomas understands other Aristotelian works to follow on the study of soul as such.

I An As It Were Abstract Consideration

The general methodological point is by now familiar, but this application of it is surprising. If living things make up a kind or type to be studied, why not inquire into the common characteristics of such things rather than make a part the subject of inquiry? Aristotle did not begin the study of physical things by isolating their form and devoting a treatise exclusively to that, writing a hypothetical *Perimorphes* or *De forma*. Rather, form was studied as a function of the whole of which it is a part. Why does the study of living things begin with what Thomas calls an as it were abstract consideration of soul?[2]

> Holding as we do that, while knowledge of any kind is a thing to be honored and prized, any kind of it may, either by reason of its greater exactness or of a higher dignity and greater wonderfulness in its objects, be more honorable and precious than another, on both accounts we should naturally be led to place in the front rank the study of the soul. (*On the Soul,* 1.1.402a1–4)

Thus Aristotle begins his treatise. The study of the soul ranks high both in the dignity of its object and in the exactness of its knowledge. These two criteria are seldom realized in the same science. Metaphysics may seek knowledge of the highest and most worthy objects, but its method is a far cry from the precision of mathematics. A science that ranks high in the worthiness of its object is likely to rank low in the exactness of its knowledge and vice versa. Thomas speaks of the two criteria as dignity of object and certainty of knowledge. Thus, not only are we seeking the knowledge of something that ranks high on the ontological scale; our knowledge of the soul is noteworthy for its certainty.

Given the disputes about living things—whether something or other is alive and indeed whether the distinction between living and

nonliving is provisional and to be overcome in an eventual unifica-
tion of the sciences—it is surprising to be told that our knowledge of
the soul is certain. "This science of the soul, however, has both, because it is certain—that he has a soul and that it vivifies him is
something everyone experiences in himself; and more noble, for the
soul is nobler than lesser creatures."[3] My certainty about the soul is
grounded in my experience of life, my certainty that I am alive. My
consciousness that I move my hand, stand and sit, open my eyes and
look is at issue here, not some deep inner experience. I am alive because of the vital activities in which I engage. The list just given is a
list of vital activities. I do not simply observe my hand move or my
foot jiggle and then wonder how to distinguish these from a moving
cloud or tumbling tumbleweed. I am aware that I bring the former
about, that I am the source of such activities. I move my fingers and
observe them move. I might do so in response to the question, "Are
you still alive?" Should someone say to us, "I thought I was alive but
I was mistaken," we would assume that he/she was reading aloud
from a ghost story. Taken in any other way, it makes no sense. Being
alive is not one of the things we can be mistaken about.[4]

My unshakable confidence that I have a soul reposes on my experience of performing vital operations: I am aware that I taste and
feel, that I understand what is said to me, that I long to be in Cincin-
nati, that I pick up the phone and call my travel agent and ask about
flights. Remember that, in *On There Being Only One Intellect,*
Thomas said that we would not ask what intellect is if we did not
have the experience of understanding.[5] In such experiences, there is
an inner and an outer experience—my awareness that I move myself about, for example, and my seeing my feet move—and when I
see the outer experience in another being, I assume the inner is
there as well. I know that you are alive on an analogy with myself. If
there were no inner experience, there would be no division in natural philosophy between the inanimate and the animate.[6]

My certainty that I have a soul is based on my certainty that I
have a different makeup from bodies that cannot perform the operations which I do. This certainty is not to be confused with the clear
and distinct knowledge of what the soul is, of course. Furthermore,
in *On the Soul,* Aristotle is not concerned with his own singular vital
activities as such; he wants to know what sets off living bodies like
himself from nonliving things. The name for that which he is seeking is "soul," and he wants a general account, however much it presupposes his personal experience of being alive. What is soul?

I The First Definition of Soul

At the outset of *On the Soul,* there arose the question as to whether
we should consider first the soul in general or its parts, that is, soul

in general or different kinds of soul. That it is a most common and universal notion of soul that should first be sought is indicated by our mode of knowing, which guides Aristotle throughout. As Thomas observes: "This is the order of teaching, that we should move from the more to the less general."[7] As it happens, Aristotle gives two definitions of the soul, and then discusses how the two relate to one another. "If one had to give a definition of soul in general, one that would fit any soul, it would be this: 'Soul is the first actuality of a physically organized body.'"[8] The route to this definition is by way of a series of distinctions or divisions. A definition assigns the thing to be defined to a type or class and shows how it differs from other things of that type. Things can be categorized most generally by means of the distinction between substance and the accidents of substance. To which class does soul fall? Substance? But "substance" has several senses: (1) it can mean matter, that which is not in itself a "this"; (2) it can mean form or essence, that in virtue of which a thing is called a "this"; or (3) it can mean the compound of (1) and (2).

Matter is potentiality, form is actuality, but "actual" can be distinguished in the way we distinguish between one who actually has some skill but is not using it and one who has it and is actually using it.

If we had to give examples of substances, we would, of course, point to the things around us: bodies, the autonomous units that have come to be, physical objects. But some bodies have life in them, others do not. "Of natural bodies some have life in them, others not; by life we mean self-nutrition and growth (with its correlative decay)" (*On the Soul*, 412a14–16). Aristotle will extend this list of vital activities, but this suffices for what he wants to say. If some bodies are alive and some are not, life cannot be explained by the fact that something is a body. Rather, it is a body of a certain kind that is alive. If two bodies are bodies of different kinds, we seek this difference in their form rather than in their matter:

> So then, since substance is threefold, namely, the composed, matter, and form, and is not the composed, which is the body having life, nor the matter, which is the body subject to life, by way of an argument from division then the soul is substance as the form or species of such a body, namely, of a physical body potentially having life.[9]

The soul, in short, is the substantial form of the living body, the actuality of a body potentially having life. Thomas explains, "He [Aristotle] says 'potentially having life' rather than simply 'having life,' because the body having life would be taken to be composite living substance."[10] This is the first definition Aristotle gives of the soul: the first actuality of a physical body potentially having life.

From the point of view of *On There Being Only One Intellect,* it should be noted that an obvious consequence of this definition is that the soul does not appear to be a thing that could exist on its own, separately from body—no more than any other substantial form could exist apart from matter. Form and matter are principles of things, not things in their own right. What a physical thing is includes form and matter, but it is neither of these alone. No more is a living thing identical with its soul: ". . . the soul *plus* the body constitutes the animal" (*On the Soul,* 413a3). Still, Aristotle states the matter cautiously:

> From this it indubitably follows that the soul is inseparable from its body, or at any rate that certain parts of it are (if it has parts)—for the actuality of some of them is nothing but the actuality of their bodily parts. Yet some may be separable because they are not the actualities of any body at all.[11]

On the face of it, it makes no sense to speak of a substantial form existing apart from its corresponding matter. But Aristotle was in the Platonic Academy for nearly twenty years, and his own reconstructed early works exhibit a view much like Plato's; the problem then was to explain how the soul ever got tangled up in the body. Death is the release of the soul, so that it can once more enjoy the kind of existence proper to it, that is, as separate from the body. Now Aristotle's problem will be to show how the human soul can continue to exist apart from its body and thus survive death. And he tells us what will be required in order to show this possibility: some vital activity is not the actuality of a bodily organ.

▌The Second Definition of Soul

Aristotle likens the definition of the soul just given to the conclusion of a syllogism, and he suggests that we look for what will explain it. Take the definition of squaring: the construction of an equilateral rectangle equal to a given oblong rectangle. But squaring can also be defined as the discovery of a line that is a mean proportional between the two unequal sides of the given rectangle, and this definition states the ground of what was first defined. The soul is the first actuality of a physical body potentially alive. Aristotle will propose another account of the soul that gives the ground. But Aristotle's example limps a bit; the second definition will not express the cause of what the first expresses, as is the case with the second definition of squaring with respect to the first. The second definition of the soul will express the cause of our *knowing* what the first definition expresses. Any clarification or explanation appeals to what is more evident than that which is clarified or explained. In the example of squaring, the second definition expresses the cause of what the first expresses. In the case of the soul, the second definition expresses the cause of our knowledge that the soul is the substantial form of the living body, but the soul itself is the cause of the operations that make it known to us.

> He [Aristotle] begins demonstrating the definition of soul that has already been given in the way mentioned, namely, through effects. And he uses this argument. *That which is the first principle of living is the act and form of living things; but soul is the first principle of living in living things; therefore it is the act and form of the living body.* Clearly this is an a posteriori demonstration. It is because soul is the form of living body that it is the principle of the acts of life, and conversely.[12]

The second definition of soul is: that whereby we first live, move, sense, and understand (*On the Soul*, 414a12–13). Thus it is made clear that it is from the various vital activities or operations that we begin. These are distinguished by their formal objects: that of sight is color; of hearing, sound; of smell, odor; and so on. The capacities to perform these operations are distinguished on this basis, with soul being the seat of these capacities or faculties or parts. The subsequent discussions of *On the Soul* move logically from this beginning. After a preliminary discussion of faculties or powers of the soul in general, Aristotle goes on to discuss the nutritive or vegetative powers, then turns to the sense powers, taking up first the five external senses, a discussion that continues to the end of book 2 and provides the starting point of book 3, in which Aristotle takes up internal senses, with the emphasis on imagination. And then comes the discussion of understanding and the passage that is the bone of contention between Thomas and the Averroists. Perhaps we should linger a bit longer over Thomas's *divisio textus*.

| The Structure of *On the Soul*

The first stage in understanding a work is to grasp its order, its division into parts, the steps of its argument. Thomas, in commenting on *On the Soul*, puts before us the structure of the work, giving us initial statements as to its parts and the order among them and, as he proceeds, refining that outline. In commenting on Peter Lombard's *Sentences* and on Boethius's *De trinitate*, the *divisio textus* comes first and is followed by *questiones* suggested by the text.[13] In his commentaries on Aristotle, on the other hand, Thomas embeds the analysis of the text in his explication of it. In both moments of his effort, he is seeking to understand the text and what the text is about rather than to take off on independent discussion of the issues it raises.

What precisely is the structure of the three books of *On the Soul* as Thomas sees it?[14] First, he distinguishes Aristotle's preface or prooemium from the text itself. The preface takes up the first chapter of the first book, 402a1–403b19, and Thomas likens it to the prooemia with which scholastics begin their accounts of classical works. "One writing a prooemium sets out to do three things, first to make one benevolent, second docile, third attentive; benevolent, by showing the usefulness of the science, docile, by setting forth the order and division of the treatise, attentive, by telling us how difficult it is" (*Sentencia libri De anima,* 1.1, lines 26–32; *In I De anima,* in *In Aristotelis librum De anima commentarium,* ed. A. M. Pirotta [Turin: Marietti, 1948], lectio 1, no. 2.). He finds that the first chapter exemplifies this.

The treatise itself is divided into two major parts: first, the discussion of the opinions of Aristotle's predecessors on the soul; and second, his view of the truth of the matter (*Sentencia,* 1.3, lines 5–9; lectio 3, no. 31). This division distinguishes the remainder of book 1 from books 2 and 3. The views of others are first narrated (403b25–405b30), and then disputed (405b31–411b30).

In the second major part of the treatise, Aristotle gives what in his view is a true account of the soul. This part in turn is subdivided into two major divisions, but they do not, as Bazán shows, correspond to the distinction between the second and third books. In the first, he determines the nature of the soul (from 412a6); in the second, its powers (from 414a29). The discussion of the powers is subdivided, with a discussion of powers or parts of the soul in general preceding a discussion of each of them in particular. The first division begins at 414a29 (chap. 3), the second division begins at 415a14 (chap. 4) (*Sentencia,* 2.5, lines 9–12; *In II De anima,* lectio 5, no. 279).

Thus far, then, we have:

A. Prooemium

B. Treatise

    1. The nature of soul

    2. Parts of the soul

        a. In general

        b. In particular

This is, as it turns out, a general overview of the whole treatise, since the discussion of the parts or powers or faculties of the soul, which begins in book 2, chapter 3, continues to the end of book 3.

The discussion of the powers of the soul is divided into two major parts, the first taking them up one at a time, the second discussing the interrelations and hierarchy among them (3.12.433b31). The discussion of the faculties of the soul one by one takes up the bulk of the treatise. This discussion is divided into four parts: in the first Aristotle discusses the vegetative; in the second, the sensitive (2.5.416b32); in the third, the intellective (3.4.429a10); in the fourth, locomotion (3.9.432a18).

The discussion of the sensitive powers, extending from book 2, chapter 5, through book 3, chapter 4, is the heftiest of the treatise. In the text as found in *The Basic Writings of Aristotle,* edited by Richard McKeon, the whole treatise runs from pages 535 to 603. The discussion of the senses runs from page 564 through page 589, or slightly more than a third of the treatise.

Thomas divides this discussion into two parts, the first dealing with external senses, the second with internal senses; this latter part begins at 424b22, which is where book 3 begins. Such editions as the Marietti divide Thomas's commentary at just this point:

> Here for the Greeks the third book begins and reasonably enough since from this point Aristotle starts to inquire into intellect. Some have held that sense and intellect are the same. It is clear, however, that intellect is not one of the external senses, which have already been treated, because it is not restricted to knowing only one sort of sensible thing. So it must be asked whether there is some other cognitive faculty in the sensitive part such that in that way it could be maintained that intellect is a sense. (*In III De anima,* lectio 1, no. 564)

In the Leonine edition, this is chapter 25 of the commentary on the second book (lines 1–12).

At this point, Thomas gives another subdivision of Aristotle's discussion of the senses. First, he says, Aristotle asks whether there is any sense beyond the five external senses already discussed. Second, Aristotle shows that intellect is in no way a sense (3.3.427a17). Third, having shown that intellect is not a sense, he determines what the intellective part is (*In III De anima,* lectio 1, no. 565; Leonine 2.25, lines 13–19).

Bazán asks whether the division given here agrees with that given earlier. Earlier Thomas divided the long part running from 415a22 to 434a22 into four sections: a discussion of the vegetative, the sensitive, the intellective, and the locomotive. The sensitive was then divided into external (from 416b32) and internal (from 424b22). Bazán suggests that the part that is being divided is book 3, beginning where the Greeks saw it beginning.

This is a most schematic presentation of the order Thomas sees in the text of the treatise *On the Soul.* One could, basing oneself on the *divisiones textus* that accompany the interpretation, develop an outline of the complete Aristotelian text.

I NOTES

1. "Rerum autem animatarum omnium quoddam genus est et ideo in consideratione rerum animatarum oportet primo considerare ea quae sunt communia omnibus animatis, postmodum uero illa quae propria sunt cuilibet rei animatae. Commune autem omnibus rebus animatis est anima; in hoc enim omnis animata conueniunt. Ad tradendum igitur scienciam de rebus animatis, necessarium fuit primo tradere scienciam de anima tanquam communem eis. Aristotiles ergo uolens tradere scienciam de ipsis rebus animatis, primo tradit scienciam de anima, postmodum uero determinat de propriis singulis animatis in sequentibus libris" (*Sentencia*, 4, lines 10–23; *In I De anima*, lectio 1, no. 1).

2. "Nam primo quidem consideravit de anima secundum se, quasi in quadam abstractione" (*In librum De sensu et sensato commentarium*, lectio 1, no. 2). This is a text we considered earlier in discussing the order of procedure in the sciences of living things.

3. "Hec autem sciencia, scilicet de anima, utrumque habet, quia et certa est (hoc enim quilibet experitur in se ipso, quod scilicet habeat animam et quod anima uiuificet) et quia est nobiliorum (anima enim est nobilior inter inferiores creaturas)" (*Sentencia*, 5a92–b2).

4. Perhaps "I thought I was dead but I wasn't" may seem a counterexample, but on reflection it makes rather than shakes the point. The I who thought she was dead is alive to the extent of exhibiting the vital activity of thinking.

5. See *On There Being Only One Intellect*, chap. 3, no. 62 (lines 28–29).

6. See the remarkable work of Charles DeKoninck, "Introduction à l'étude de l'âme," written to introduce Stanislas Cantin's *Précis de psychologie thomiste*, Editions de l'Université Laval (Quebec: Presses Universitaires, 1948), vi–lxxxiii.

7. *Sentencia*, 68, lines 26–29; *In II De anima*, lectio 1, no. 211. Thomas adds: "as the Philosopher shows at the outset of the *Physics*."

8. *Sentencia*, 72, lines 60–65; *In II De anima*, lectio 1, no. 233.

9. *Sentencia*, 70, lines 216–23; *In II De anima*, lectio 1, no. 221.

10. *Sentencia*, 70, lines 223–26.

11. *On the Soul*, 413a3–9. In the continuation of the passage, we read, "Further, we have no light on the problem whether the soul may not be the actuality of its body in the sense in which the sailor is of the ship." This openness to the Platonic metaphor may strike us as false eirenism and/or disingenuous, but Aristotle may be taken to be stressing the difficulty of these matters and his unwillingness to plunge ahead as if all were perfectly clear even at the outset of the inquiry.

12. *Sentencia*, 79, lines 106–16; *In II De anima*, lectio 3, no. 253.

13. *Expositio super librum Boethii De trinitate*, ed. Bruno Decker (Leiden: Brill, 1959).

14. Bernardo Bazán, in his review of the Leonine edition of the *Sentencia libri De anima*, 540–41, gives a sketch of Thomas's division. He does this in the course of asking whether or not Thomas accepts the Greek beginning of book 3. See also *Tommaso d'Aquino Commentario al "De anima,"* ed., trans. Adriana Caparello (Rome: Abete, 1974).

I Aristotle's Analysis of Cognition

Quick answers as to what Thomas's account of cognition is would include "having the form of another as other" or "having a concept which represents something that is." To say that these are obscure in the extreme so stated is not to say that they are false, but we may feel no particular impulse to accept them as anything other than the technical jargon of a particular school of philosophy. Thomas got these accounts from Aristotle, and he did not consider the teaching of Aristotle to be one school of philosophy, as if there could be several such schools, all of them internally coherent but quite different from one another. But this in turn might seem only to indicate Thomas's fierce loyalty to Aristotle, and we can imagine fervent Kantians and Humeans who would consider what they hold about knowledge not simply as a possible account but as *the* account. This has been called the scandal of philosophy, and the search for a way to overcome it once and for all has been high on the agenda of philosophy since Descartes. What commended Aristotle's approach for Thomas was that it began with things more easily grasped by us—although they were often confused generalities—and moved in the direction of greater and greater precision. Later, accounts are commended because they repose on what is more easily grasped and are shown to follow from what is more easily grasped. Not that the specific is deduced from the general; rather, we proceed from more general to ever less general accounts.[1] It is, therefore, significant that the *Physics* stands at the beginning of inquiry into natural things; what was established there has application to, and is determined and specified in, subsequent works.

I Cognition and the External Senses

The most obvious instance of this method thus far is the way in which the analysis of living things in *On the Soul* borrows from and specifies the analysis of physical objects in the *Physics*. The living body, like any physical thing, is composed of matter and form because it comes to be as the result of a change. Soul is that which is presupposed by the activities and operations which give rise to the distinction between living and nonliving physical objects. But a thing's form is the basis of its properties and accidents. Soul thus emerged as the substantial form of living bodies.

But the analogy with becoming as analyzed in the *Physics* continues as *On the Soul* progresses. Vital operations are occurrences, changes, and when sensation is analyzed as a becoming, an account of it emerges that commends itself against that background. From not seeing something, one comes to see it. From not feeling something, one comes to feel it. Becoming was seen to involve a subject that, from not having a form, comes to have it. When sensation is regarded as a becoming, it will be seen as the acquisition of a form on an analogy with physical becoming. But it is an analogy, not a metaphor. In the case of physical change, the acquisition of a form by matter results in a new instance of the kind specified by the form. But when I see an apple and am said to receive the form of the apple analogously, the obvious difference is that this becoming does not result in a new instance of the kind, another apple—not even the apple of my eye.

> By a "sense" is meant what has the power of receiving into itself the sensible forms of things without the matter. This must be conceived as taking place in the way in which a piece of wax takes on the impress of a signet-ring without the iron or gold; we say that what produces the impression is a signet of bronze or gold, but its particular constitution makes no difference: in a similar way the sense is affected by what is colored or flavored or sounding, but it is indifferent what in each case the *substance* is; what alone matters is what *quality* it has. (*On the Soul*, 2.12.424a17–24)

In commenting on this passage from Aristotle, Thomas observes that the principle involved seems to be true generally of the effect of a cause, namely, that since the cause acts through its form rather than its matter, the effect is similar to the agent in form. Thus the reception of form without matter does not seem peculiar to sensation.

The difference lies in the way that the form is received. If the form is received in the effect in the same way that it exists in the agent, the form is not received without matter. True, it is not numerically the same matter in effect and agent, but the form exists in matter in the same way in both. Thomas explains:

> Sometimes the form as received in the patient exists in another way than in the agent, because the material disposition of the patient for receiving is not the same as the material disposition in the agent. Thus the form is received in the patient without matter, insofar as the patient is assimilated to the agent in form but not in matter. In this way sense receives form without matter because the form exists differently in sense than in the sensible thing. It has natural existence in the sensible thing, whereas in the sense it has an intentional and spiritual existence."[2]

The example of the gold signet ring's impression in wax bridges the gap between natural change—with the form existing in the same way in agent and patient—and the way in which sense and the sensible thing have the same form—with sense having the form without the matter that accompanies it in the sensible thing. Although wax is not gold, it is equally material, and we end up with numerically different instances of the image. But when the sense is acted upon and receives a form, it receives it into a physical organ— eye, ear, the corresponding section of the brain. The difference thus seems to evaporate, and Thomas's characterization of the sensed form's mode of existence as "intentional and spiritual" seems decidedly premature. This suggests just the sort of thing that Thomas seeks to avoid, namely, that sensation, as something involving the soul, takes place separately from the body. Sensing is the actuality of a corporeal organ and thus involves matter essentially. Perhaps Thomas should have stayed with his observation that there just is not all that much difference between natural changes and sensation.

Indeed, if it were simply a matter of external observation, the distinction might never be made, and sensation could be analyzed as simply a special case of natural change. But, as we have seen, questions about life arise from our experience of our own vital activities, of which we have both internal and external experience. My experience of seeing or touching is not simply to be altered by another body but also to have or grasp it in some way, to be aware of it because of the alteration that takes place. Feeling warm in the sense of uncomfortable and feeling the warmth of an object are palpably different things, and both differ from the way in which fire heats water. It is not Aristotle's task to prove that sensation exists or that it is different from physical change. He starts from such distinctions as from the principles of the discussion, and the clear suggestion is that the denial of those starting points is something that could be dealt with, although it is not the task of natural philosophy to take up such challenges to its principles.

Having given an account of how the reception of form in sensation differs from any physical change, which could be described as the reception of the agent's form by the thing acted upon, Aristotle is now concerned lest what he is saying about sensation should be taken to be the same as what he will eventually say about intellection, whose immateriality is not to be confused with that of sensation. That is why he insists that the capacity to sense has its seat in a bodily organ, the two being related as form to matter. A sign of the intimate union of sense power and sense organ is that sound can be so great as to destroy hearing and a color so bright that we are blinded by it.

But is that peculiar to sensation? Does not a loud sound have effects on nonliving bodies as well? Obviously. In much the same way, light and color affect nonliving bodies, reflected in water, off walls, to say nothing of mirrors. If inanimate bodies can be affected by objects of the senses—color, sound, smell, etc.—what happens to Aristotle's account of the difference between sensation and physical change?

> Must we not, then, admit that the objects of the other senses also may affect them? Is not the true account this, that all bodies *are* capable of being affected by sounds and smells? . . . Is not the answer that, while the air, owing to the momentary duration of the action upon it of what is odorous, does itself become perceptible to the sense of smell, smelling is an *observing* of the result produced? (*On the Soul,* 424b14–18)

The answer comes down to this, that only sense is affected by the object of sense—smells are smells only to those who have the sense of smell, color is color only to those who have the sense of sight. Nonetheless, things that do not have senses can be accidentally affected by the objects of sense, that is, not as an object of sense, but insofar as, say, the movement of air is involved in sound and a physical object can be affected by it. But it is not affected by sound as such.[3]

What then are we to understand by Thomas's claim that in sensation the form of the sensed thing is received, but not in matter, and therefore sensation involves immateriality and spirituality? The very phrasing of the question makes clear that sensation is being analyzed on an analogy with physical becoming, i.e., a substance comes from not having a certain quality to have that quality. Sensation is approached as a becoming—as an instance of someone's from not seeing X, coming to see X; from not hearing Y, coming to hear Y; and so on. If the controlling sense of becoming involves a subject or matter, a privation in that subject, and the form of which the subject was deprived, and the change is the acquisition by the subject of the form it did not previously have, then sensation will be said to involve the acquisition of a form. That this is not simply another instance of physical change is clear to us from our experience of what happens when we see and hear. It is not simply that we undergo a physical change; what is peculiar to sensation is that it makes us aware of a quality or form in something else. That is what Thomas meant by calling the form as it exists in sense *intentional:* it is a sign of the form in the thing sensed, it is that whereby we are aware of the form in the physical thing. If the form as sensed were received in matter in the same way as the form exists in the sensible thing, the result would be a physical change and the production of another instance of the form-in-matter. But the color of the apple is in the apple; the color as seen is in the eye, not by coloring the eye, not by producing a new instance of the color, let alone another apple. To say that the form is received immaterially is to employ an adverb that negates the way the form is in matter in the physical thing that is sensed. When we grasp or receive the colors of things—see them—the colors take on a different mode of existence in sense. But, clearly, as sensed, the form exists in matter, namely, in the physical organ of sensation. The use of "immaterial," in short, is quite controlled here. It says what it says and it does not say what it does not say.

| Internal Senses

Aristotle bridges his discussion of the external senses and intellect with a discussion of internal senses, beginning with the observation that we sense the difference between a color and taste, say, red and sweet, and it cannot be either sight or taste that does this. Thus, if this difference is sensed, the sense in question cannot be one of the external senses, but a common sense that, Aristotle says,

> . . . asserts thus—both now and that the objects are different now; the objects therefore must be present at one and the same moment. Both the discriminating power and the time of its exercise must be one and undivided. (*On the Soul,* 426b27–29)[4]

Most of Aristotle's predecessors had assumed that thinking and sensing are identical. Having given an account of the activity of the senses, he is in a position to describe thinking, pointing out its dissimilarities with sensation. He suggests that practical thinking cannot be identical with sensing, since sensing is everywhere in the animal world, whereas only a portion of that world contains beings who engage in practical thinking. Moreover, speculative thinking must be distinguished from sensing because the former may be true or false, whereas the grasp of the special objects of sense is always free from error. He is also concerned to distinguish both sensing and thinking from imagining. This leads Aristotle into an extended discussion of imagining, after which he returns to mind and thinking.

It is important to have at least this schematic understanding of the wider context of the passages disputed in the controversy to which the *De unitate intellectus* contributes. The discussion of mind arises out of the discussion of the faculties of the soul involved in sensing and then out of the discussion of internal senses, which, however different from the external senses, are senses. The activity of the senses may be described as immaterial when we contrast the way a form is acquired in a natural change with the way a form is acquired in the change from not sensing to sensing. Throughout the discussion of sensation, external or internal, it is clear that a bodily organ is always involved, that sensing is the actuality of that organ and thus essentially involves matter. That being the case, there seems to be no possibility that the soul, which engages in such activity, could exist apart from the body, without which its activity is impossible.

What, then, is thinking? As Aristotle perceives it,

> If thinking is like perceiving, it must be either a process in which the soul is acted upon by what is capable of being thought, or a process different from but analogous to that. The thinking part of the soul must therefore be, while impassible, capable of receiving the form of an object; that is, must be potentially identical in character with its object without being the object. Mind must be related to what is thinkable, as sense is to what is sensible. (*On the Soul,* 429a12–17)

The manifestation of what thinking is will accordingly come about by way of analogy. In the *Physics,* Aristotle said that prime matter, the subject of the change whereby a substance comes into being or passes out of being, is known by analogy. Analogy with what? With the subject of the change whereby a substance acquires an attribute it previously lacked. When the substance is some stuff such as clay and the attribute is shape or form, the terminology becomes matter and form and change, understood first as accidental change, as the matter's acqustion of a form. If the coming into being of a substance is understood after this pattern, there will have to be a subject that, from not being conjoined with the form that makes a substance to *be* and to be what it is, comes to be conjoined with it, the result being a substance.

In accidental change the form acquired by the matter causes it to be in a certain way that it previously was not, e.g., to be white, to be here, and so on, but it does not make the subject *be* in a fundamental sense. The subject exists as to what it is, e.g., a person, prior to the change whereby the skill of playing the piano is acquired. One is said to have become a musician, a pianist, but not to have become a person as the result of such a process. If a substance is to come to be as such, the subject or matter cannot itself be a substance. If it were, the form acquired would modify it but would not cause it to be substantially. So if substantial changes occur—and they do—and if, as changes, they require a subject, and if that subject cannot be a substance (since then the change would be merely an accidental one), let us call that subject *prime matter* to signal its difference from the subject of accidental change, and let us call the form acquired—the one that makes a substance to be a substance—substantial form.

That is what Aristotle means when he says prime matter is known by analogy. So, too, thinking is to be understood by analogy with sensing:

Mind : thinkable :: sense : sensible.

A sense cannot sense everything but rather only things that fall within the range of its proper object: for the sight, color; for hearing, sound; and so forth. But anything is a possible object of thought. From this Aristotle draws the conclusion that the mind cannot have a nature; in order for mind to be able to become anything, it must itself be no determinate nature, "for the copresence of what is alien to its nature is a hindrance and a block." Mind is a capacity rather than a nature.

> Thus that in the soul which is called mind (by mind I mean that whereby the soul thinks and judges) is, before it thinks, not actually any real thing. For this reason it cannot reasonably be regarded as blended with the body; if so, it would acquire some quality, e.g., warmth or cold, or even have an organ like the sense faculty; as it is, it has none. (*On the Soul*, 429a23–27)

The first characteristic of mind arrived at by this contrast with sense is that it is a capacity, not a nature. A sense is capable of becoming only what falls under its proper object; mind is capable of knowing anything. If it is capable of all forms, potential in their regard, it cannot actually be some form, that is, have a determinate nature. From this Aristotle deduces that the mind cannot be blended with body.

Strong stimulation of a sense renders the sense less capable of acting. A light of great intensity blinds us, an extremely loud noise deafens us. But "in the case of mind, thought about an object that is highly intelligible renders it more and not less able afterwards to think objects that are less intelligible: *the reason is that, while the faculty of sensation is dependent upon the body, mind is separable from it*" (*On the Soul*, 429b3–4).

Aristotle next makes a distinction that was first encountered at the outset of the treatise. One who learns geometry can be said to have a mind that, from being potentially in possession of this science, now actually has it. But this actuality that terminates the process of learning is compatible with a person's not actually thinking of what she has learned. The accomplished geometer *can* do geometry even when she is not actually doing it, but the actuality involved in her use is different from that first acquired with the science.

Mind can come to know itself insofar as it knows itself thinking, thinking bearing on some object that actualizes the mind.

Mind relates to its objects in a way analogous to that in which sense relates to sensibles. The objects of the two are now distinguished on the basis of a distinction between flesh and what it is to be flesh. Flesh here means *this* flesh, a particular instance of the kind. If sensed, flesh is grasped through its color, this singular instance of color; to know what color is pertains not to sense but to some other faculty.

> Now it is by means of the sensitive faculty that we discriminate the hot and the cold, i.e., the factors which combined in a certain ratio constitute flesh: the essential character of flesh is apprehended by something different either wholly separate from the sensitive faculty or related to it as a bent line to the same line when it has been straightened out. (*On the Soul*, 429b14–17)

The objects of thinking are called abstract (*ton en aphrairesei onton* [429b18]), and "to sum up, insofar as the realities it knows are capable of being separated from their matter, so it is also with powers of mind" (429b21–22). Mind does not have as its object *this* flesh or *that*, but the nature of flesh as this would be expressed in a definition. "Thisness" is a feature of the nature as enmattered; for the nature to become an object of mind, it is separated or abstracted from that which is true of it as *this* instance or *that;* such aspects are set aside, left out of the account.

An obvious problem arises. If mind is wholly impassible, yet thinking seems inescapably to involve the mind's being acted upon, how can thinking come about? Interaction seems to require community among the things which interact. Another problem to be faced is how mind can be one of its own objects. If mind itself can be an object of thought and all thinkable things are, as thinkable, the same in kind, it seems to follow that either mind belongs to everything, or mind and all other realities share some common element that makes them thinkable.

Aristotle's response to the first difficulty recalls that mind is potentially all things but actually none of them until it thinks. "What it thinks must be in it just as characters may be said to be on a writing-tablet on which as yet nothing actually stands written: this is exactly what happens with mind" (*On the Soul*, 429b31–430a1).

In response to the second problem, Aristotle distinguishes objects which involve no matter and those which must be disengaged from their matter in order to be thought. The latter are in their natural condition potential objects of thought, but the potentiality is realized in the mind when the actuality of thinking and the actuality of being thought are identical. Why is not mind always thinking of those things which involve no matter? Here Aristotle merely notices the difficulty, postponing discussion of it until the following chapter.

| Active and Passive Mind

Aristotle continues analyzing soul on an analogy with what has gone before, now recalling a most general feature of the natural world, namely, that there is a matter which is potentially all things and a productive cause which makes them all. We find somewhat the same thing in the soul. The mind, as we have been discussing it thus far, is like prime matter in the physical world.

> And in fact mind as we have described it is what it is by virtue of becoming all things, while there is another which is what it is by virtue of making all things: this is a sort of positive state like light; for in a sense light makes potential colors into actual colors. Mind in this sense of it is separable, impassible, unmixed, since it is in its essential nature activity. (*On the Soul,* 430a14–18)

We have before us now the background and the key text of the dispute carried on in the *De unitate intellectus.* Now we must look at the interpretation that Thomas contests.

I NOTES

1. Thomas distinguishes the *modus demonstrandi* from the *modus determinandi,* the latter being the movement toward ever more specific knowledge of the subject. Cf. *In I Physicorum,* lectio 1.

2. "Quandoque uero forma recipitur in paciente secundum alium modum essendi quam sit in agente, et ideo forma recipitur in paciente sine materia in quantum paciens assimilatur agenti secundum formam et non sencundum materiam; et per hunc modum sensus recipit formam sine materia, quia alterius modi esse habet forma in sensi et in re sensibili: nam in re sensibili habet esse naturale, in sensu autem habet esse intentionale siue spirituale; et ponit conueniens exemplum de sigillo et cera, non enim eadem est dispositio cere ad ymaginem, que erat in ferro et auro" (*Sentencia,* 169, lines 45–59; *In II De anima,* lectio 24, nos. 553–54.

3. Thomas distinguishes and develops these two moments of Aristotle's argument. Cf. *Sentencia,* 170, lines 126–52; *In II De anima,* lectio 24, nos. 558–60.

4. Thomas observes, "Considerandum est etiam quod licet hoc principium commune immutetur a sensu proprio, quia ad sensum communem perveniunt immutationes omnium sensuum propriorum" (no. 612).

▮ Averroes or Aquinas?

Thomas's argument with Averroes begins in earnest with the interpretation of Aristotle's definition of soul at the outset of book 2 of *On the Soul*. Does this definition apply to all kinds of soul? Is it possible to give a definition that will permit us to predicate "soul" univocally of all the species of soul? Aristotle makes the attempt: "If, then, we have to give a general formula applicable to all kinds of soul, we must describe it as the first grade of actuality of a natural organized body" (412b4).

Here is Averroes's commentary:

> "If then something universal, etc." That is, if then it is possible to define the soul with a universal definition, no definition is more universal than this, nor more appropriate to the substance of soul, namely, that the soul is the first perfection of an organic natural body.[1]

Why does Aristotle introduce this as if in doubt? "Perfection in the rational soul and in the other powers of soul is said almost with pure equivocation, as will be clarified later. That is, one can express the doubt that the soul has a universal definition."[2] An account of the soul cannot be given that would apply univocally to all souls. How then? Almost purely equivocally. We are thus warranted to doubt whether a general account can be given and are prepared to doubt that the account given is meant to apply to all souls. Nonetheless, as if grudgingly, Aristotle says that if it were possible to give a universal account, this would be it.

Thomas counters this in number 4 of *On There Being Only One Intellect* by invoking what Aristotle says later:

> From this it indubitably follows that the soul is inseparable from its body, or at any rate that certain parts of it are (if it has parts)—for the actuality of some of them is nothing but the actualities of their bodily parts. (413a4–7)

Here is the text in the Arabo-Latin version:

> Quoniam autem anima non est abstracta a corpore, aut pars eius, si innata est dividi, non latet; est enim quarundam partium perfectio. Sed nichil prohibet ut hoc sit in quibusdam partibus, quia non sunt perfectiones alicuius rei ex corpore. (*Commentarium magnum*, text 11, 147.1–6)

Here is the text Thomas had:

> Quod quidem igitur non sit anima separabilis a corpore, aut partes quedam ipsius, si partibilis apta nata est, non immanifestum est: quarundum enim actus partium est ipsarum. At vero secundum quasdam nichil prohibet, propter id quod nullius corporis actus anima.

Thomas finds this argument in the text:

1. The soul is the act of the whole body, and its parts are acts of bodily parts.

2. An act or form is not separated from that of which it is the act or form.

3. Manifestly soul cannot be separated from body, the whole or any of its parts—if it has parts.

4. It is clear that some parts of the soul are body, the whole or any of its parts—it if has parts.

5. But with respect to some of its parts, nothing prevents the soul from being separated, because some of its parts are not the acts of parts of the body, as will be proved below concerning intellect.[3]

What does Averroes make of it? *"Sed tamen nichil prohibet,* etc." ("However, nothing prevents, etc."). It is not clear that all parts of the soul are inseparable from body, since someone might say that some part of it is not the perfection of a bodily member or that, although it is a perfection, nonetheless some perfections can be abstracted, like the sailor from the ship. Because of these two objections, then, Averroes says, this definition does not make clear that not all parts of the soul cannot be abstracted: *"Propter igitur hec duo non videtur manifestum ex hac diffinitione quod omnes partes animae non possunt abstrahi"* ("On account of these two things therefore it does not seem clear from this definition that not all parts of the soul can be abstracted"; *Commentarium magnum,* 148.27–29). Three negatives. In other words, the definition does not exclude there being parts of the soul that can be abstracted or separated. Alexander, Averroes notes, says that from this definition it appears universally true that parts cannot be abstracted. *"Et nos loquemur de hoc quando loquemur de virtute rationabili"* ("And we will speak of this when we speak of the rational power"; *Commentarium magnum,* 148.31–32).

In Thomas's view, Aristotle's text clearly says that the definition of the soul given applies to the human soul, some of whose parts may not be the actualities of bodies. "We have now given an answer to the question, What is soul?—an answer which applies to it in its full extent" (*On the Soul,* 412b10). That intellection is not an actuality of body will be proved below, and that later proof is taken to connect with this text.

The example of the sailor and the ship refers, Thomas says, to Plato, something he learned from Plotinus and Gregory of Nyssa—Greeks, not Latins, he adds pointedly—and the suggestion is that the soul is not the form of the body but rather its mover. This may

still be wondered about because the truth has not yet been established fully.

But Aristotle, Thomas says, begins immediately to remove the
basis for such a doubt by drawing out the implications of the obvious
truth that the animate is distinguished from the inanimate because
it is alive, that is, lives, manifests vital activities. Aristotle will now
establish that the soul is the substantial form of the living thing by
arguing with reference to vital activities. That "soul is first act of a
physically organized body having life in potency" is demonstrated
from "soul is that whereby we first live, move, sense, understand."

In his commentary on chapter 3 of book 2 (lectiones 3, 4), Thomas
goes to some lengths to discuss this demonstration and the point of
it. If understanding is one of the vital acts thanks to which we know
that we are alive and if that whereby we first perform such an activity is soul, which is the substantial form of the body, intellect must
be a part or faculty or power of that soul.

What does Averroes take the implications of this second definition of the soul to be?

> Since the definition does not suffice to give us knowledge of
> each part of the soul . . . , he [Aristotle] begins here to demon-
> strate the way to knowledge of definitions proper to each part
> *in rebus ignoratis* and the reason why definitions are insuffi-
> cient in such things. (*Great Commentary,* 149)

Actually Averroes introduces a parenthesis between the parts of the
sentence above:

> Since this definition is common to all parts of the soul and is
> said of them in many ways, and such definitions do not suffice
> for perfect knowledge of a thing (that requires univocal not
> equivocal universals), knowledge of each of the parts placed
> under this definition by means of proper (specific) knowledge
> must next be sought, since the definition is not predicated of
> them univocally.[4]

Thus it is the equivocal character of the first definition that calls for
this further inquiry. The definition does not apply equally to all
souls or express something that is predicable and true of all, but the
parts of the soul have to be taken up independently.

It may be the case that when Averroes says that "soul" applies
equivocally or almost purely equivocally to intellect that he is deny-
ing both that "soul" is univocally predicable of all souls and that it is
predicable of intellect in what Thomas would call an analogous fashion. Averroes's use of "equivocally" in saying that substantial form
and accidents are said to be in a subject equivocally suggests this
(*Commentarium magnum,* 133.32–33). The use of *multipliciter* ("in
many ways") in the parenthetical remark just quoted might support

this. In any case, as we shall see, Thomas will argue that "soul" is univocally common to vegetative soul, sensitive soul, and intellectual soul.

According to Ovey N. Mohammed, Aristotle's phrase, "If, then, we have to give a general formula . . . ," warrants Averroes's exemption of intellect from the reach of the general formula given.[5] The key question is whether Aristotle's remark—that a part of the soul may not be the actuality of the body when the soul has been defined as the actuality of body—implies that "soul" is said equivocally of that which is the actuality of body and of that part which is not the actuality of body. If this were an open question in Aristotle, unclarified in the rest of *On the Soul,* Mohammed might reasonably say that scholars are free to interpret as they will. But it is Thomas's contention that what Averroes says is manifestly incompatible with the rest of the text. Mohammed may be right in saying that Averroes is here constrained by the Koran, but that does not seem immediately relevant (Mohammed, 88). "In other words, within the perspective of the Qur'an's monistic conception of man, his observation may be interpreted to be the systematic clarification of his own position as an Aristotelian philosopher of Islam" (Mohammed, 89).

Is it really unclear whether Aristotle speaks of intellect as a power of the soul? Has he not included understanding among the vital operations which enter into the second account of soul, that whereby we first live, move, sense, and understand? Averroes appeals to Aristotle's remark at 413b24–27 ("We have no evidence as yet about mind or the power to think; it seems to be a widely different kind of soul, differing as what is eternal from what is perishable; it alone is capable of existence in isolation from all other psychic powers") and thinks that this leaves the matter in doubt.

This is the passage Thomas discusses at the end of number 7 as well as in number 8 of *On There Being Only One Intellect.* How should Aristotle be understood here? It is not yet clear whether intellect is a soul or part of the soul, and if it is a part, whether it is separate in place or only definition. Thomas explicitly denies the interpretation that intellect is called soul equivocally or that the definition given does not apply to it (8.149–56). That intellect is eternal and other powers perish with the living thing seems a large difference, certainly, and we may indeed wonder whether intellect is not a different kind of soul. How can an imperishable power be the power of a soul that also has perishable powers? Are they powers of one and the same soul?

This is the question that separates Averroes and Thomas. Averroes finds in Aristotle doubt as to whether his definition of the soul can apply to the intellect. If it does not, then, as Mohammed observes, the intellect is not a kind of soul but rather something other than soul. At this juncture in book 2, Thomas's reading seems more justified than Averroes's. Aristotle speaks of intellect as a part or faculty of the soul, as a faculty of our soul, which is the substantial form of our body. The passage at 413b24–27 follows on a paragraph that asks whether one part of the soul is separate from another in account alone or also in location (413b13–24).[6] The answer to this question with respect to the intellect is that Aristotle does not yet have evidence to answer it. He is not wondering whether the intellect is a part of the soul. Intellect is a part of a soul that also has vegetative, locomotive, and sensitive powers, and it is that soul which is said to be the form of a physical body. Lest someone suggest that intellect here has some lesser meaning, Thomas reaches ahead and cites book 3, 429a23.[7]

Thomas is not through with book 2, however, suggesting we dwell on it a little longer in order to grasp what Aristotle is saying about the soul. Having defined the soul, Aristotle distinguishes its powers, identifying the vegetative, sensitive, appetitive, locomotive, and intellective (414a31–32). He then compares the way in which "soul" is said of kinds of soul to the way in which "figure" is said of species of figure, saying that just as there is no figure apart from the kinds of figure, so, too, there is no soul apart from the various kinds. Thomas takes this to mean that we need not look for any soul other than those mentioned of which the term might be predicated.

In book 3, Aristotle begins his treatment of intellect by identifying it as that part of the soul by which the soul thinks (429a10–12) and links the discussion to that begun at 413b13–24. Having discussed the other powers of the soul, he can turn now to the intellect. Thomas invites us to admire the orderliness of the Aristotelian tractate. There were two matters left unsolved in book 2: first, whether the intellect is separated from the other parts of the soul in location or only in account; and, second, how intellect differs from the other parts of the soul (nos. 15–16, lines 267–306). The first question is restated at 429a11–12, the second at 429a12: "we have to inquire (1) what differentiates this part, and (2) how thinking can take place." Clearly, Thomas observes, we are going to be told how intellect operates; the text does not lead into the question of whether or not the intellect is a substance existing apart.

The comparison of thinking with sensing underscores the fact that Aristotle is speaking of activities that have their source in soul:

> If thinking is like perceiving, it must be either a process in which the soul is acted upon by what is capable of being thought, or a process different from but analogous to that. The thinking part of the soul must therefore be, while impassible,

> capable of receiving the form of an object; that is, must be po-
> tentially identical in character with its object without being its
> object. (429a13–16)

The sense is the sensed object in potency, but each sense is in potency to a limited range of things, namely, those which come under
its formal object, e.g., color, taste. But intellect is in potency to anything whatsoever; we can know anything that is. For this to be possible, intellect must be free of all admixture (429a18). Why? "For the
co-presence of what is alien to its nature is a hindrance and a block:
it follows that it too, like the sensitive part, can have no nature of its
own, other than that of having a certain capacity" (ibid.). If it were of
the nature of seeing to see blue, we could not see other colors. So, too,
if it were the nature of mind to know some nature X, we would be
unable to know non-X.

   In this discussion, Aristotle makes use of what Anaxagoras said
of Mind or Nous. But Anaxagoras was apparently speaking of a
separate substance, not a human capacity. Does this not lend cre-
dence to Averroes's assumption that Aristotle is speaking of something other than a part or faculty of the soul? This is excluded by
Aristotle's statement, "Thus that in the soul which is called mind (by
mind I mean that whereby the soul thinks and judges) is, before it
thinks, not actually any real thing" (429a22–24). That the intellect
is unlike the powers which Aristotle has discussed thus far is clear
when he adds, "For this reason it cannot reasonably be regarded as
blended with the body: If so it would acquire some quality, e.g.
warmth or cold, or even have an organ like the sensitive faculty: as it
is, it has none" (429a24–27). That it has none is developed from the
implications of the Platonic description of the soul as "the place of
the forms."

   By likening intellection to sensing, Aristotle has shown how
they are unlike. In impassibility, first of all: the sense can be destroyed by an overwhelming sensible, but intellect is not destroyed
by an overwhelmingly intelligible thing. The sense's union with an
organ explains this. Thus it is clear that the intellect, which is potentially all things, is a power of the soul, which is the form of body, although intellect does not have a bodily organ as do the other powers
of the soul (no. 26). Mohammed, like Averroes, is misled by the remark, "the reason is that, while the faculty of sensation is dependent
upon the body, mind is separable from it" (429b4–5), taking this to
mean that the mind is a substance existing separately from the body
(Mohammed, 56). The meaning is, Thomas maintains, that intellect
has no organ. Only that interpretation fits the context (nos. 24–25).

   How can it be that the soul, which is the form of body, should
have a power that is not the power of a bodily organ? Thomas says

that this is not difficult to understand. First, he gives an argument from hierarchy. The powers of the soul, as we move up from vegetative through the sensitive, external, and then internal, are progressively less immersed in matter, and their activities are less like material change. No wonder, then, that the highest natural form, the human soul, should have a power whose activitity is not the act of an organ (no. 27). This is not to say that the soul, which has the power of intellect, exists elsewhere than in the body; rather, the activity of its intellect is not the actuality of some bodily organ.

Is this a fanciful addendum to Aristotle's thought? In our opusculum, Thomas invokes texts from book 2 of the *Physics* (nos. 29–30) that indicate how Aristotle saw the human soul as the pinnacle of the natural philosopher's inquiry, a form in matter, yet in a way separate from it. Nothing prevents a form, which is the actuality of the body, from having a power whose activity is not the actuality of an organ.

But how can something incorruptible be the form of a corruptible body? Thomas refers his reader to the *Metaphysics,* 12.3, where we read that, while the shape of the bronze sphere exists at the same time as the bronze sphere, some forms may survive their composites: "...the soul may be of this sort—not all soul but the reason; for doubtless it is possible that *all* soul should survive" (*Metaphysics,* 1070a25–27). Is Aristotle speaking of agent intellect, of possible intellect, or both? Both, says Thomas, since neither employs a bodily organ (no. 36). Thomas reminds us of the statement at the outset of *On the Soul:* "If there is any way of acting or being acted upon proper to soul, soul will be capable of separate existence" (403a10–12). He sees this as negation of the conclusion of an argument whose premises are:

1. A thing's level of being is manifested by its mode of action.
2. Forms, all of whose activities intrinsically involve matter, are such that it is not they, the forms, which act so much as that the composite acts through the form.
3. Such forms have no activity proper to them (no. 37).

Thomas continues: "Forms with activities according to some power or potency of them which does not intrinsically involve matter have existence of themselves and not just through the existence of the composite as with those other forms, it is rather the composite that exists through the form" (no. 38). That is why, when the composite is destroyed, the form is not.

Here we have the basis for Thomas's teaching that the soul has existence of itself. This is neither an intuition nor a deliverance of revelation but a consequence of showing that thinking is an immaterial activity.

Thomas's opponents invoke Aristotle's remark in *On the Generation of Animals,* that "intellect comes from outside and it alone is divine" (2.3.736b27–28), to argue that, since no form that is the act of matter comes from outside but rather from the potency of matter, the soul cannot be the form of matter. But why does Aristotle say this of soul? "Nothing of the corporeal is involved in its activity" (736b27–737a1). But such forms give existence to the composite rather than exist because of the composite. If coming from the potency of matter meant simply that matter is in potency to the soul, there is no difficulty. But since the human soul differs from other souls and substantial forms, it cannot be said to be educed from the potency of matter in the same way they are, i.e., such that they exist only when the composite of which they are the form exists. That is why Aristotle gives another account of the soul's coming into being. But what is coming into being is the form of a body, albeit one unlike other souls and forms (no. 46).

It may be worth noting that Thomas's opposition to Averroes on the matter of the soul is based on the *Great Commentary* in Latin. Some have asked whether Averroes is an Averroist by appealing to writings that Thomas would not have known. Whatever the outcome of that discussion, there can be no doubt that the Averroes of the *Great Commentary,* as Thomas knows it in Latin, holds the views that Thomas contests. Averroes in Latin was clearly the father of Latin Averroism.

I NOTES

1. "*Si igitur aliquod universale,* etc. Idest, si igitur possibile est diffinire animam diffinitione universali, nulla diffinitio est magis univeralis quam ista, neque magis conveniens substantie anime; et est quod anima est prima perfectio corporis naturalis organici" (*Averrois Cordobensis Commentarium magnum in librum Aristotelis De anima,* 138.1–15. Subsequent references to this text will be made parenthetically in this section.

2. "Perfectio enim in anima rationali et in aliis virtutibus anime fere dicitur pura aequivocatione, ut declarabitur post. Et ideo potest aliquis dubitare, et dicere quod anima non habet diffinitionem universalem" (*Commentarium magnum,* 138.18–22).

3. "Quia enim ostensum est quod anima est actus tocius corporis et partes sint actus parcium, actus autem et forma non separatur ab eo cuius est actus uel forma, manifestum est quod anima non potest separari a corpore uel ipsa tota uel alique partes eius, si nata est aliquod modo habere partes: manifest est enim quod alique partes anime sunt actus aliquarum parcium corporis, sicut dictum est quod uisus est actus oculi. Set secundum quasdam partes nichil prohibet animam separati, quia quedam partes

anime nullius corporis actus sunt, sicut infra probabitur de hiis que sunt circa intellectum" (*Sentencia,* 76, lines 141–53; *In II De anima,* lectio 2, no. 242).

4. ". . . quoniam hec diffinitio est universalis omnibus partibus anime et dicta de eis multipliciter, et tales diffinitiones non suffciunt in cognitione rei perfecte cum fuerint universales univoce, nedum cum sint universales multiplices; querendum est enim post ad sciendum unamquanque partium que collocantur sub illa diffinite cognitione propria, cum diffinitio non dicatur de eis equivoce" (*Commentarium magnum,* 149.15–21).

5. "Here, attentive to the conditional clause which prefaces the definition, Averroes notes that Aristotle leaves the question as to whether the intellect is a power of the soul unanswered. Therefore, speaking in his own name, he asserts that since the soul is the first perfection of the body, to speak of the perfection of the rational power and of the other powers of the soul involves some equivocation. And this observation again shows that Averroes is aware that there is a disparity between soul and intellect" (Ovey N. Mohammed, *Averroes' Doctrine of Immortality* [Waterloo: Wilfred Laurier University Press, 1984], 87–88).

6. Mohammed, in his own survey of what he calls "The Aristotelian Anthropology," understands the question in the way in which Averroes does. "But having defined the soul as the form or actuality of a body, Aristotle ceases to be consistent. While maintaining the essential correlativity of body and soul, he now suggests that there may be parts of the soul which are separable from the body "because they are not the actualities of the body at all" (55).

7. Mohammed summarizes the Aristotelian doctrine as follows: "In Book II of the De Anima, Aristotle has two lines of thought in conflict. After defining the soul as the form of a natural body, Aristotle asks us to entertain the possibility that a part of the soul may not be the perfection of a body. We have seen that it is Aristotle's concern with the intellect which prompts this suggestion, a suggestion which creates an ambiguity as to whether or not the intellect is a part of the soul. Averroes solves the problem in harmony with revelation by insisting that any power of the soul must be perfected by matter. That is, he interprets the intellect to be a power sui generis which is, strictly speaking, not a part of the soul. Thus, Averroes' solution is consistent with the monistic conception of man found in Aristotle's own philosophy and in the Qur'an. Furthermore, by making soul and intellect distinct, Averroes is in accord with Aristotle's suggestion that the intellect is external to man and comes to him 'from the outside' and with the Qur'anic doctrine of the creaturehood of man" (91–92). It is hard to see what basis Mohammed has for saying that Averroes's interpretation is consistent with what Aristotle says in book 2. The passage about intellect "coming from without" is discussed below.

▮ Is "Soul" Equivocal?

A central pillar of the Averroist interpretation as we find it in the *Great Commentary* is that Aristotle uses "soul" equivocally when he speaks of intellect as soul. The definition of the soul given at the outset of book 2 of *On the Soul,* which makes it clear that the soul is the substantial form of a physical body having life in potency, cannot, in Averroes's view, apply to the intellect.

Unless this is meant as an account of Aristotelian usage, it could scarcely have figured in a controversy over what Aristotle meant. It seems clear that Averroes, and such modern interpreters of Averroes as Mohammed, take what Averroes is saying here to be at least a defensible account of what Aristotle's usage in *On the Soul* is. Thomas Aquinas rejected this *as an interpretation of Aristotle* early and late.

> If as he [Averroes] says "soul" were predicated equivocally of intellect and the rest, he [Aristotle] would first have divided up the equivocation and then defined, since that is his practice. Otherwise he would have been proceeding equivocally, which is out of place in a demonstrative science.[1]

Gauthier traces this error of interpretation to Alexander and finds it to have been received opinion among ancient and modern commentators until Marcel DeCorte challenged it in 1939.[2] An oddity of Averroes's stand is that he considers himself the foe of Alexander, whom he reads as maintaining a univocal definition of soul.

Aristotle asks, at the outset of *On the Soul,* whether all souls are of the same kind and, if they are not, whether they differ specifically or generically. A feature of discussions of the soul up to this time, he writes, is that only the human soul is considered.

> We must be careful not to ignore the question whether soul can be defined in a single, unambiguous formula, as is the case with animal, or whether we must not give a separate formula for each sort of it, as we do for horse, dog, man, god; in the latter case the "universal" animal,—and so too with every other common predicate—being treated as nothing at all or as a later product. (402b5–9)

If soul is like animal, it will be a generic term predicable of many specifically different things. The accounts we give of those species— horse, dog, man—enable us to predicate them of numerically different things. Both the generic term and the specific term are predicated univocally, according to the definition at the outset of the *Categories.*[3] The unity of the generic term is due to human understanding and answers to no unit in reality. This seems to be Aristotle's meaning when he says that it is either later or nothing.[4]

This question figures among those which Aristotle lists at the outset of *On the Soul* as those to which we hope to get answers, but even there Thomas observes that Aristotle wants both a common definition of the soul and definitions of each of its types. The sequel bears out this interpretation, since in book 2 Aristotle says he wants to give the most general possible definition of the soul (412a5–6). Having formulated it, he says it applies to soul in its full extent (412b9). In keeping with what he has said of generic accounts, moreover, he characterizes the definition as figurative or descriptive (413a9–10).

Aristotle compares the way "soul" is said of types of soul to the way in which "figure" is common to different types of figure:

> It is clear therefore that the definition of "soul" is common in the same way as that of figure, for there is no figure apart from triangle and those which are consequent on it; no more is there any soul apart from those mentioned. For should there happen to be a notion common to figures which belongs to all of them, it is proper to none of them. So too with the aforementioned souls. Therefore it is foolish to seek a common definition of these or other things which would be the proper definition of none, just as it is foolish to seek the proper and atomic while ignoring the common definition. Souls are related in the same way to what is said of them as are figures; for that which is consequent always contains in potency what is prior, both in figures and in souls; as triangle is in square so is the vegetative in the sensitive. (414b20–32)

This passage raises the question whether likening "soul" to "figure" in some way alters what was suggested by likening it to "animal." The order of priority and posteriority among figures suggested to Alexander that the common term cannot mean the same thing as was said of each of them. That is why he denied that "soul" is univocally common to all the kinds of souls. D. W. Hamlyn takes an Alexandrine stance in his comment on the passage.[5]

The different types of soul are known and named from their parts, faculties, or powers, and if we confine ourselves to the nutritive, sensitive, and intellectual faculties, we see that the plant soul has only the nutritive power, the animal soul has both the nutritive and sensitive, while the human soul possesses nutritive, sensitive, and intellectual powers. There is, consequently, an ordering of the prior and posterior among souls similar to that in figures. For, although the triangle is only a triangle, the square contains the triangle in potency, i.e., by dividing the square we can obtain triangles. Does this entail that neither "soul" nor "figure" are predicated univocally?[6]

If it is the case that whenever things which admit among themselves priority and posteriority have a common name, they are like the things called "being" and "good," that is, they are *pros hen legomena* (and are called by the common name with reference to one of them which is thus prior to the others, as Alexander says), then the verdict for things called "soul" seems clear. Alexander refers to the *Nicomachean Ethics* (1096a17ff.) for confirmation of his interpretation.[7] Tricot invokes *Metaphysics* (1019a2ff.) as well.[8] In both texts, it is clear that the hierarchy existing among the things sharing a common name excludes univocity. It looks as if we must agree with Alexander and Averroes and dozens of others that "figure" and "soul," like "good" and "being," are *pros hen* equivocals.

This interpretation presents difficulties, however, particularly when 414b20–32 is compared with its evident parallel at the beginning of *On the Soul,* 402b1–9, where the community of "soul" was likened to that of "animal." If Alexander is right, why would not "animal" be a *pros hen* equivocal when said of horse, dog, man, etc.? But Alexander would not draw that conclusion. Tricot is puzzled:

> It is certainly difficult, and to understand it we must suppose, with Alexander, that Aristotle there gave a fictive example, since, in truth, dog, man, and god are in the genus *zoon,* which is a univocal term.[9]

It is, of course, not rare for Aristotle to give an example that is not perfectly adequate to the problem he is treating, but one wonders if Alexander's interpretation takes sufficiently into account the polemic against Platonic Ideas latent in 402b1–9 and 414b20–32. As Tricot observes, the point made is that there could be a genus if something like a Platonic Idea, a separate *ousia,* existed.[10] Moreover, if the example of "animal" raises difficulties, "figure" and "number" raise deeper ones. For, while it is perfectly clear that no figure exists which is not triangle or square, etc., and no number which is not two or three, etc., this does not prevent there being a generic and univocal notion of figure and number. What presents difficulties is the hierarchy among figures and numbers, but we have to ask ourselves if priority and posteriority exclude a genus and univocity. This is surely true in the case of "being" and "good," but is the same true of "figure" and "number"?[11] *Metaphysics* 999a6ff. seems to suggest that subalternate genera are always related in a hierarchical fashion and that only the things under the *species specialissima* are not ordered in this way. This poses difficulties when we recall that the species of a genus are "simultaneous" and are said not to admit of priority and posteriority (*Categories,* 14b32–15a8).

What does Thomas Aquinas have to say about Aristotle's definition of the soul? As already mentioned, he says that Aristotle wishes to give a common definition of the soul, that is, a definition common

to all types of soul. He sees the key passage at 414b20–32 as, first,
showing Aristotle's difference from Plato. Plato would have it that
"animal" names a separately existing substance by participation in
which sensible particulars exist, thus giving priority to what
Aristotle regards as an abstraction. What the generic term signifies
has no unity apart from the abstractive activity of the human mind.
That unit presupposes and thus is later than the individuals in
which the nature is found. As found in the individuals it is real.

In conformity with what we have seen to be the methodology of
natural science, Thomas sees the formulation of a common definition as a first step, with progress consisting in gaining more and
more clear knowledge of the various kinds of living things in their
specific distinctness.[12]

In order to understand our key passage, then, we must observe
that Plato held that universals exist; he was not, however, indis-
criminate in doing this. Thus, if things are so related that one follows on the other (*quae se habent consequenter*), no common Idea of
them was posited. The examples are figures and numbers. There is
an order among the species of number, for two is the cause of all subsequent numbers; so, too, the species of figure are so ordered that
triangle is prior to square, square to pentagon, etc.[13] Where there is
no such order among things receiving a common name, an Idea is
posited. For example, individual people are not ordered as are numbers and figures, so there can be an Idea existing apart from
Socrates and Plato. It will be noticed that Thomas's example is of
individuals and their species, whereas numbers and figures are species of something more common, presumably their genus. This could
suggest that individuals are related to species differently from the
way species are related to genus, but not that univocity is necessarily excluded from the generic notion. Thomas continues his comments in terms of Platonic separation:

> Therefore he [Aristotle] says that it is clear that there is one
> definition of soul in the same way there is one definition of fig-
> ure. For just as there is no figure which is not triangle and the
> others consequent on it, which would be an Idea common to
> them all, so in the present case there is no soul existing as it
> were outside the parts mentioned.[14]

What would a figure existing apart from triangle and those following on it be? Any existent figure is a figure of a determinate kind.
This is applicable to any genus: there is no animal *in rerum natura*
that is not a man or horse or dog, etc.; but this does not prevent the
formation of a generic notion univocally common to them all. Its
unity and community derive from our mode of understanding.

How can we move from such considerations to the soul and its parts? These parts are precisely faculties or potencies: the vegetative, sensitive, appetitive, locomotive, and intellectual powers (414a31–32). The only way the move can be made is by claiming that no soul is to be found that does not have at least one of these parts, from which it is denominated such-and-such a kind of soul. However, although there is no separately existing figure, a *common* notion can be formed that applies to all of them, though it is not the *proper* notion of any of them.

> It is ridiculous, then, for a man to seek one common definition, whether in souls or other things, which does not belong to each of the souls which exist particularly in the real order, nor is it fitting for a man to seek a definition of soul according to each species of soul and forego the definition common to them all.[15]

What, then, is the similarity of soul and figure? The species of figure are such that what is prior is potentially in the posterior. Just as the triangle is potentially in the square, so the vegetative is potentially in the sensitive soul, and so on.

Is this a denial that "soul" is said univocally of vegetative, sensitive, and intellectual soul? If Thomas thought that "soul" were said according to an order of prior and posterior (*per prius et posterius*) of the kinds of soul in the way "being" is said of substance and the other categories, he would conclude that "soul" is an analogous term.

It is not always sufficiently appreciated that there is no one-to-one correspondence between Aristotle's use of *analogia, kat'analogian,* and *analogià* and Thomas's use of *analogia, secundum analogiam,* and *analogice.* In commenting on Aristotle, Thomas will often speak of analogy where there is no occurrence of *analogia* or its cognates in the text. Relevant to our discussion is the way in which Thomas comments on Aristotle's statement in the *Metaphysics* that "being is said in many ways but with reference to some one nature and not equivocally" (*"to on legetai pollaxos, alla pros hen kai mian phusin kai oux homonumos,"* 1003134a–35). This prompts Thomas to one of his most extensive statements on what it means for things to be named analogously (*In IV Metaphysic.,* lectio 1, nos. 535–36). Aristotle never used *legetai kat'analogian* ("said according to analogy") as equivalent to *legetai pollaxos pros hen* ("said in many ways but with reference to one"), but for Thomas something *multipliciter dictum* ("said in many ways") is said *analogice* whenever it is not a question of pure equivocation. What is more, things said analogously are related *per prius et posterius.* Our question thus becomes: When things related as prior and posterior, or *consequenter* ("sequentially"), receive a common name, is that name never said univocally of them? Are "figure" and "number" and "soul," in the uses we have been examining, examples of what Thomas calls analogous terms and Aristotle would call *pros hen* equivocals?

The passage in the *Nicomachean Ethics* to which Alexander appeals seems to bear out his interpretation. There Aristotle rejects the Platonic Idea of the Good by invoking against Plato his own rule: "The originators of this theory, then, used not to postulate Ideas of groups of things in which they posited an order of priority and posteriority (for which reason they did not construct an Idea of numbers in general)" (*Nicomachean Ethics,* 1096a18–20). He goes on to argue that, since good is found in each of the categories, good things are prior and posterior and cannot be the basis for an Idea of Good. In commenting on this, Thomas makes clear that it is the priority and posteriority among goods that prevents a common notion; consequently, "good" is not a univocal term.

> There is not one definition common to the different categories, for nothing is predicated of them univocally. Good, like being, with which it is convertible, is found in each category. . . . Therefore, it is clear that there is not some one good that could be an Idea or common definition of all good things; if there were, that good could not be found in all the categories, but only in one. (*In I Ethic.,* lectio 6, no. 81)

This linking of "good" and "number" certainly permits continuing the linkage to include "figure" and "soul." Nonetheless, Thomas elsewhere disputes Alexander's interpretation of things that are *ta ephexhs* ("one after another in line").

Aristotle divides speech (*logos*) into affirmative, negative, and composite (*On Interpretation,* 17a8–9). The affirmative is said to be prior to the others. What does that mean? Thomas, in commenting on this, first recounts Alexander's view that this is not a division of a genus into its species but rather of a multiple (that is, for Thomas, an analogous) name into its diverse significations: "A genus is said univocally of its species, not according to prior and posterior; that is why Aristotle did not wish to say that being is the common genus of all things, because it is first predicated of substance and then of the nine accidents."[16] Surely Alexander's interpretation is reasonable if the presence of prior and posterior (*proteron kai hysteron*) in beings prevents "being" from signifying univocally, and the same with goods and "good." Must not the same be true of "speech" here and elsewhere of "soul" and "figure"? What Thomas has said in commenting on the *Ethics* may not have prepared us for his rejection of Alexander here.

One of the things that fall under something predicably common can be prior to the others in two ways, Thomas observes. First, because of their proper definitions or natures; second, because of their partaking of the definition of what is common to them. The first sort of prior and posterior does not prohibit the univocity of the genus, "as is manifest in numbers, in which two taken in its proper definition is prior to three, yet they share equally in the definition of their genus, namely, number: three is a multitude measured by one every bit as much as two is" (*In I Periherm.*, lectio 8, no. 6). The second sort of prior and posterior prevents there being a univocal genus. This happens with "being" and "good." Being is not the genus of substance and accident "because in the very notion of being, substance, which is being in itself, has priority over accident, which is being in or through another" (ibid.). Thomas concludes that affirmation is prior to negation in its proper notion, but this does not prevent "speech" from being a genus univocally common to it and negation.

What is here said of "number" can be said of "figure" and thus opens the way to Thomas's view that Aristotle intends "soul" to be taken as univocally common to the kinds of soul, even though in their proper notions, the vegetative is prior and the others consequent on it, in the way described earlier.[17]

Although thinking is not the actuality of any bodily organ, mind or intellect is a faculty of the human soul, which, like any soul, is the first act or substantial form of a physically organized body.

Thus Thomas rejects Averroes's contention that "soul" is said only equivocally of intellect, whether "equivocally" be taken in a complete sense—as Averroes seems to want—or whether "equivocally" be taken in the sense synonymous for Thomas with "analogously." Thomas shows on Aristotelian grounds why we must interpret the community of Aristotle's definition of the soul to vegetative, sensitive, and intellectual souls to be univocal.

▌N O T E S

1. "Si autem, ut ipse dicit, *anima* aequivoce dicitur de intellectu et aliis, primo distinxisset aequivocationem, postea definivisset, sicut est consuetudo sua. Alias procederet in aequivoco. Quod non est in scientiis demonstrativiis" (*II Summa contra gentiles,* cap. 61).

2. Gauthier, preface to *Sentencia libri De anima, Opera omnia,* 45/1 (Rome, 1984), p. 228*. The reference is to M. DeCorte, "La définition aristotélicienne de l'âme," *Revue thomiste* 45 (1939): 460–508. See too my "Le terme 'âme' est-il équivoque ou univoque?" *Revue philosophique de Louvain* 58 (1960): 481–504 [English version in *Studies in Analogy* (The Hague: Nijhoff, 1968)]. Characteristically, Gauthier introduces a few zingers into his account, saying of the *De unitate intellectus,* "ici encore, l'exégèse du texte est subordonnée au but cherché, mais avec plus de mesure" (p. 229*). This suggests that the point sought is other than exegetical, which is unfounded unless Gauthier wishes to contest the reading Thomas offers as the clear sense of Aristotle. The implications for the discussions of Averroes elsewhere are clear enough. This is to undermine Thomas's stature as an interpreter of Aristotle, an unworthy task for his editor and a doomed one in any case.

3. "On the other hand, things are said to be named univocally which have both the name and the definition answering to the name in common" (*Categories,* 1a7–8).

4. See Charles DeKoninck, *Introduction à l'étude de l'âme,* xxxii–xxxvi. Thomas sees the remark as anti-Platonic in intent (*Sentencia,* 6–7, lines 186–230; *In I De anima,* lectio 1, nos. 9–13).

5. "It is to be noted that Aristotle does not say that it is impossible to produce *any* definition of figure and soul; the point is that if you do, it will not be informative about figures and souls. These are not correlative species under a genus; there is no proper genus, just as there is no proper genus of being over and above the categories" (D. W. Hamlyn, trans. and ed., *Aristotle's De anima* Books II and III [Oxford: Oxford University Press, 1968], 94, *ad* 414b20). According to this view, "soul" is said with controlled equivocation, with a focal meaning, of the different kinds of soul. It would be, in Thomas's terminology, an analogous term.

6. Tricot gives us Alexander's interpretation: "Aristote se demande s'il existe une notion (ou une définition) générique de l'âme. Il répond par le négative, en raison de l'impossibilité où nous sommes de donner une définition commune des choses qui, comme c'est le cas pour les différentes variétés d'âmes, admettent entre elles de l'antérieur et du postérieur. Il en sera comme pour la figure géométrique, laquelle n'existe pas en dehors des différentes variétés de figures et donc la définition générique ne peut s'appliquer qu'à ces variétés" (*ad* 414b20–32).

7. *Aporiai kai luseis,* I, XIb, *Suppl.* 2.2.22–24.

8. J. Tricot, ed., *Aristote De l'âme* (Paris: Vrin, 1947), 84 n. 1.

9. "Elle est assurément difficile, et pour le comprendre il faut supposer, avec Alexandre, qu'Aristote a donné un exemple fictif, puisque, en vérité, le chien, l'homme et dieu rentrent dans le genre zoon qui est un terme univoque" (*ad* 402b1ff.).

10. "En résumé, l'âme est un *pollaxos legomenon.* Elle n'admet pas de définition commune proprement dite, mais ses espèces doivent être définies séparément. Et d'une manière générale, n'est pas un genre toute notion *epi pollon,* mais seulement ce qui répond à une *ousia* réelle, à une nature commune . . ." (*ad* 402b1ff.).

11. G. Rodier, *Aristote Traité de l'âme,* commentary first published in 1900 and reissued by Vrin, Paris, 1985, takes up our problem both at 402b5ff., 15–20, and at 414b20ff., 216–20, in the first discussion taking Alexander as his guide, and in the second bringing the views of many commentators to his reader's attention.

12. *Sentencia,* 2.1, 14–29; *In II De anima,* lectio 1, no. 211.

13. Ibid., 74, 232–81; lectio 5, nos. 295–98.

14. Ibid., 248–54; no. 296.

15. Ibid., 260–70; no. 297.

16. This is Thomas's account of Alexander. *In I Periherm.,* lectio 8, no. 5.

17. In "Le terme 'âme' est-il équivoque ou univoque?" I discuss the treatment of this in a large number of Thomistic texts.

▎ "This Human Being Understands"

In his commentary on *On the Soul,* which Gauthier characterizes as serene, Thomas makes this highly significant remark about the Averroistic misinterpretation:

> There are many other things which could be said against this position and we have gone into them at length elsewhere. But one thing suffices against it: the position entails that this human being does not understand.[1]

Any theory or account that prevents us from saying that this singular human being understands is invalid. The reason is that it is not gainsayable that this person understands. The statement may seem uncertain if we imagine ourselves observing someone and wondering if he or she is thinking. Yes or no? We could be wrong.

Thomas, we remember, when he commented on Aristotle's remark that the study of the soul ranks high both in certainty and in dignity of subject, explained what seems to be the surprising claim of certainty by saying this means that the pursuit of knowledge of the soul rests on the irrefragable fact of our experiential certainty that we are alive. What the soul is, is obscure in the extreme, and questions and doubts almost immediately come to mind when the topic arises, questions and doubts that Aristotle lays out at the beginning of the treatise. But our ignorance of what precisely soul is in no way diminishes our certainty that we are alive. That there is a soul is as certain as that we perform vital activities.

If this were taken to mean that we are initially and unshakably certain that we have a spiritual and immortal soul, it would be a silly claim. Because philosophical and religious teachings about the soul will doubtless pop into our minds upon hearing the word, we may think that Aristotle and Thomas are beginning with the certainty that *those* accounts of the soul are beyond question. On the contrary, our initial certainty is shrouded with obscurity.

No wonder, then, that Thomas begins chapter 3 of *On There Being Only One Intellect*—the chapter devoted to developing rational arguments that the intellect is a faculty of the soul, which is the form of body—with a reminder of that experiential certainty on which the whole inquiry rests.

He notes that the conjunction of Aristotle's two accounts of the soul forms an argument. The soul is the substantial form of body because it is that thanks to which we first live and understand (no. 61).

> The power and irrefutability of this demonstration is clear from the fact that whoever wishes to differ with it necessarily says what is absurd. That this individual human being

understands is manifest, for we would never ask about intellect unless we understood, nor when we ask about intellect are
we asking about anything other than that whereby we understand. (no. 62)

Our experience of life is precisely the experience that we think,
want, move ourselves, see, hear, and the like. These are not merely
inner experiences, as we have seen. The human being is by nature a
political animal, Aristotle has said, and a central feature of this is
our ability to talk. We communicate, enter into community with the
world and one another, through language. The individual who experiences his/her own vital activities learns the names for them. This
human being understands but does not invent the term "soul." He
learns that it is the name for that in him which enables him to perform vital acts.

That is, the first principle of our vital acts must be the form of
body, Thomas remarks, an argument that depends on the prior
proof that form is that whereby anything first acts.

1. A thing acts insofar as it is actual.
2. A thing is actual thanks to form.
3. A thing acts thanks to form.

In order for the overall argumentation to work, there must be a
conflation of soul and intellect. But intellect is a power of the soul.
Elsewhere, Thomas has argued against identifying the essence of
the soul with any of its powers or faculties. Since soul is act, if the
essence of soul were the immediate principle of operation, one who
actually has a soul would always actually perform the vital act in
question. To be alive and to think would be identical. But soul as
form is the term of the process of generation, the actuation of a potency; that it might then be in potency to activities is explained not
by its essence but by its powers, parts, faculties, or potencies. That is
why soul is called *actus primus* and is ordered to the second act of
activity thanks to its powers.[2] How, then, can Thomas identify soul
and intellect? It is a *façon de parler*. Just as the sensitive soul is
sometimes called sense, so the intellectual soul is sometimes called
intellect, named from its chief power.[3]

The force of "This human understands" is that the person who
thinks is engaged in an activity, the source of which is within, and
that source is primarily form. One who wishes to deny this has to
come up with some other account of the claim that it is the individual human being who thinks. And people have tried in various
ways to do this.

Notice that Thomas does not suggest that his opponent begins
with the *denial* of "This person understands." Far from it. The rival
account is meant to explain what it means to say that the individual

human thinks. The force of Thomas's rebuttals is that the explanations remove what was to have been explained.

If Thomas's opponent wishes to say that the principle of the activity of thinking is not form, he must show how the activity of the principle can be said to be the activity of this individual. This is what he might say:

But an objector might say that this principle, which is the possible intellect, is only equivocally called a soul; it is really a separate substance. Its activity of thinking is attributed to you and me insofar as it is hooked up with us by way of the phantasms in us. Thus the intelligible species, which is as form and act to the possible intellect, has two subjects: one my phantasms, the other the possible intellect. Since the possible intellect is linked to me via my phantasms, when it thinks, I think.

To this Thomas replies, first, that intellect would thus be mine episodically, and this goes counter to the view that it characterizes us from birth. That is why the natural philosopher sees the study of intellect as the culmination of his science. According to Averroes, thinking can be attributed to me insofar as I imagine, and the separate intellect is linked with my images. Second, says, Thomas, the intelligible species exists only potentially in images and becomes actual when it is abstracted from them. Thus the intelligible species is the act of the possible intellect only when abstracted from phantasms; but this separates rather than links intellect and images.

According to Thomas's third objection, even granting that the numerically identical intelligible species is the form of possible intellect and at the same time in the phantasms, we still could not say that this individual thinks. The intelligible species is that through which something is thought, and the intellectual faculty is that whereby one thinks. Likewise, the sense image is that thanks to which something is sensed, and the sense power is that thanks to which one senses. Thus the color of the wall, whose sensible species is actually in sense, is seen; it does not see. It is the animal that has the power of sight that sees. Thomas then draws an analogy: My phantasms are to possible intellect the way the color of the wall is to sight. The intelligible species abstracted from my phantasms are in the possible intellect, and the sensible species of the wall's color is in sense. And, just as it is that which has the power of sight that sees and the wall that is seen, so the possible intellect thinks, and my phantasms are what is thought.

Thomas pursues his quarry in chapter 3, addressing his opponent's efforts to speak of the possible intellect as a mover rather than a form. His arguments are always aimed at showing that the simple truth, "This individual human thinks," cannot be uttered if the proposed view is held.

8
8

2

08 I PART FOUR

In light of chapter 3, the remark that Thomas made in the commentary on *On the Soul* becomes almost ironic. To say that one thing alone suffices to counter the Averroist position, namely, that were that position true, we would be prevented from saying that an individual human person thinks, turns out to be the upshot of a whole series of arguments rather than an argument in and of itself. The arguments begin with a claim, the truth of which is nongainsayable, namely, that this man thinks. It is nongainsayable because no one can think that it is not true, since they would then exemplify what is allegedly rejected. Thus Thomas assumes that his opponent is as committed as he himself is to the truth of "This man thinks." Thomas's arguments are instances of the *reductio ad absurdum*. If what you say is true, you cannot maintain what you must maintain: This man thinks.

In the passage from the commentary on *On the Soul* cited above, Thomas mentions that he has gone into this matter at considerable length elsewhere. Indeed he has. Already in commenting on the *Sentences* of Lombard, Thomas discusses "Whether the intellective soul or intellect is one for all men" (*II Sent.*, d. 17, q. 2, a.1). He notes that some post-Aristotelians have held both that the agent intellect and the possible intellect are substances separate from the human soul. He counters the first by appealing to Anselm, but when he gets to the possible intellect, he notes that while some regard it as a separated substance, others multiply it by the number of people. But there are three ways of doing the latter. Alexander takes possible intellect to be a kind of *praeparatio* or readiness to receive the impression of the agent intellect, *and* asserts that it is a corporeal power. Having attributed this to Alexander, Thomas comments: *"sed hoc non potest stare etiam secundum intentionem Aristotelis"* ("but this cannot stand even according to the intention of Aristotle"). Aristotle explicitly rejects the view that the intellect is mixed with the body. Others identify possible intellect and the cogitative power. Thomas attributes this view to Avempace and says that it is impossible because of what Ariostotle says in book 3 of *On the Soul*. In both these interpretations of Aristotle, intellect would be something that could corrupt and cease to be. A third way is attributed to Avicenna: we each have a possible intellect, but there is one agent intellect for all. In the *Commentary on the Sentences,* at the place cited above, Thomas writes: "With respect to possible intellect, his opinion is what we hold according to the Catholic faith, although he errs along with others concerning agent intellect."

There are two ways of holding the view that there is but one possible intellect for all people. Averroes describes the first way as the teaching of Themistius and Theophrastus, and he rejects this way. Thomas then gives the view of Averroes. Both agent and possible intellect are separated substances, but intelligible species or concepts are not eternal. In the course of his discussion, Thomas says, *"et hoc est contra intentionem et verba Philosophi"* ("and this is against both the intention and the words of the Philospher") and *"quod est contra Philosophum"* ("which is contrary to the Philosopher"); and, having drawn attention to a few absurd consequences of the view, he adds, *"et plura alia absurda non difficile est adducere"* ("and it would be easy to cite many other absurdities").

Very early on, then—the *Commentary on the Sentences* being early—we find Thomas quite independent vis-à-vis the tradition of Aristotelian interpretation. He is certain that something has gone wrong if it conflicts with the faith, but he is contesting the accuracy of the reading of Aristotle as well.

By the time he wrote the *Summa contra gentiles,* Thomas was a practiced critic of Avicenna and Averroes. His treatment of them is threefold. What they say conflicts with faith; what they say conflicts with Aristotle; what they say conflicts with reason. It would be possible to show that every argument marshaled in *On There Being Only One Intellect* puts in an appearance in the group of chapters in book 2 of the *Summa contra gentiles* devoted to the same matters, that is, chapters 59 through 79. By contrast, the treatments in the *Summa theologiae* seem perfunctory (Ia, q. 76, a. 2; q. 79, aa. 1, 4, 5). Averroes goes unmentioned, and the dispute is taken to be largely between Plato and Aristotle, with Thomas siding with Aristotle.

The *Disputed Question on the Soul* is thought by some to antedate Thomas's return to Paris in 1269. Article 3 asks "whether the possible intellect or intellective soul is one for all," and of the twenty-two arguments that are put forth in favor of an affirmative answer, twelve purport to be based on Aristotle, with nine taken from *On the Soul.* The first of the two *sed contra*'s invokes Aristotle in favor of a negative answer. The body of the article examines and rejects Averroist positions without mentioning Averroes by name; Thomas's arguments would be familiar to one acquainted with his earlier writings. In responding to the twenty-two objections, Thomas never makes his point by questioning the Aristotelian reference; but when he rejects the opposed view, he is setting forth what he takes to be the view of Aristotle as well as the truth of the matter. This is clear from his procedure in other works.

The *Disputed Question on Spiritual Creatures* is often located during Thomas's second Parisian professorate. Article 9 poses the question whether the possible intellect is one for all people. Seventeen arguments are adduced on behalf of an affirmative answer, and they invoke Augustine, Cyprian, and Anselm more than they do

Aristotle, although one of them purports to be based on *On the Soul*.
There are three arguments advanced against the presumed an-
swer—three *sed contra*'s; one cites the Apocalypse, the second
Augustine, and the third invokes Averroes!

In the body of the article, Thomas begins by situating the doctrine of agent and passive intellect in Aristotle's *On the Soul*. After a
few remarks on agent intellect, he turns to the possible intellect and
cites the interpretation of Averroes. "However, that this position is
contrary to faith is easy to see, for it takes away the pains and re-
wards of future life. But it must be shown through true principles of
philosophy that this position is in itself impossible." He then proceeds to draw three impossible conclusions from the assertion that
there is one possible intellect for all. And then he adds, "And it is also
obvious that this position conflicts with the words of Aristotle"
*("manifestum est etiam quod haec positio repugnant verbis
Aristotelis"*). Aristotle begins his treatment of intellect in *On the
Soul* by calling it a part of the soul, that is, a faculty or power. As
Thomas says in the same article of the *Disputed Question on Spiritual Creatures*,

> Wishing to inquire into the nature of the possible intellect, he
> [Aristotle] prefaces it with a doubt, namely, whether the intel-
> lective part be separable from the other parts in subject, as
> Plato thought, or by definition alone. And he says this:
> "Whether existing as separable or inseparable in place but ac-
> cording to definition." From which it is clear that if both of
> these be positive, his view concerning possible intellect stands.
> But it cannot be that it is separate in definition alone, if the
> foregoing position is true. Wherefore, the foregoing opinion is
> not the teaching of Aristotle. Afterward he says that possible
> intellect is that whereby the soul thinks and understands, and
> many other similar things, from which he manifestly gives us
> to understand that possible intellect is something of the soul
> and not a separated substance.

Thomas's reply to the sixth objection gives us a long response but a
short form of his rejection of Averroes's interpretation of *On the
Soul*. The discussion betrays none of the edginess of earlier discussions, however; indeed, it turns more on the rivalry of Platonic and
Aristotelian views on universals. In the reply to the eighth objection,
Averroes is said to have been led astray (*deceptus fuit*), but this is
more of a matter-of-fact observation and rhetorically distant from
On There Being Only One Intellect, where Averroes is called the
perverter of Peripatetic philosophy. If this is a later work, we can
conclude that serenity broke through again.

| NOTES

1. *Sentencia,* 3.1, 353–57; *In III De anima,* lectio 7, no. 695.
2. *Summa theologiae,* Ia, q. 77, a. 1. "Nam anima secundum suam essentiam est actus. Si ergo ipsa essentia animae esset immediatum operationis principium, semper habens animam actu haberet opera vitae; sicut semper habens animam actu est vivum. Non enim inquantum est forma est actus ordinatus ad ulteriorem actum, sed est ultimus terminus generationis."
3. Ibid., q. 79, a. 1, ad 1m.

| Double-Truth Theory

In the penultimate paragraph of *On There Being Only One Intellect,* Thomas cites a shocking remark of one of those whose teachings he has been criticizing: "Through reason I conclude necessarily that intellect is numerically one, but I firmly hold the opposite by faith" (123). It is easy to share Thomas's horror, and one need not be a Christian to do so. Thomas draws out the implications of the quoted remark. The author cited obviously means to say that he finds no difficulty in this thesis: Faith consists of propositions, some of whose opposites are necessary truths. But the opposite of a necessary truth is something both false and impossible. Faith, accordingly, consists of giving one's assent to propositions one knows to be both false and impossible. If the one saying this is a believer (as presumably the author whom Thomas quotes is), he has put himself in the position of simultaneously giving his assent to a proposition and to its contradictory opposite. He is violating the most fundamental law of reasoning: a proposition and its contradictory cannot be simultaneously true, or, symbolically, -(p.-p). The author cited wants the contradictory opposites to be simultaneously true. For example, he wishes to affirm as a matter of religious belief that the world had a beginning in time while simultaneously affirming that it is necessarily true that the world did not have a beginning in time. Both of these cannot be simultaneously true, but it is because this author expressed his confidence that they could be that his position has been described as the "double-truth" or "two-truth" theory.

Who was the author of the quoted remark? It has yet to be tracked down to any master whose writings have survived. However, since it is unthinkable that Thomas would have invented the quotation, someone among his Latin Averroist opponents must have written these words, or said them, and what he said was then written down.

Was Siger of Brabant the author of the remark that Thomas quoted? Did Siger of Brabant hold the double-truth theory? We have no textual basis on which to answer the first question in the affirmative. The answer to the second question may very well be, as Etienne Gilson insists, negative. But negative answers to these two questions do nothing to settle whether the double-truth theory was maintained in Paris in the late 1260s. The quotation that Thomas gives us is as good a statement of the theory as one could ask. On the safe assumption that he is accurately quoting, the double-truth theory, far from being a fabrication of historians, may be taken to be historically established.

Gilson, perhaps the greatest historian of medieval philosophy of the twentieth century, seems to say that no medieval master held the double-truth theory. That goes far beyond exempting Siger of Brabant and Boetius of Dacia, on the basis of the writings of the two men that we have, from holding the theory. Unless Gilson questions that the quotation at the end of *On There Being Only One Intellect* expresses that theory, and proves that Thomas is not quoting someone who said or wrote those words, it is difficult to see how he can make so sweeping a claim.[1]

Albert Zimmermann argued that we find the double-truth theory maintained in the Aristotelian commentary of Ferrand of Spain.[2] Van Steenberghen reviews Zimmermann's arguments and rejects them. His own verdict, which he calls a "historical fact," is as sweeping as Gilson's: "The first and most important conclusion which follows from our investigation is this: *No one in the Middle Ages defended the double-truth theory.* No one maintained that two contradictory propositions can both be true at the same time" (*Thomas Aquinas and Radical Aristoteliansism,* 106). Apparently Van Steenberghen also thinks that the remark quoted by Thomas Aquinas is either spurious or does not express the double-truth theory. But surely there can be no doubt of the latter. To believe *p* is true and to hold that its contradictory opposite can be shown to be necessarily true is precisely the double-truth theory.

That no one can *coherently* hold the double-truth theory is, of course, true. Perhaps our historians have adopted their position by deriving a negative historical fact from the demands of coherence. Since it cannot be simultaneously true that Thomas quoted one of his contemporaries and that there was no such contemporary to quote, it must be a historical fact that the double-truth theory was held by someone in the thirteenth century.

What redeems Gilson and Van Steenberghen is that their generalization stems from a close study of the writings of Siger of Brabant. They provide solid grounds for doubting that Siger held the double-truth theory, however much he may seem to have flirted with it. Moreover, one of the charming aspects of the story of the conflict between Siger and Thomas is that Siger developed in the direction of the positions on faith and reason, philosophy and theology, that Thomas held. Siger becomes a species of Thomist. No wonder Dante assigns to Thomas the task of praising Siger in the *Paradiso.*[3]

I NOTES

1. A convenient summary of the discussion can be found in Fernand Van Steenberghen, *Thomas Aquinas and Radical Aristotelianism,* 93–109.

2. A. Zimmermann, "Ein Averroist des späten 13. Jahrhunderts: Ferrandus de Hispania," *Archiv für Geschichte der Philosophie* 50 (1968): 145–64.

3. See Gilson, *Dante et la philosophie* (Paris: Vrin, 1939), 308ff. Ernest Fortin, in his adventurous *Dissidence et philosophie au moyen âge* (Paris: Vrin, 1981), devotes a chapter to the double-truth theory, with particular reference to Dante. See chap. 8, "La théorie de la double vérité," 165–76.

Anscombe, E. A. "Aristotle." In *Three Philosophers,* by Peter Geach and Elizabeth Anscombe. Oxford: Oxford University Press, 1961.

Averroes. *Averrois Cordobensis Commentarium magnum in librum Aristotelis De anima.* Edited by F. Stuart Crawford. Cambridge, Mass.: Medieval Academy, 1953.

Barbotin, Edmond. *La théorie aristotélicienne de l'intellect d'après Théophraste.* Paris: Vrin, 1954.

Bataillon, L.-J., O. P. "Les conditions de travail des maîtres de l'Université de Paris au XIIIᵉᵐᵉ siècle." *Revue des sciences philosophiques et théologiques* 67, no. 3 (1983): 417–32.

Bazán, Bernardo Carlos. *Siger de Brabant: Quaestiones in tertium De anima, De anima intellectiva, De aeternitate mundi.* Louvain: Publications Universitaires, 1972.

———. Review of Leonine edition of the *Sentencia libri De anima. Revue des sciences philosophiques et théologiques* 69, no. 4 (1985): 521–47.

———. *Siger de Brabant: Écrits de logique, de morale, et de physique.* Louvain: Publications Universitaires, 1974.

Berti, Enrico. *Le ragioni di Aristotle.* Rome: Laterza, 1989.

Boyle, Leonard, O.P. *The Setting of the* Summa Theologiae *of Saint Thomas.* Toronto: Pontifical Institute of Mediaeval Studies, 1982.

Brady, Ignatius , O.F.M. "Background of the Condemnation of 1270: Master William of Baglione, OFM." *Franciscan Studies* 30 (1970): 6–48.

———. "Questions at Paris, c. 1260–1270." *Archivum Franciscanum Historicum* 61 (1968): 434–61.

Cajetan, Cardinal Thomas de Vio. *Commentari in De anima Aristotelis.* Edited by P. I. Coquelle, O.P. Rome: Angelicum, 1939.

Caparello, Adriana, trans., ed. *Tommaso d'Aquino Commentario al De anima.* Rome: Edisioni Abete, 1974.

Clark, Stephen R. L. *Aristotle's Man.* Oxford: Clarendon Press, 1975.

Crowe, Michael. "Peter of Ireland: Aquinas's Teacher of the *Artes Liberales.*" In *Arts libéraux et philosophie au moyen âge,* 617–26. Montreal: Institut d'études médiévales; Paris: Vrin, 1969.

DeCorte, Marcel. "La définition aristotélicienne de l'âme." *Revue thomiste* 45 (1939): 460–508.

———— *La doctrine de l'intelligence chez Aristote.* Paris: J. Vrin, 1934.

DeKoninck, Thomas. "La 'pensée de la pensée' chez Aristote." In *La question de Dieu selon Aristote et Hegel,* edited by Thomas de Koninck and Guy Planty-Bonjour, 69–151. Paris: Presses Universitaries de France, 1991.

DeKoninck, Charles. "Introduction à l'étude de l'âme." Preface, S. Cantin, *Précis de psychologie thomiste.* Editions de l'Université Laval. Quebec: Presses Universitaires, 1948, vii–lxxxiii.

Elders, Leo. *Aristotle's Theology.* New York: Humanities Press, 1972.

————. "Le commentaire de saint Thomas sur le *De anima* d'Aristote." In *Autour de saint Thomas d'Aquin,* 1:55–76. Paris: Fac Editions, 1987.

Evans, J. D. G. *Aristotle.* New York: St. Martin's Press, 1987.

Fabro, Cornelio. "Dall'*Ente* di Aristotele all'*Esse* di San Tommaso." In *Tomismo e pensiero moderno,* 47–102. Rome: Laterna University Press, 1969.

Festugière, A. M. "La place du 'De anima' dans le système aristotélicien d'après St Thomas." *Archives d'histoire littéraire et doctrinal du moyen âge* 6 (1931): 25–47.

Fortin, E. L. *Dissidence et philosophie au moyen âge.* Paris: Vrin, 1981.

Furth, Montgomery. *Substance, Form and Psyche: An Aristotelian Metaphysics.* Cambridge: Cambridge University Press, 1988.

Gauthier, René A., O.P. "Notes sur les débuts (1225–1240) du premier 'Averroisme.'" *Revue des sciences philosophiques et théologiques* 66, no. 2 (1982): 321–73.

————. "Le traité *De anima et de potenciis eius* d'un maître ès arts (vers 1225)." *Revue des sciences philosophiques et théologiques* 66, no. 1 (1982): 3–55.

Giele, M., F. Van Steenberghen, and B. Bazán, eds. *Trois commentaires anonymes sur le Traité de l'âme d'Aristote.* Louvain: Publications Universitaires, 1971.

Gilson, Etienne. *Dante et la philosophie.* Paris: Vrin, 1939.

————. *History of Christian Philosophy in the Middle Ages.* New York: Random House, 1954.

Hamelin, Octave. *La théorie de l'intellect d'après Aristote et ses commentateurs.* Paris: Vrin, 1953.

Hyman, Arthur. "Aristotle's Theory of the Intellect and Its Interpretation by Averroes." In *Studies in Aristotle,* edited by Dominic O'Meara. Washington, D.C.: Catholic University of America Press, 1982.

Keeler, L. W., S.J. *Sancti Thomae Aquinatis Tractatus De unitate intellectus contra Averroistas.* Rome: Gregorian University Press, 1936.

Lear, Jonathan. *Aristotle: The Desire to Understand.* Cambridge: Cambridge University Press, 1988.

Lloyd, G. E. R., and G. E. L. Owen, eds. *Aristotle on Mind and the Senses.* Proceedings of the Seventh Symposium Aristotelicum. Cambridge: Cambridge University Press, 1978.

Mansion, Suzanne. *Etudes aristotéliciennes.* Louvain-La-Neuve: Editions de l'Institut Superieur de Philosophie, 1984.

Maritain, Jacques. *The Dream of Descartes.* New York: Philosophical Library, 1944.

————. *The Degrees of Knowledge*. Trans. G. B. Phelan. New York: Charles Scribner's Sons, 1959.

McInerny, Ralph. *Boethius and Aquinas*. Washington, D.C.: Catholic University of America Press, 1990.

————."Le terme 'âme' est-il équivoque ou univoque?" *Revue philosophique de Louvain* 58 (1960): 481–504. [English in *Studies in Analogy*. The Hague: Nijhoff, 1968.]

Mohammed, Ovey N. *Averroes' Doctrine of Immortality*. Waterloo: Wilfred Laurier University Press, 1984.

Moreau, Joseph. *De la connaissance selon saint Thomas d'Aquin*. Paris: Beauchesne, 1976.

Nemesius of Emessa. *De natura hominis*. In Patrologia Graeca, edited by J. P. Migne, vol. 40. Paris: Garnier, 1857.

Nussbaum, Martha Craven. *Aristotle's De motu animalium*. Princeton, N.J.: Princeton University Press, 1978.

Phillipe, M. D. *Initiation à la philosophie d'Aristote*. 1954. Reprint. Paris: La Colombe, 1990.

Rist, John M. *The Mind of Aristotle*. Toronto: University of Toronto Press, 1989.

Robinson, Daniel N. *Aristotle's Psychology*. New York: Columbia University Press, 1989.

Rodier, G. *Aristote: Traité de l'âme*. Commentary. 1900. Reprint. Paris: Vrin, 1985.

Sellars, Wilfrid. "Aristotelian Philosophies of Mind." In *Philosophy for the Future,* edited by Sellars, McGill, and Farber, 544–70. New York: Macmillan, 1949.

Slakey, Thomas. "Aristotle on Sense Perception." *Philosophical Review* 70 (1961): 470–84.

Sorabji, Richard. *Aristotle on Memory*. Providence, R.I.: Brown University Press, 1972.

Thomas Aquinas. *Sancti Thomae de Aquino Opera omnia iussu Leonis XIII P.M.* Edited by the Leonine Commission. Rome: Commissio Leonina, 1882–.

————. *Expositio super librum Boethii De trinitate*. Edited by Bruno Decker. Leiden: E. J. Brill, 1955.

————. *De ente et essentia*. Edited by Roland-Gosselin. Paris: J. Vrin, 1948.

————. *De ente et essentia*. In *Opuscula philosophica*. Edited by R. Spiazzi, O.P. Turin: Marietti, 1954, 1–18.

————. *In Boetium De trinitate et De hebdomadibus expositio*. Edited by M. Calcaterra, O.P. In *Opuscula theologica,* 2:291–408. Turin: Marietti, 1954.

————. *In librum Boethii De trinitate quaestiones quinta et sexta*. Edited by Paul Wyser, O.P. Fribourg: Société Philosophique; Louvain: Nauwelaerts, 1948.

————. *In librum De causis expositio*. Edited by C. Pera, O.P. 2d ed. Turin: Marietti, 1972.

————. *Scriptum super libros Sententiarum*. Edited by Mandonnet and Moos. Paris: Lethielleux, 1929–33.

————. *Super librum De causis expositio*. Edited by H. D. Saffrey. Textus Philosophici Friburgensis, vol. 4/5. Fribourg: Société Philosophique; Louvain: Nauwelaerts, 1954.

————. *Thomas von Aquin in librum Boethii De trinitate quaestiones quinta et sexta*. Fribourg: Paulusverlag, 1948.

Tugwell, Simon, O.P. *Albert & Thomas: Selected Writings.* The Classics of
    Spirituality. New York: Paulist Press, 1988.
Van Steenberghen, Fernand. *Maître Siger de Brabant.* Louvain: Publica-
    tions Universitaires, 1977.
———. *Thomas Aquinas and Radical Aristotelianism.* Washington, D.C.:
    Catholic University Press, 1980.
———. *La philosophie au XIIIème siècle.* Louvain: Publications Universi-
    taires, 1966.
Vanni Rovighi, Sofia. *L'antropologia filosofica di San Tommaso d'Aquino.*
    Milan: Vita e Pensiero, 1982.
Veatch, Henry B. *Aristotle.* Bloomington: Indiana University Press, 1974.
Verbeke, G., ed. *Themistius: Commentaire sur le Traité de l'âme d'Aristote.*
    Translated by Guillaume de Moerbeke. Leiden: E. J. Brill, 1973.
———. "Themistius et le 'De unitate intellectus' de S. Thomas." *Revue
    philosophique de Louvain* 53 (1955): 141–64.
Wedin, Michael. *Mind and Imagination in Aristotle.* New Haven, Conn.:
    Yale University Press, 1988.
———. "Tracking Aristotle's Nous." In *Human Nature and Natural Knowl-
    edge: Essays Presented to Marjorie Grene,* edited by A. Donagan,
    A. N. Perovich, Jr., and M. V. Wedin, 167–97. Boston, Mass.:
    Reidel, 1986.
Weisheipl, James, O.P. *Friar Thomas d'Aquino.* Rev. ed. Washington, D.C.:
    Catholic University of America Press, 1983.
Zedler, Beatrice H. *Saint Thomas Aquinas On the Unity of the Intellect
    against the Averroists.* Translation of Keeler edition. Milwaukee,
    Wis.: Marquette University Press, 1968.

INDEX

Faith: Christian, 1, 19, 143; mysteries of, 160; and philosophy, 19; preambles of, 160, 161, 162; and reason, 155–63, 210; revelation of, 97, 161
Festugière, A. M., 169
First man, 117
Five Ways, 161
Form: educed from potency of matter, 65; and matter, 49, 51, 73, 87, 95; reception of, 180
Fossanova, 13
Franciscans, 3, 6

Gauthier, R., 2, 8, 9, 13, 14, 51n, 61n, 197, 203, 205
Gerard of Abbeville, 6, 7
Giles of Rome, 14
Gilson, Etienne, 212–13
Glossa ordinaria, 5
God, 127, 143, 159
Good, 137
Gosvin de la Chapelle, 13
Gratian, 5
Great Commentary (of Averroes), 8, 190, 195, 197
Greeks, 23, 77, 79, 141, 159, 177
Gregory IX, 5
Gregory of Nyssa (Nemesius of Emessa), 23, 53, 93, 95, 189

Heavenly bodies, 137
Henry of Ghent, 14
History of Animals, The, 164
Hugh of St. Victor, 5
Human knowledge, order of, 164

Illumination, 87
Imagination, 131
Immaterial, 99
Immateriality, 181, 183
Immortality (incorruptibility) of soul, 19, 51, 53
Individual and species, 105
Individuated by matter, 121, 123
Innocent IV, 2
Intellect: agent, 35, 51, 61, 71, 73, 75, 83, 103, 135; as capacity, 41, 185; and imagination, 35, 73; incorruptibility of, 139; and intelligible forms, 39, 41, 73, 185; as part of soul, 27, 29, 67, 69, 91, 125, 149; passibility of,

37, 39, 43, 113, 186, 192–93; possible, 8, 10, 35, 51, 61, 73, 75, 81, 83, 103, 105, 115, 208, 210; practical, 77; separability of, 37, 55; speculative, 35; unmixed, 39
Intelligible: possible and actual, 71, 117, 119, 131, 186–87, 194, 209; species, 81, 83, 85, 115, 117, 119, 207
Intention, 131
Intentional mode, 181, 182

Jaeger, Werner, 170
John Fretel, 14
John of Huy, 14
John Pecham, 7
John XXII, 12

Keeler, Leo W., S.J., 17, 19n, 35n
Knowing, analogy with becoming, 179
Koran, 191, 196

Latin Averroism, 1, 8, 155
Latins, 23, 141, 143
Learning and discovery, 113, 115, 135
Legere, disputare, praedicare, 3
Lewis, C. S., 17
Liberal arts, 4, 7, 159
Life, levels of, 25
Logica vetus / logicus nova, 4

Macrobius, 93
Magister artium, 7
Magister regens, 3, 6, 155
Mansion, Auguste, 170
Marietti edition, 35n, 177
Matter and form, 49, 51, 73, 87, 95
Medieval education, 12, 158
Mendicants, 6
Metaphysics, passim
Meteorology, 11, 164, 165
Mohammed, Ovey N., 191, 192, 196, 197
Montecassino, 2
Montesangiovanni, 2
Moral philosophy, 97, 109
Moving and being moved, 89
Multipliciter dicitur, 190, 201
Mysteries of faith, 160

Naples, 2, 4, 12
Nations at University of Paris, 10
Natural philosopher, 49, 61, 83, 166–69
Natural things, 165
Nazarius, John Paul, 163
Necessity and probability, 135
Nicomachean Ethics, 3, 4, 7, 8, 93, 137, 199, 202
Numerically one, 105, 107, 111, 121

On Being and Essence, 4, 156
On Generation and Corruption, 164, 165
On Interpretation, 202
On Minerals, 165
On Sense and the Sensed Object, 164, 166, 169
On Sophistical Refutations, 157
On the Generation of Animals, 63, 79n, 150, 195
On the Heavens, 164, 165
On the Principles of Nature, 4, 156, 167, 168, 170
On the Soul, passim
On the Trinity, 169
Order of learning, 165, 185
Order of Preachers (Dominicans), 2, 3
Organ, sense and intellect, 41, 43, 45, 47, 55, 59, 75, 97, 99, 149, 181, 193
Orvieto, 4, 9, 13

Paris, 1, 3, 5, 6–9, 168
Parmenides, 168
Passibility of sense and intellect, 37, 39, 43, 113, 186, 192–93
Pauson, John J., 170
Peripatetics, 19, 71, 79, 139, 141, 150
Person, 1
Peter of Ireland, 2, 13
Phantasms: abstraction from, 83, 119, 186, 207; and thought, 61, 81, 97, 111, 115, 207
Philosopher, The (Aristotle), 23, 89, 111, 115, 123
Philosophy: Christian, 163; and faith, 19; moral, 97, 109; scandal of, 179; and theology, 156–59

Physical objects, structure of, 16ι 69
Physics, 11, 12, 49, 61, 63, 83, 111, 139, 164, 165, 167, 168
Plato, 4, 23, 27, 67, 93, 103, 123, 131, 141, 157, 169, 174, 189, 199, 200, 202, 209
Plotinus, 23, 93, 189
Poetic argument, 157
Possible intellect, 8, 10
Posterior Analytics, 169
Potency and act, 65
Practical thinking, 183
Preambles of faith, 160, 161, 162
Prime matter, 167
Principles or starting points, 157
Proclus, 156
Prooemium, 176
Proper object, 185
Pseudo-Dionysius, 8

Quiddity, 49, 131

Rashdall, Hastings, 13, 15
Reception and receiver, 119
Reductio ad absurdum, 162, 208
Revelation of faith, 97, 161
Rhetoric, 97
Robert Kilwardby, 8
Robert of Neuville, 14
Rodier, G., 204

Santa Sabina, 1, 2, 4
Scandal of philosophy, 179
Science, 115
Sciences, distinction of, 169
Self-evident principles, 135, 157
Self-understanding, 117, 133
Sense: possibility of, 37, 39, 43, 113, 186, 192–93; in potency to sensibles, 37
Senses: external, 179–83; internal, 183–86
Sentences of Peter Lombard, 2, 3, 4, 5, 19n, 156, 175, 208, 209
Separation: from body, 29, 61; in definition and in place, 27, 29, 35, 185
Siger of Brabant, 8, 9–13, 103n, 212–13
Simon de Brion, 10
Simon of Brabant, 10
Simplicius, 93

I N D E X